TEEN MOTHERS

CITIZENS OR DEPENDENTS?

TEEN MOTHERS

CITIZENS OR DEPENDENTS?

Ruth Horowitz

THE UNIVERSITY OF CHICAGO PRESS
Chicago and London

Ruth Horowitz is professor of sociology at the University of Delaware.

The University of Chicago Press, Chicago 60637
The University of Chicago Press, Ltd., London
© 1995 by The University of Chicago
All rights reserved. Published 1995
Printed in the United States of America

04 03 02 01 00 99 98 97 96 95   1 2 3 4 5

ISBN: 0–226–35378–8 (cloth)

Library of Congress Cataloging-in-Publication Data

    Teen mothers—Citizens or Dependents? / Ruth Horowitz.
    Includes bibliographical references and indexes.
      p.   cm.
    1. Teenage mothers—Services for—United States.   2. Welfare
recipients—Education—United States.   3. Public welfare
administration—United States.   I. Title.
HV700.5.H67   1995
362.82'94—dc20   94-16034
                                                               CIP

Contents

Preface

Controversy concerning welfare policies is growing. Some social scientists and policymakers blame the welfare system and the social services it provides for creating long-term dependency. More darkly, some see existing programs as an instrument of the powerful, designed to control and disenfranchise the poor. More positively, the welfare system has been viewed as an attempt to expand effective rights of citizenship to all people. In all views, however, the system is seen as not working. The formulation of proposals to modify or reconstruct the existing welfare system, and the evaluation of such proposals, requires the kind of extensive and textured understanding that social science research can provide. Much of the existing research, however, focuses only on the macrolevel. It explores general patterns of welfare provision and use. Less frequently encountered are studies of the operation of the welfare system and social service programs at the microlevel of human interaction in the provision of services.

This book seeks to help fill this gap. It concerns the construction of relationships among social service providers and their clients, teen mothers in this case, and what those relationships say to the clients about themselves and about their role in the wider society. Part of the reason for concern with teen mothers is that teens who become mothers tend to be in the group who remain on welfare for longer periods than most (Ellwood 1986). Between one-half and two-thirds of those who entered the welfare rolls between the mid 1960s and the late 1970s were on welfare for only one or two years and about one-sixth used it for eight or more years, while the median was less than four years (Duncan et al. 1988).

The research upon which the book is based consists of participant observation of a year-long social service program for teen mothers who had failed to graduate from high school. The program was experimental and funded for a year through a grant for "disadvantaged workers" to provide education to obtain a GED (General Education Development diploma) and job readiness training. During the year, I spent most days attending classes and talking informally with the young women and staff after class and during lunch breaks. This book focuses on what went on—what days in the program were like. As an ethnography, it steers away from generalizations about what kind of program may or may not work. It does suggest, however, why some programs may be more successful than others. It focuses on the relationships between personnel and participants.

One of the insights that this work offers arises from my observation that the social service providers in the program had two distinct approaches to their jobs; they communicated different views regarding the identity of their clients, as teen mothers in the program and as to how the teens did and should fit into the wider society. I refer to the first group of social service providers as the arbiters and the second as the mediators.

The arbiters attempted to develop the program as though it were a formal job site by constructing a hierarchical relationship with the clients and trying to establish unquestionable authority based on their success and that of their friends in the wider society. They communicated a view of the world as rigidly segmented between the public world of work and the private world of friends, family, and the local community. The young women were seen as clients and students, and their lives as welfare recipients, girlfriends, and mothers were relegated to the private world of "dirty laundry."

The mediators worked to create a community of women who could talk about issues important to them. Their authority was embedded in experience and through the provision of information that was presented to the young women as choices they could either use or discard based on their own assessment of its worth. The mediators emphasized making decisions and taking account of how others (both those in the local community and in the wider society) may view their actions. To the mediators, being a mother was critical and was at least as important as being a good student or client. For them, the world was not readily divisible into public and private worlds but consisted of an evolving series of front and back stages. According to the mediators' view, one needs critical awareness of the situation and readiness not only to adapt to what is going on but readiness to change the direction of the interaction.

The book is divided into three parts. The first part, chapters 1 and 2, analyzes how the program started, my research role, and how helping relationships may be developed in the delivery of social services. Part II, chapters 3 through 8, explores the construction of identities and relationships within the program. Each chapter analyzes an element of the worker-participant relationship. The third part of the book, chapters 9 and 10, explores the consequences on the services delivered of the two staff perspectives on the relationship between the individual and society and explores the possibility of voluntary social service programs which increase self-regulation through increased participation in a larger diversity of social worlds.

I wrote this book with three different audiences in mind, each as important as the next. The first audience comprises the social service personnel who are faced daily with the problems of trying to make social welfare programs work and, in that effort, are forced to define what it means for such a program to work and how that can be accomplished. I believe they may find helpful illumination in the account of the varying struggles the social service providers had as they tried to establish relationships with the teen mothers. The service providers have the most difficult job: they are the ones who, most pointedly, are asked to produce some observable change. They have to translate general policies and theories of social work into the daily program interactions. Working with people who face trouble and problems almost every day is, of course, a difficult, trying task. It is my hope that this book may provide workers with some helpful insights about the interactive nature of their work.

Another important audience for this work is comprised of those who develop policies and programs for the welfare state. They may be interested in the gaps that this fieldwork study reveals between the established policies and program proposals which appear on paper and the program in action. Nor was the program in action a uniform affair. This book shows that the different approaches of the program staff to the establishment of relationships, particularly in matters of authority, may effect outcomes. Setting up a GED and job readiness program is only the beginning of a program to decrease dependency and move the participants toward the work force and greater participation in the social world. This book shows that much is communicated to clients and not all messages are formal or consistent with developing independence. The phenomenon of disconnections among policies, the delivery of services, and various informal messages, I call "loosely coupled cultures."

The third audience is sociologists. This book raises questions about citizenship and alternative paths for becoming a contributing member of society in a welfare state. It examines different models that people, in this case staff members, use to inform the way they see themselves and others interacting with the wider society. And it focuses on the construction of power in social relations and of meaningful social identities of both staff and participants.

In sociology there is renewed interest in citizenship and the welfare state. My interest in this area began after I left graduate school and began to reread the works of Morris Janowitz. I did not fully appreciate his analysis until I looked closely at the program analyzed in this book and tried to see "what was really going on," a major task for any ethnographer. This research attempts to add its microlevel analysis of everyday life to more general issues of social control and self-regulation that are some of the most important questions that Janowitz addressed.

Several people read parts of this book while it was still in manuscript and helped to improve it. I am deeply grateful to my colleagues and friends who listened and read and commented. Especially, I note my thanks to Anne Bowler, Mark D. Jacobs, Peter K. Manning, and Dmitri N. Shalin who each read the entire manuscript and held many fruitful conversations with me, often at times when I could not yet coherently capture the complexities presented by my data. Thanks are also due to Saul Hoffman, Sherryl Kleinman, and two of my graduate teaching assistants, Stefanie Field and Rika Schmitt, who also supplied helpful criticisms. Kathryn A. Kraynik helped significantly to smooth the prose. Of course, I remain solely responsible for such errors and shortcomings as remain.

The teen mothers were very cooperative and supported me in this endeavor. I truly enjoyed talking with them and sharing lunches and confidences. Some of the staff were more cooperative than others. It was difficult to have an extra person around who did not have to influence the teens to do anything and was not responsible when things did not go as planned. Some of the staff were admirable in their willingness to include me in the program and their lives.

My husband, William T. Allen, supported and encouraged me throughout. His impatience with sociological jargon and his willingness to listen were helpful in developing my analyses as clearly as possible.

PART ONE

Issues in Program Development

CHAPTER ONE

Getting to Know Project GED

Two months after the program started, I was excluded from the staff meetings of Project GED, which were held every Friday, by Roberta[1] (the coordinator and job readiness teacher who replaced Sarah[2]) because they "needed to let their hair down." They agreed to let me back in after several meetings. A month after Mr. Harrison (he replaced John after the first five-month session) began as the GED (General Educational Development diploma) teacher, he asked me not to attend his classes. A similar event occurred when Ivy (the counselor) told Amy[3] (a volunteer who taught the family life class) that she could not attend her class to see a film on rape. Roberta again told me I could not attend the staff meetings, this time because they were talking about "intimate details of the girls' lives."

Georgia (a state representative), angered by the staff's lack of co-operation with each other, with me, and with the research staff, called a special meeting. Wilma (the overall part-time coordinator), Roberta, Ivy, and Mr. Harrison appeared to forget that the funding was for a demonstration project. Mr. Harrison argued that research was not a valid activity and that he had said so in his graduate classes. He claimed he never would have taken the job if he had known about the research component. The second argument he made was to claim that I would breach the confidentiality of what the young women told me, which would hurt them very much. Here Ivy jumped in and

1. All of the names, including that of the program, have been changed except my own. All of the staff were black except as indicated otherwise.
2. Sarah was white and left for a permanent job after several months.
3. Amy was white and had no training in social work and very little experience. She was often assisted by Becky who had years of experience as a service provider.

3

expressed her fears that they would be hurt by anything that I wrote. Roberta made a third argument that they (the staff) were very different when I was not around and that there was a lot that I did not know about them. She explained that they were really not who they seemed. I reiterated that I was not doing an evaluation of their work. Mr. Harrison and Roberta demanded that I talk to the participants again because the participants were not aware that I was planning to write a book and were innocent and defenseless.

The next day the staff assembled the ten or so teen mothers who were present and informed them that I had something to say. When I explained I was writing a book that they would be in, the participants replied they were well aware of what I was doing and liked to talk to me. Several claimed that they knew about me from the previous participants (first session). One said, "We trust her and say anything in front of her, even the dirty stuff." They invited me to lunch after the meeting and told me to ignore the staff. I think it was clear to them that I was seriously shaken by the staff's behavior. We left the building and crossed the street to the sub shop and then ate lunch and waited outside for Jenna (the behavior modification teacher), who had not attended the meeting, and for the afternoon class. That afternoon we had an active discussion about male/female relationships.

The changes in Project GED personnel contributed to the continuing debate about the program's aims and the best ways to achieve them, often resulting in tension and conflict among staff, between staff and participants, and between me and some of the staff. The broad intent of this program was to change the teen mothers; to get them off welfare and head them toward jobs. What this change meant for the teens and how it should be accomplished was not clearly defined when the program started and was never agreed upon by all the staff or the participants. Importantly, this site represented a "natural experiment" about different approaches to policy and staff/client interaction embodied by two distinct, and often conflicting, orientations of staff members. These points of conflict reveal the different perspectives of the staff and their effects on the teens and are the focus of this book, a study of the daily interactions and rituals of staff and participants.

Project GED

The program was housed in an inner-city community. The problems of this small city are similar to those experienced in the older industrial cities. Most new jobs are for white-collar and low-wage service workers, and the number of well-paid blue-collar jobs has declined. The minority is poorer than the white population, though there is a sizable black middle class. Most of the poor blacks live in segregated neighborhoods, but busing has lessened school segregation, if not racial tensions and conflict. Many of the participants in this program, then eleven or twelve years old, were among the first to be bused. The state has a high rate of births to teen mothers. In a call for proposals, a state agency designated a one-year federal block grant for the "disadvantaged worker" to include teenage parents. A consortium of four agencies with some experience with teen mothers developed a proposal. Georgia, a representative from the state agency, explained to me that the consortium was funded because the group claimed that they had access to and could attract teen *mothers and fathers* and both *blacks and whites* to the program.

The heads of the four agencies and some of the state officers established the broad outline of the program. The "charter"[4] provided some of the possible parameters for the program and was established prior to hiring the staff. According to a news release put out by the state, this pilot program was

> designed to increase employment readiness and self-sufficiency. . . . The agencies will be testing approaches to build motivation, basic skills, confidence and responsibility in managing daily life. Services such as parenting, budgeting and day-care will be paired with instruction in work readiness, basic math and English and career exploration . . . We hope to learn enough to apply the results to some ongoing efforts that will be effective in helping members of these groups become more independent and self-sufficient.

The last statement accounted for the presence of researchers.

At the first staff meeting, before the participants arrived, Georgia emphasized the charter of the organization. She started by saying that "we must document all outcomes" and continued with five basic points she deemed essential to changing the behavior of the teen mothers: (1) "changing attitudes by increasing self-esteem," (2)

---

4. A charter is "the concept to which organization members orient in their dealings with one another and with nonmembers to establish the limits of legitimatizable action. . . . [A] charter can be said to represent the constraints on a member's freedom of action that he or she experiences or depicts as exterior, objective and given" (Dingwall and Strong 1985, 217). To some extent, the charter defines the range of legitimating accounts concerning the purpose of the organization and what the organization is intended to do.

"breaking the welfare cycle," (3) changing attitudes toward work prior to obtaining jobs for them, (4) teaching basic skills such as filling out applications and organized shopping, and (5) training the clients in coping skills for everyday life, such as budgeting and self-sufficiency in getting around outside of the community. Georgia also argued that communication and coordination among the staff were crucial for success and that the program would fail if each staff member pursued his or her own goals: "You may have to step beyond your job description. You need to problem solve and see what works."

The relationship between the state employees and the project developers (the heads of the four consortium agencies) was never smooth and many of those agency directors who had worked on the proposal had minimal contact with the program after it started. The minimal communication had significant effects on the project development and implementation, leaving its mark on intra-staff relations, staff-client relations, and the content and organization of the program.

The heads of the four agencies originally proposed that eighty participants attend the program for the entire year so that each one would move through the components of the program in sequential steps: several months of GED training; several more of job readiness; a sequence of parenting skills; and a segment called behavior modification that included consumer education, group counseling, birth control information, and a variety of other topics intended to increase self-esteem. Instead, the state representatives, headed by Georgia, decided that two groups of forty clients participating for five months each would be more successful. Each component would have several class periods each week. Several of the agency directors declared that this change would doom the project to failure because five months was too short a period to have sufficient impact.

It took longer than anticipated to hire the full-time staff: a coordinator-job readiness teacher (after the first month of the program, Sarah left for a more secure job and was replaced by Roberta), a counselor (Ivy), and a GED teacher (John was replaced after the first session by Mr. Harrison). The overall administrator, Wilma, was already a staff member in the agency where they located the program and was to dedicate only a small part of her time to the program. The behavior modification teacher (Jenna, with the help of Esther) had release time from her agency and had been involved in the initial stage of writing the program proposal. She had money to bring in a variety of resource people to complete her component. Parenting classes were taught by a volunteer (Amy, and sometimes Becky) from another of the four coordinating agencies. Amy, Becky, and Sarah were the only white staff.

One week after the coordinators hired the staff, Georgia told them to start the program even though they had recruited and found day-care for only fourteen participants. The state representatives attended only sporadically and monitored the program largely through the staff's provision of data: attendance statistics and weekly written reports. Without much on-the-scene direction by those who were funding the program or those who developed the original proposal and with the vague articulation of the limits of the organization, the staff were relatively free to construct their own *mission* or "what we are here for" (Dingwall and Strong 1985, 217), which was not necessarily consistent with the *charter*. In fact, more than one *mission* developed. At first the set of goals and objectives were very specific:

1. To test all who qualify for the GED program within two weeks;
2. Assess the readiness of the students to take the GED test (this would be conducted on a monthly basis);
3. Successfully instruct 50 percent to pass the GED test;
4. If the GED is passed, recommend attendance at an institution of higher learning or involvement in a vocational skill;
5. Graduation.

The flyer they designed and handed out around the community specified the eligibility criteria and content of the program. It advertised for "teenage parents, sixteen to nineteen years of age, not in school." The pamphlet listed the following components of the program: "learn parenting techniques and job seeking skills; explore careers, improve basic skills, reading and math; prepare for GED exam; and behavior modification." While these statements provided some of the limiting accounts for the staff, they were not necessarily consistent with the behavior or accounts of daily activities as the program developed. Nor were the accounts or actions of the individual staff members necessarily congruent.

A major focus of this book will be the split between the staff members. Two distinctive orientations toward the program and participants developed after the departure of Sarah as coordinator and job readiness teacher. These orientations not only affected and were reflected in the staff/participant relationships but also were embedded in the views that the staff communicated to the young women about the wider society and their relationships to it. The staff whom I refer to as arbiters created relationships based on hierarchy and social distance and viewed the program as equivalent to a work site where obeying the boss was critical for success and separate and distinct from family life. Mediators, on the other hand, tried to create a community of women and mothers; they emphasized the difficult dilemmas and interconnections between the world of work and the worlds of family and friends and decision-making skills. They attempted to explore the diverse social worlds *with* the young mothers. The two distinctive orientations created tension and conflicts both among the staff and between staff and participants. Roberta, Ivy, John, and Mr. Harrison interacted as arbiters, while Jenna, Esther, Amy, Becky and others Jenna brought in to help out tended to follow the orientation of mediators. This book will explore the dilemmas posed by and the differing reactions of the participants to the two distinctive orientations.

A Participant-Observer in an Evaluation Context

This book is based on participant observation of the year-long program. While the reader should not regard this analysis as an evaluation, my role as a researcher in the program was linked by some of the arbiters to that of the evaluators who administered several questionnaires, and they viewed my presence and actions as evaluation research.[5] My participation began when the evaluation researcher asked me to attend a meeting Georgia called to discuss the evaluation process[6] with the proposal writers several weeks prior to the

5. None of the evaluation results will be presented here. The samples were very small and the manner in which the young women filled out the tests appeared to invalidate the results. I watched them fill out the surveys. Most worked hard and spent most of the time on the first few questions and then randomly filled in the rest in a few minutes. This occurred both on the self-esteem tests and the reading and math tests. The control group data were gathered by the coordinator/job readiness staff person, Roberta, who did not believe that research was important. Most of the control group sample was institutionalized and, in my opinion, differed greatly from those attending the program, only one of whom had been in a detention facility. While most of the program participants had been involved in minor delinquencies, the majority were not extensively involved in such activities.

6. Despite Peter Rossi's (1978, 574) claim that "the expected value for any measured effect of a social program is zero," the state officials decided to evaluate this program and three others in order to demonstrate to the legislators that their expenditures had some merit. The evaluation team collected attendance data, self-esteem measures, and academic achievement scores. They also attempted to gather control group data.

The debate continues whether the failure of evaluations of social service programs to demonstrate success lies in the model that explains what is wrong with the individual or institution, the way the treatment is formulated to correct that problem, the manner in which the treatment is delivered to the clients, or the evaluation techniques

start-up of the program. The evaluator suggested to the group that I act as a participant observer in the project and be permitted to observe the program on a daily basis. I explained that I wanted to explore the daily routines of the program, not evaluate staff members. The people attending the meeting were receptive to my inclusion as a researcher and expressed more confidence in developing an understanding of program dynamics from participant observation techniques than from survey instruments. It is important to note that most of the staff had not been hired prior to this meeting and, as the program directors of the cooperating agencies had little communication with the staff hired later, my presence may not have been clearly explained to the workers.

During my year in the field, I generally attended for the entire day, two, three, or five days a week, depending on my teaching schedule. During four months I attended daily. I sat in on classes, went on field trips, and ate lunch in the program or at a local sub shop with the participants. After the termination of the program, I occasionally saw some of the young women in the grocery store or walking downtown. On the first day, when the workers met the participants, I told the participants I was planning to write a book about the program. Like all of the female staff members in the project, I was introduced by my first name. Sarah told the young women that I was a university professor and was not paid for attending. During the classes I took down as much of the discussion as I could, but I did not take notes during informal talks and wrote the field notes when I came home or while waiting for a class to start.

A researcher who studies groups that may develop conflicting interests is in a difficult position between developing closeness and maintaining distance. Distance allows the researcher not to be identified exclusively with any particular group or orientation, permits

---

themselves. According to Rossi (1978), to conduct a good evaluation of a program one must be relatively sure that the treatment designated is related to the way the "cause" of the problem has been defined, that the service provided is appropriate, and that it is being delivered appropriately. To study how the services are delivered, it is necessary to examine what actually occurs between workers and participants on a daily basis. With some exceptions (for example, Deutscher 1977; Fry and Miller 1975), there are few examples of the use of participant observation in evaluation research (Rossi 1978).

One study found that "Project Redirection," a comprehensive program involving most centrally medical care for the mothers and babies and birth control counseling but also education and employment-related services (Polit, Kahn, and Stevens 1985, 59), had some positive effects on employment, parenting skills, and the child's cognitive development but not on education and further pregnancy. Most programs appear to have generally short-term effects on the young women's reproductive or economic futures (Vinovskis 1988; Weatherley et al. 1985).

the researcher to move readily among several groups, and aids objectivity. It is often argued (Brogan and Taylor 1983; Emerson 1983; Miller 1952) that taking sides within a setting undermines objectivity and contaminates the research site. However, the maintenance of distance raises the question of whether the researcher can penetrate the formal role structure. A second position advocates taking an insider or membership role so that the researcher can accurately experience what the subjects do and understand their way of life (Adler and Adler 1987; Hunt 1984; Jules-Rosette 1978). Thus, alliance and membership status with one group would be expected in order to experience what its members did and to produce insights and analysis that might otherwise be unavailable. However, alliance with one group may place a researcher in difficult situations if more than one group interacts in the setting. She must choose among groups.

Neither approach is completely satisfactory to study an organization in which workers and participants may have different interests. Membership in one group may limit access to the other. Membership as a staff member would have been the only possibility for me as I am neither a teen nor a mother. In fact, several of the mothers of the teenage participants were younger than I. As a staff member, however, I would not have been privy to the participants' viewpoints. Distance, on the other hand, while facilitating movement between the groups and aiding insights into the formal role structure, proves less effective for discovering the informal aspects of organizational action and revealing their more hidden meanings and feelings. Increased intimacy, thus, is necessary, and roles which help encourage that intimacy are critical.

A middle ground which assumes that the appearance of any new person in an organization will affect the others in the setting made more sense here. A balance was needed. I could not be a shadow; however, what the nature of my role should be was unclear and I had to negotiate continually. The various members of Project GED attributed different identities to me and dealt with me in part in terms of those identities. The researcher asks not only why particular identities are given to her, but also how those identities affect what is observed. "Objectivity" through distance is not sufficient nor is experiencing what the "natives" do totally practical or possible. As the relationship between data and theory remains problematic, only close examination of how and from what perspective the data is gathered will allow us to begin to understand how the analysis is created.

Not only did I continually have to negotiate identities with the arbiters, mediators, and participants, but the different relationships with them were sometimes in conflict. However, from each of the positions I negotiated or was coerced into taking, I had a unique view of the others which gave me additional means of discovering the meanings of conduct. It allowed me to compare what I saw from each perspective. The particular view depended upon my relationship with each group at the particular time and the identities we negotiated. The program looked very different from the arbiter's and mediator's perspectives as did the lives of the teenage mothers. The lives of the teens also looked different from inside versus outside of the program. While the different positions within the setting gave me distinctive vantage points for examining behavior and discerning the meanings of action, I was pressured into choosing sides after several months. In fact, I found myself in a similar relationship to the arbiters as the young women found themselves. Instead of totally forgoing "objectivity," it provided an additional dimension to the fieldwork, allowed me to enter further into the informal world of the program, and increased my understanding of the social interactions between arbiters and teens. The various identities had consequences both for the data I collected and my analysis of the data, as I have actively used my different relationships with each of the groups to understand their positions within the organization and the meaning of their actions (Horowitz 1986; Katz 1983).

My identity not only changed over time but varied between the arbiters and mediators and between workers and participants. At some points I was permitted to participate freely, but on more than one occasion, the arbiters tried to limit my participation or kick me out of the program. To the arbiters my presence was linked to their evaluation and this made them very uncomfortable; however, the mediators tended to view me largely as a resource and fellow staff member. To many of the participants, I was an additional resource but not a staff member.

At First a Useful Presence
During the first several weeks, the program was chaotic and all of the staff considered my presence useful. I learned names immediately and the workers persuaded me to help with a variety of tasks: scoring achievement tests, thinking up activities, helping with math assignments, and making the participants feel at home. In the classes, the personnel included me in discussions and asked me to voice an opinion or talk about my experiences. While the staff ate lunch apart from the participants, no one questioned me when I started to eat lunch with the young women or when I talked with them prior to the start

of classes. At the end of each day and during staff meetings they asked me for advice about the program or a particular participant. For example, when I reported that several of the young mothers wished to join the armed forces and expressed my doubts about their eligibility, the coordinator, Sarah, immediately arranged for a recruiter to visit and explain recruitment criteria. As an extra resource I was appreciated.

The participants understood that I was not a staff member, but an interesting resource to have around; one of the young women told me that I did not act like a social worker and, when a woman came to observe the program, the participants immediately and correctly identified her as one. Within a short time, the participants felt they could talk to me quite freely. One young woman remarked in a "rap session," "we can say anything in front of Ruth."

With the Arbiters: From Resource to Intruder
Several events occurred that were instrumental in changing my position relative to the arbiters so that I became an undesired intruder instead of an additional resource. Roberta was hired to replace Sarah as coordinator and, two months later, she had the program running more smoothly, that is, without the daily chaos and according to a strict time schedule. The participants' attendance decreased and mine increased. I became more visible and less necessary. While I had never aspired to staff-membership status and had rarely initiated suggestions or helped without someone asking me, I had been drawn slowly into a resource-staff role and was accepted both by the mediators and the participants as such. This was problematic to the arbiters because I was not a staff member, had more education (a very important criteria of status in their eyes), and was white (they made a great deal out of saying that it did not matter to them and they always discussed their white friends, but they always made comparisons and expressed sensitivity at being perceived as black and different in the white middle-class society).

The arbiters began to see me as an evaluator. A month after Roberta took over as coordinator and job readiness teacher, Roberta told me not to attend staff meetings because they "needed some time to let their hair down." Recovering from their objections to my attendance took some change of behavior on my part and more active participation than I wished. When asked formally what I thought of the program, I responded with a positive report, but even after I took over the GED class when John did not show up, Roberta failed to tell me about a suspension she had made the previous day. The teens discussed it with me the next day. Several weeks later the staff discovered that they needed my statistical skills to improve the presentation of their attendance data to the state. After I completed that task I was told I could return to the next staff meeting. Everyone became as overtly friendly and chatty as they had been before.

The next three months went very smoothly with the arbiters. I participated marginally in some of the group discussions, attempting only to add a few informational comments when asked. I would occasionally help someone with a math problem or correct a paper. When John was absent for a three-week period, I helped organize the work. The staff also discussed John's inappropriate behavior with me, and we commiserated about the failure of those whom the staff saw as having the authority to take a stand on the issue of his prolonged and unexcused absence. It was not clear who had that authority. Wilma rarely observed at the program and was running several others in the building. Some thought that she had the authority to do something.

By the time the first session was over, my relationship with the arbiters seemed to have settled down to a reasonably easy acquaintanceship. Everyone discussed what they were going to do during their week off and they commiserated with me because I had my regular teaching schedule. In the week that the staff had to recruit and prepare for the new group, I had lunch with Ivy and Roberta and then went with them to a public housing project to hand out leaflets and try to talk several young women into joining the program.

The arbiters redefined my role as that of an intruder after Mr. Harrison took over as GED instructor at the start of the second session. They began to examine my comments carefully and to make changes in their conversational content with me. Conversations after work became increasingly centered on clothes and home decoration. While these were major topics of discussion with other staff members, it became clear that they no longer wanted to discuss the program or the participants with me. They regarded me as an intruder they wished would leave. This is reflected in my exclusion from meetings and then the GED classes.

Seeing the Teens from the Arbiters' Perspective: The Limitations of
Formal Roles
The formal roles, first as resource person and then as an intruder, limited what I could see to the more formal, overt activities of the

program. I did try to develop some intimacy with the arbiters; I spent time gossiping with them after the program and occasionally ate lunch with them. However, the young women claimed the arbiters gossiped about them all of the time so that if I had spent more public time with them, I might have been suspected of joining in on the gossip. The participants explained to me that they knew I was not a part of it because I was with them most of the time.

When I was in an arbiter-defined position, I saw some of what they saw. The formal nature of the arbiters' relationships with the participants, however, limited what they saw. In the arbiters' classes, the participants seemed to know what they wanted and rarely expressed intimate information or their fears about their future. If a young woman said, "I'll be a nurse" and sounded convinced that that was what she wanted, the arbiters evaluated her as assured and likely to make it. Expressed certainty was rewarded even though the young women had little idea about what becoming a nurse entailed and were sometimes just mentioning a particular job because they had an idea of what it was. Often after private meetings with the arbiters about a job, they expressed to the other participants total confusion about what they were required to do to obtain such jobs and what the jobs entailed.

The arbiters were not interested in the lives of the participants outside of the program and such things were never discussed in classes. As the staff members were trying to make the perfection of the presentation of self the most important skill to get a job, one might not realize how much the young women had invested in their relations with men and in being mothers. The young women were quite successful at using impression management skills, but their sense of who they were was invested in identities outside of the program, identities which remained largely hidden in interactions with the arbiters.

I gained a very different perspective on the young women when I went with them into the streets and attended the classes given by the mediators. The following example demonstrates the importance of a multifaceted view of the participants; one that could not be achieved solely through the "resource" role. One young woman who was evaluated highly by the arbiters and regarded as one of the most successful clients was also involved in many fights and had been to court on more occasions than any of the other participants. She was the only one who had spent time in a juvenile detention facility. When asked about drugs, she told Ivy that she knew little and did not use them; however, out in the street, when we were walking down "pushers' alley," she knew all of the drug dealers by name.

With the Mediators: A Continuing Resource to Staff and Seeing
the Teen World as Tense

Jenna, a mediator, helped to structure my relationship with her and the young women in class in a manner different from the arbiters. I was slowly brought into the discussions and asked to reveal things about my life that were pertinent to the discussion. My relationship with Jenna and the young women became an egalitarian exchange of experiences in which part of each of us became integrated into the same social world despite significant differences in our prior experiences. In these classes, my relationships with the young women was similar to that of Jenna's. Over time, Jenna and I began to talk more informally and had increasingly long and personal discussions of our lives and views.

The relationship that Jenna, and other mediators, established with the participants permitted her, and consequently me, to see aspects of the young women's lives that they would not talk about with the arbiters or among themselves. During discussions with the mediators, the participants often talked about being hurt by their boyfriends' treatment of them and by the failure of the fathers of their babies to stay with them through the birth of their babies. One cried as she demanded to know why men never loved women as much as women loved men. They also discussed their dreams of the future and apprehensions about handling the world and failing to achieve their dreams of a husband who was employed, a home, a well-educated child, and a good job for themselves. The young women rarely discussed these difficult situations informally among themselves outside of class and Jenna had to push them to open up in her sessions.

With the Participants Outside of the Program: Friendly Exchanges

My relationships with the young women outside of the "classroom" was different than my other roles and permitted me to enter a small portion of their social world. They were much more complex people than their participation in the classes demonstrated. I went with some of them to their houses, ate lunch with them, wandered around the community with them, and sometimes took them to appointments at doctors' offices which were difficult to reach by public transportation. I talked about some of my experiences and showed them where I lived.

Slowly I became more of a "real" person to them but always different. We exchanged help and information. We shared lunches and talked while walking in the community. Occasionally, when I realized that someone had no money for lunch, I offered them some of my lunch and, in return, they always offered some to me when I had none. I did not offer to loan money until someone offered to loan me money when I said that I was not going to eat that day. They thought that I had no money. Loans I made for lunch were always repaid. In general, we had a balanced reciprocity relationship (Sahlins 1972). On the one hand, I would tell them about my life when they talked about their own so that nothing was ever entirely one-sided. On the other hand, I was not like them; I was a professor from the white middle-class world. This was dramatized when five black participants and I were walking through "pushers' alley" and a man turned to the young women and asked who I was. They introduced me to several of the dealers as their teacher, Ruth. I was not part of the world of teenage mothers.

The informal relationship developed with the young women outside of the official parameters of the program was different from any of the worker/participant relationships and was different from my relationship with them in class. It allowed me to see different aspects of the young mothers' lives and to reinterpret their actions within the program. From the perspective of the arbiters, the young women were becoming successful at manipulating their presentation of self and, from the perspective of the mediators, they did not have very good control over their lives. What they talked about among themselves at lunch and walking around the community created distinct impressions.

They often sounded tough when they talked of parties and fights that they had had or had observed outside of the program. They never talked of such things in any of the classes and one of the young women, facing serious assault charges in Superior Court, never mentioned it in the program. She told me about it while we were standing around waiting for the van to arrive to take them to pick up their children from day-care. Even the participant who was considered one of the best clients, had the best attendance record, dressed in what the arbiters thought an excellent style, and was very close to getting her GED, fought one weekend and had scratches up and down her arms. She covered these with a long-sleeved shirt. When she failed to show up for the GED exam, she told the staff that her father had gotten into an accident on the way over. The arbiters thought she was trying to put something over on them and did not continue to support her. They did not realize, or perhaps acknowledge, the possibility that she was so nervous and afraid of failing that she could not take the test after what seemed to the arbiters to be a relatively minor upset. I could see this fear from the discussions in class with the mediators, and she had told me she was terrified she did not know enough to pass the test.

My visits into their world made it clear that they were much more complex individuals than their public behavior in the program demonstrated. Not only were they able users of impression management, but they could also maintain a tough face in public and appear in control of most situations. Only in a few situations did I see that control break down outside of the discussions in Jenna's classes.

Our Shared Marginality and Dependency Created by the Arbiters
The relationship I developed with the young women in the classroom was possible in part because of my relationship with them outside of the program. It permitted me to see what was going on in the program not only from the perspective of the mediators and the arbiters, but also from the perspective of the young women. They discovered they could be as much a help to me in the program as I was to them, which made it even clearer that I had no control in the program either, particularly during the second session. After the meeting the arbiters called so that I might reiterate to the participants that I might put anything they said into a book, they told me to ignore the arbiters because they did not care what those workers said. The young women saw that I respected them and had no influence with the arbiters.

Within the program I began to find myself in a similar relationship to the arbiters as the participants, but it was not the same as the young women's—I had more job status and societal acceptance than the arbiters, while the young women did not. There were a number of similarities that made us experience our relationships with the arbiters as similar. We continued in the program voluntarily because we wanted something from it; we had to follow the same rules and schedules set up by the arbiters; and we had to ask permission to deviate even slightly.

Permission was *granted* by the arbiters in a similar manner whether it was for the participants to take a sick child to the doctor or for me to attend a particular session. It made me feel totally helpless. The superior attitudes and the desire for total control came through clearly to all of us. The atmosphere became so strained that toward the end of the program during the summer months, Jenna would immediately accept the suggestion that we have our discussion in the park. As we left the building, the mood of the group changed and we all smiled. Being treated by the arbiters like the young women in the program not only helped me to create a stronger alliance with the participants, but also permitted me to experience, if only in passing, what they must have felt with the arbiters. My position within the program as a non-social worker who was being harassed by the arbiters created the situation which allowed me to develop an "ally" style relationship with the young women and experience a little of what they did.

My relationships varied over time and differed among the groups. While my relationship with the arbiters was tenuous, it permitted me to better understand the experiences of the young women with those staff members. My relationship with the mediators allowed me to see another facet of the young women's lives that they rarely expressed on their own. Outside of the program I saw another side of their experience, invisible within the program. I even served as a staff member during two days when Roberta and Ivy went to a conference and John failed to show up and developed a better understanding of what it was like to be a staff member who was supposed to direct changes in the lives of others rather than a researcher who was not responsible for others' conduct.

Scope of the Book

This book focuses on what is happening on the level of staff/participant interaction: the daily practices, symbols, ordinary rites and ceremonies in a social service program. It is not intended to add to the argument about the intended functions of social service and welfare programs by those who create and fund them, but to understand the experiences of the young women. The "intent" of policy on the federal or state level may be translated in many ways when the policies are operationalized on the microlevel of the delivery of the services. I will argue that what is central to the experiences of the participants is the way the staff work to construct the program, how staff negotiate their relationships with the participants, and what the staff communicate about individuals and their relationships to the wider society, in addition to practical skills.

This book raises a number of questions concerning how social control operates on the microlevel and to what end. First, it raises questions about the social service program as a mechanism of social control. It is a people-changing organization whose stated goal is to have the participants change their behaviors outside of the organization, that is, to make them self-sufficient. At the level of the organization's relationship to its environment, questions arise as to how the staff is guided in its efforts. What messages are communicated to them and what kinds of controls are exerted on their actions by supervisors? And how do their views of "professionalism" and their experience guide them? On the level of program organization, what types of relationships do workers construct with the participants in order to effect meaningful and lasting change? How do the staff try to get the participants to go along? How do the participants interpret and respond to those efforts? How do the definitions of the situation of the participants constrain their own actions within the program?

Second, there are normative questions concerning the content of the messages sent to the participants and how they are interpreted. To what ends are these efforts in social control directed? Are they attempting to move the participants toward a more central role in the wider society by increasing their choices and options or are the staffs' actions reinforcing the participants' positions on the periphery of society? How are the participants supposed to change what they are supposed to do with their lives? What are the participants learning about what their social relations should be like in the world outside of the program, both in the local community and in the wider society? Is becoming a compliant program participant more important to the staff than being a good mother or a dedicated girlfriend? Is being a welfare recipient a short-term measure until one can become self-sufficient or a stain on one's moral character? Are we dealing with teenage girls or young adults? Is being someone's girlfriend outside of the program a positive factor that can be harnessed to help independence and self-sufficiency or is it part of one's "dirty laundry" that must be kept hidden from the public?

Third, some questions concern commitment to the organization. Why do the participants remain in the program? What are the benefits for the participants? Was a program identity and purpose ever developed in which self-interest could be merged with collective interests? Did a shared sense of social or cultural order develop? Did the young women go along with the program because they were so compelled or because they wanted and needed something the program had to offer? Under what kinds of circumstances did the young women fail to go along and take an active stance against the staff? In what types of situations do participants accept or reject challenges? To what extent did the program nudge them out and when did situations outside of the program draw them out?

Several themes emerge from these questions: Hierarchy and egalitarianism, impression management and the "real me," persuasion and authority, social control as socialization and social control as the ability to regulate oneself, dependence and autonomy, and the communication of folk theories of the relationship of individuals to the wider society.

This book is organized according to the identities employed in the construction of staff/participant relationships and activities in the program. The different appraisals and evaluations of these identities by the mediators, arbiters, and the teen mothers is illustrated by focusing first on those identities thought important by the arbiters and then on those by the mediators. The tensions created by the different ways of appraising and evaluating identities as the staff/participant relationships are negotiated are explored in each chapter as the young women attempt to assert their own priorities and establish their own identities. Each chapter begins with a scene from the program that illustrates the major themes in each chapter.

Chapter 2, "Contested Organizational Cultures: Helping and Authority," focuses on the macrolevel research of the effects of welfare on recipients and the importance of examining social service programs at the microlevel. I argue that the intent of the policy at the federal or state level is loosely coupled to what actually is communicated to those who use such services. What is communicated is as dependent on the construction of social relationships between personnel and participants as on the content of the particular class or program.

Arbiters and mediators construct their identities very differently, both in the program and outside. Chapter 3, "Social Service Providers' Problems of Social Identity" explores the differences in the ways the mediators and the arbiters define their experiences and how these differences are related to how they try to construct personnel/participant relationships.

Chapter 4, "Social Distance as a Strategy of Compliance," focuses on how the arbiters attempt to gain control over the organization and culture of the program and to establish the client identity as dominant for the participants. While the arbiters are reasonably successful at compelling the young women to be "good clients," their claims of competency—having achieved much in the wider society—and threats of expulsion are not totally successful in maintaining the subordinate and dependent status of the clients; they revolt and often refuse to give the client identity precedence.

Chapter 5, "Classroom Failure without Redress" tries to answer the question: When the goal of completing a GED is universally recognized as demonstrating competency, is that a sufficient reason to compel commitment to continued learning when the teachers fail to demonstrate that the program is a priority for them or that they are competent to teach? The teachers, all arbiters, were able to create a culture of competition but were less successful in involving the young women as students. Moreover, this created a situation in which the students had few ways to respond to the indignities they experienced.

"Sex and Boyfriends: Your Dirty Laundry or Dramatic Dreams," chapter 6, explores the importance of the boyfriend/girlfriend relationship. It shows how the mediators are able to develop the type of relationship with the young women that allows them to be very critical of some aspects of their relationships. The mediators focus on the "future-oriented self" and show the teens how working and independence will better enable them to achieve the type of relationship they dream about.

For these young women motherhood is what allows them to express their authentic selves. Chapter 7 examines the evolution of intention to become a mother, the importance of motherhood, and the dangers that the young mothers experience in their interactions with the social service providers in the wider society. The young mothers perceive that it is very risky to show that they may not be perfect mothers as they see that anyone connected to social services can take away their children. As a result, they are very canny in their revelations about the need for any help and the family life teachers were not very successful in eliciting the discussions they desired as they were not perceived as sincere.

The following chapter, "Changing Welfare From Stigma to Scholarship: The Arbiters versus the Mediators," deals with the issue of the meaning of welfare and how the arbiters and mediators create very different meanings for welfare use by young teen mothers. The arbiters create an empty role of "worker to be" and communicate that welfare use is deviant. The mediators, on the other hand, are able, through placing themselves in the same moral community as the young women, to criticize use of welfare while developing a positive identity as a temporary user of welfare.

Chapter 9, "Backstage Links to Public Empowerment" surveys the staff's folk theories of the relation of individuals to the larger worlds and the relationships among the larger worlds. For the arbiters, the world is divided neatly into the public and private spheres, whereas the mediators divide the social worlds into a series of back and front regions. These models are communicated to the young women in the program and indicate how the staff think they should organize their lives.

In conclusion, chapter 10, "The Embodied Reason of Welfare Reform," examines the possibility of voluntary social service programs for increasing social control through increased active participation in a larger diversity of social worlds, that is, social control as self-regulation.

With the continual contest between the mediators' and arbiters' views of the organizational culture, this program became a "natural experiment" about different approaches to policy and the delivery of services as embodied in the two approaches. The participants moved carefully between them: making choices, getting into conflicts, tuning in and out, and dropping out or holding on for reasons that were often not obvious to all the staff.

CHAPTER TWO

Contested Organizational Cultures: Helping and Authority

Some social workers and teen mothers alike experience a lack of control over their social worlds and concurrently experience others as attempting to control them. They may, in turn, try to control someone else's life. Other teens and social workers feel they are in control of their lives and do not try to manipulate others. While many of the young women enrolled in this program felt helpless and saw others as trying to control their lives, the staff were divided between those who experience the social world as outside of their influence and those who feel they have some control and influence. After failing to show up for an entrance exam to a trade school one of the participants wished to attend, Bobbie explained,

> My mom forgot to wake me this morning but the kids got me up in enough time. My youngest was crying and both had wet diapers. I called my sister who was supposed to take care of them when I went to take the test but she said that she had to go out. I called the babies' father but he had some business so I tried my grandmother but she wasn't feeling well. It was already late by then, so I couldn't go.

Not only does the world appear beyond their control, but others seem to try continually to direct their lives for them.

> My mother is always trying to tell me how to raise my daughter. She says that I can't go out at night now because I got to take care of the baby but she goes out when she wants to. Then this social worker says that I better go back

to school but I got no one to take care of the baby and I always gets into trouble at school.

On the other hand, one young woman after three months in the program, signed up for professional training, obtained a loan to pay the
tuition, and started a two-year program without specific help or much
encouragement from the staff.

Some of the staff find themselves in similar situations of little control and power. An arbiter frequently mentioned to me how poorly
she was treated by sales people in department stores despite her efforts to present herself as conventional and middle class.

They always ignore me. One time I was standing there with
several things that I wanted to buy but I had a few questions. I think I wanted a blouse in another color or something. This girl looked at me, I saw her staring at me but
she wouldn't come over. I gave up and drove home in my
new car.

For these staff, the experience is different in the program. The same
workers who experience much of the social world as beyond their
control attempt to develop significant control within the program:
over what the other staff members and participants should and
should not do in the program.

While social experiences are linked to position in the social structure, that link is not necessarily tight. People in similar situations do
not necessarily experience them in the same manner. The mediators
feel much more in control of their social worlds. One explained,
"When I graduated from high school I left the area and took a job that
paid well. I had my daughter but her father was not the man I wanted
to marry and I decided I needed more education so I returned home
to go to school." These people make their own paths. These different
experiences are reflected in the manner in which they offer help and
work to construct the staff/participant relationship. The staff send
particular messages to the participants about social relations in the
wider society and how they are and should be connected to the social
world outside of their local community. Efforts by the staff to redirect
the lives of others may provide a basis for increasing independence
and self-regulation or may reinforce dependency and subordination.

Social experiences, so poignant on the microlevel, are intricately
linked to more macro social processes of social control through the
institutions in which people interact. For the staff members, the program is a place of work and establishes their position in the world of

employment, while for increasing numbers of teen mothers, participation in a social service program is one of the major links they have
beyond the local community to the wider society (Gartner and Reissman 1974). For both service providers and participants it may become
a central institution. The staff serve as links between the program
and its environment of state officials and programs and as translators
and communicators of program goals and rules to participants. The
participants are participants in an organization through which they
experience some connections with the larger world and through
which they hope to gain what is necessary to participate increasingly
in the wider society. What occurs in that organization is critical to all
but especially to those who have little power through access to traditional economic, social, and cultural options in this society, the teen
mothers.

Some sociologists argue that the provision of welfare confirms recipients on the periphery of society, but disagree as to why this occurs. Even those sociologists who see welfare and social service programs as potentially incorporating the poor into the mainstream
disagree on how and why change is possible. Some see the programs
as largely necessary for provision of instrumental skills and think that
the focus of resources should be largely on the provision of employment opportunities with sufficient pay to support a family (Wilson
1987). People will conform to American work habits when they have
the skills and jobs that pay enough to support a family. Others view
programs as potentially providing new values more consistent with
those of the wider society and feel the need to focus on resocialization. Young people and the poor need to be socialized to conform to
middle-class standards. Still others see the need for developing a society's ability to regulate itself (Janowitz 1975, 1978; Shalin 1986, 1988);
welfare extends financial support to all who need it, and voluntary
social service organizations provide some possibility for expanding
membership in the society and developing a unique self capable of
transcending a given social order. On the microlevel, empowerment
is necessary for the subgroup to regulate itself. In Meadian terms, the
generalized other must be increased so that the individuals can take
both a critical attitude toward themselves and the society while accepting the basic norms and values of the group. By becoming a participating member of various groups and developing a unique self
capable of transcending a given order, one can increase creative potential (Shalin 1986, 1988).

There is constant tension in any society between social order,
group differences, and an individual's independence. These different

views of the intent of social service programs express different views of the relationship between social order and individual conformity. Social order may mean conformity to a specific set of norms and values or maintenance through a constant series of negotiations embedded in situational exigencies and basic values. How much does a society need to provide for meaningful and clearly articulated roles? How much does the individual need to fit herself into such roles so that others can accept her as a full or complete member of the society? How can a social service program provide help and help to do what?

These questions have no easy answers and the existence of these dilemmas implies that we as a society have not fully achieved answers to moral questions about where we would like to be or which way we should move as a nation. What we do and do not do in our social welfare programs reflects, in part, our lack of a clear vision.[1] It is essential to carefully examine what social service programs communicate to their participants about themselves and what their relationships are and should be to the social world beyond the local neighborhood, the program, and the family. It is only by developing an understanding of what occurs at the microlevel of daily experience that we will begin to understand how the provision of social services affects people's lives.

To develop an understanding of what occurs on the microlevel of daily routines of social service programs, it is necessary to focus on (1) the organization's relationship to its environment; (2) how the staff of the organization translates the messages communicated by those controlling the money and designing the services; (3) how social service providers develop what "help" is, how it is communicated to those whom they serve, and in what particular type of relationship help is provided; (4) how the staff try to influence the participants to go along with their wishes; and (5) how the clients interpret the communications of the staff and act upon those interpretations. Organizations do not exist independently of their environments, nor do their environments totally control the nature of the organization and the messages sent to and interpreted by the participants in the organizations.

This analysis is embedded in specific images of organizations

1. Moreover, the differing interpretations by sociologists of the intent of welfare programs is embedded precisely in these dilemmas. In a sense, the extreme variations in sociological perspectives on the welfare system both reflect and may be a source of the diversity of views of what our social service programs *should* do. Not only do we have different ways of examining the social world, but that social world may be expressing different things in part depending upon the historical period and the level at which the phenomenon is examined.

and interaction. First, organizations more closely resemble "loosely coupled systems" than rational bureaucracies. This image is particularly valid for social service delivery systems with the many layers of policies and officials and the frequent lack of communication and supervision among the levels. Policy established at the federal or state level may not be tightly connected to communications by the line personnel to the people in or using the programs. Additionally, programs make up only one aspect of people's experiences. The personnel and participants are embedded in histories of experiences and these are brought to bear in interpreting and making sense out of what is going on in the program, thereby contributing to the experience within the ecological boundaries of the program. We know that even in total institutions in which the system is organized to strip people of their prior identities and thereby control inmates' lives, it is impossible to do so completely (Goffman 1961; Thomas 1984).

Second, most social service programs are oriented toward changing people or dealing with people whom this society has described as deficient. They are organizations for the small percentage of the population who have failed to get a hold on the American dream, are viewed by many as unfairly draining the resources of others, and are stigmatized. Any organization that wishes to change "core selves" is a moral organization (Kleinman and Fine 1979). It is an attempt to make people into what much of the society defines as productive or good citizens—people who work and pay taxes. Project GED was one such organization, but the staff could not collectively agree on the direction of change or how it should be accomplished. They never agreed on what "help" was, how it should be offered, and how to get the clients to go along.

Third, not only do sociologists develop models of and for behavior, but so do most people. The diversity of the models is exemplified in the messages sent by the arbiters and mediators to participants in their daily interactions and the different workers' stories about the world around them, especially the world of work. These distinctive folk models become especially clear as workers try to move participants off welfare and into the world of employment.

Social Service Programs and Organizational Metaphors

Much more of consequence occurs in social service organizations than the transfer of skills and information. As an organization that teaches only skills, it might be equivalent to that of a factory that produces cars or bolts. The product here is human change, which involves significant experiences, feelings, relationships, and interpretations both on the part of those to be changed—the participants—and on the part of those who are supposed to help and direct the change—the personnel.

What is the best metaphor to use to explore this type of organization on the microlevel? "Metaphors are ways of seeing things or naming them in terms of something else (usually a label or set of systematically related categories, taxonomies, or theories)" (Manning 1977, 209). Sometimes these metaphors obscure a portion of reality; at other points, they are revelatory. Many no longer regard the bureaucratic metaphor as particularly useful, especially for small social service organizations. That is, viewing organizations as rational efficiency models with relationships ordered by the structuring of roles, division of labor, rewards, job descriptions, authority of office, and evaluation no longer provides sufficient insights into many organizations. This metaphor for social service agencies generally was replaced in the 1960s by the human service model. Human service organizations were differentiated from other formal organizations by the raw materials (human beings), the problematical and ambiguous nature of the goals, the indeterminate technology, the staff-client relationship, and the lack of reliable and valid measures of effectiveness (Hasenfeld and English 1974). This metaphor, however, is not a general one for organizations as it distinguishes human service organizations largely by function—the processing and changing of human beings. As a metaphor, it places organizations that deal with people in a separate category from those producing inanimate products and obscures some of the similarities that all organizations possess. The organization is still regarded as structured, hierarchical, and goal-oriented, and not as negotiated by all participants. It is not as much a different approach to the study of organizations as an attempt to distinguish a type of organization.

Social service programs are made up of a continuous series of tasks, events, and interactions among personnel, among participants, and between participants and personnel. Increased evidence shows that groups are ordered through continuous negotiations both within (Maines 1977; Strauss 1978) and between organizations (Altheide 1989). This approach focuses on the actors' perspectives on the organizational experience (Fine 1984) and especially on the nonrational and noneconomic aspects of the organization. Structure is a relationship between people in the organization rather than a "social fact." Moreover, the structure is continually under revision, the negotiations are based on the way people perceive the structure in which they are embedded (Manning 1977), and people make continual adjustments to their situations (Fine 1984).

Of particular interest is the development of the concept of "loose coupling,"[2] alluded to earlier, which is particularly useful in understanding the possibility of the lack of a strong relationship between the stated mission and charter of the organization and what actually goes on.

> Loose coupling implies a lack of connection, or *slippage*, between organizational niches and the behaviors that are intended to bind organizational goals to organizational practices. The concept is useful to illustrate the degree to which individual discretion occurs, for example, in interpreting, enacting, negotiating, modifying, or simply ignoring explicit organizational policies. (Thomas 1983, 244)

Not only can the stated goals of the program become to some degree separated from daily interactions, but, as occurred in Project GED, the segments of the program can become separated until there is more than one "program" within the organization. Additionally, staff discussions at meetings about individual participants and their particular needs can become only loosely related to personnel's individual programming for and treatment of those participants on a daily basis.

It may be useful to merge the negotiated order and culture metaphor. The negotiated order metaphor focuses on the importance of meaning for understanding organizations (Fine 1984); however, it emphasizes the negotiations (Day and Day 1977; Hall and Hall 1982; Strauss 1978) more than the symbolic aspects of social relationships (Meyer and Rowen 1977; Smircich 1983a and 1983b; Van Maanen and Barley 1985). The negotiated order metaphor obscures some of the drama of organizational participation and the stability and repetitive nature of some of the interaction by not emphasizing the rituals, stories, and ceremonies that sometimes stop the flow and other times smooth the flow of daily life in the organization. The organizational culture metaphor focuses more closely on stories, rituals, symbols, and rules (Louis 1980a and 1980b) but often not on how the meanings are negotiated and evolve continuously. This metaphor tends to focus on the culture created by those in power, that is, unproblematic static

2. Weick (1979, 111) describes loose coupling: "if one of the variables is disturbed, the disturbance will tend to be limited rather than to ramify." It occurs when separate systems have little in common.

meanings determined by people in power. Culture is not seen as a possible means of those in a subordinate position to gain power (Kertzer 1988) nor as negotiated.

Focusing on the culture permits understanding of the expressive aspects of social relations and actions. Through an examination of the ritual actions that provide some of the forms for communication, both in terms of propriety and of certainty, one can see some of the more stable aspects of daily interaction. A ritual act is one that occurs with some regularity at a specific time or place and in a similar form with particular elements and with a high degree of convention (Manning 1977, 304). Ritual conduct may express something about the state of the individual, about the social order, and about what gives meaning to that order or the justification for that order (Manning 1977). It provides an understanding and interpretation of the social world. It is different than specific information provided to enable someone to do something.

Loosely Coupled Cultures
To understand what was going on in Project GED, it is useful to integrate the metaphors of negotiation and culture. The cultural perspective needs a better means to deal with the possibility of different groups within an organization creating alternative cultures, lack of agreements that are never resolved, continual negotiations and conflicts, and subordinates creating their own cultures. Symbols are what create the meat of ritual and they can be ambiguous or multivocal (Kertzer 1988). More than one group can participate in a ritual, but each constructs meaning differently and no agreement is necessarily achieved. Both those in power and those with less power contribute to culture and on either side use symbols to gain power. It is possible for alternative cultures to be under continual negotiation within one organization.

There is the possibility of a loosely coupled negotiated culture. Acts and social relations are negotiated but agreement on what they mean is not necessarily achieved. Culture and action are problematically related and cultures may be loosely connected. Meanings of, for example, the mission statement were negotiated but never worked out and more than one culture arose within the organization that was not segmented by position within the organization but by approaches to getting off welfare and views of the relationship between the individual and the social world—what that is and what it should be.

Developing shared cultures is problematic. Cultures may conflict or be only loosely connected. Cultures are often messy and loosely connected to what people do. On some occasions, even with a shared culture, all of the people cannot live up to the expected level. Sometimes agreements are achieved about when not to live up to one's shared understandings, but on other occasions this shared understanding is not achieved. People have to make choices about how to structure their experiences and make sense out of their lives; they do not all agree and, often enough, cannot even live up to their own standards. Here we will focus on various efforts to develop shared understandings: how efforts are made, when efforts come to fruition, when efforts fail, how these efforts are viewed from different sides, when deviations are excused, and when agreements cannot be lived up to.

Moral Embeddedness of Social Service Programs

Were poverty just a situation of having no money and were raising a child as a teen outside of the marriage relationship just an example of early single motherhood, perhaps social service programs could exist largely as instrumental, skill developing organizations. That they cannot exist solely as such can be illustrated by the public focus on teen mothers.

During the last decade, the media has focused the public's attention on teen mothers as a problem. Often cited is the figure of one million teen pregnancies and one-half million births. The rate of increase in the number of teenage mothers leveled off through most of the 1980s, and only then did authorities begin to recognize and publicly discuss teen motherhood as a major social problem. In a survey conducted in mid-1985 by Louis Harris Associates for Planned Parenthood Federation of America, 84 percent of the adults over eighteen considered births to teenagers to be a serious problem (*New York Times*, 5 November 1985, p. A12). Newspapers and news magazines continue to publish articles discussing the often related issues of teen and unwed motherhood. Headlines include "Now, One in Six Is Born out of Wedlock," "Unwed Mothers Accounting for Third of New York Births," "Reaching Out to Unwed Teen-age Fathers," or "Fight on Teen-age Pregnancy Asked."

The number of births to teen mothers every year does appear staggering, especially when compared to other Western nations where the rates of sexual activity do not differ significantly from that of the United States but where rates of pregnancy and teen motherhood are less than half of those in the United States (Jones et al. 1986; Katz

1989). For example, births to teen mothers (aged fifteen to nineteen) in the United States in 1985 were four times higher than in France, almost five times higher than in Sweden, and not quite twice as high as Britain (*Child Trends*, November 1988). Despite the disparity between the United States and other Western nations, the rate of births to teens decreased from 90 per 1,000 in 1955 to 50.6 in 1986. However, the rate began to climb again and increased to 58.1 in 1989 (*Child Trends*, January 1992).

Births to teens are not new, but some of the patterns are; moreover, the consequences appear important. What has changed most significantly is the increase in births to teen single mothers. Of all births to women under the age of twenty in 1986, 61 percent were to single mothers, that is, 49 percent of all births to white teens and 90 percent to black teens. This percent has doubled since 1970 but has increased more rapidly for whites than blacks (*Child Trends*, November 1988; Moore, Simms, and Betsey 1986). The birthrate of unmarried adolescent (aged fifteen to nineteen) black women dropped 13 percent between 1960 and 1970, while among whites it increased 27 percent. Nonetheless, for blacks, the births per 1,000 women between the ages of fifteen and nineteen rose from 76.5 in 1960 to 90.8 in 1970 and then declined to 83.0 in 1980 and increased to 92.0 in 1989; for whites, the rate rose from 6.6 in 1960 to 10.9 in 1970 to 16.0 in 1980 and to 22.0 in 1989 (Katz 1989). The trend of births to single mothers continues to grow. In 1987 the total percent of teen births to single mothers increased to 64 percent (*Child Trends*, September 1989).

Becoming a teen mother appears to have significant consequences. Indications are that teen mothers are more likely to drop out of school, to earn less, and to receive more welfare than those who delay child bearing (Card and Wise 1978; Hofferth 1987; McCarthy and Menkin 1979; Moore and Burt 1982; Moore and Waite 1977), though the differences are not as great as one might expect as many do graduate from high school and do work (Furstenberg, Brooks-Gunn, Morgan 1987). Additionally, teen mothers are more likely to have more children, to have low birth-weight babies (Children's Defense Fund 1985; *Child Trends*, November 1988), to have children closer together, and to have more out-of-wedlock births (Ford 1983, 268); however, Rank (1989) found that women on welfare between the ages of eighteen and forty-four had lower fertility rates than women who were not on welfare. Importantly, many come from families with few resources and they need other help.

All of this information, significant in and of itself, barely touches upon the variable in the "social problem" that is instrumental to the

/many/

success or failure of any (social service program intended to "help" solve the problem portrayed by the statistics. The local culture, and the more general culture of society at large, imbues the statistics with moral attributions, and an absence of moral attributions is not representative of the experiences of the poor or young single parents (Matza 1966; Waxman 1983).[3] Being jobless in a society that respects individual achievement and initiative and believes that anyone who tries and works hard enough can earn a living reflects upon one's moral character and may impact on daily interactions, particularly those of welfare recipients. Becoming a teen mother and not marrying also has moral significance where the expectation is that a woman should grow up and marry prior to having children. Any social service program that is set up to help a group of single teen mothers, most of whom receive welfare, is very likely to be perceived by the public as a moral organization.

Moreover, organizations are not autonomous from local cultures. Organizations are embedded in larger contexts and those worlds tend to penetrate the organizational boundaries. Organizations are generally permeable if not directly linked to their environments and people bring in interpretations of everyday life with which they make sense of actions within the organization. Not even the negotiations of prison cultures are impervious to understandings brought in from the outside (Giallombardo 1966; Thomas 1984). Both personnel and

---

3. Much of that focus may be based on or promote misconceptions of the data. Katz (1989, 216) has summarized some of the public *misconceptions* about teen mothers that exist despite contradictory data:

1. Adolescent pregnancy is an epidemic which shows no signs of abating.
2. The epidemic is spreading fastest among blacks.
3. Unmarried black mothers (especially adolescents) consume most of America's social welfare budget and drain public resources.
4. America's adolescents become pregnant so often for two primary reasons: they start to have sex earlier than their counterparts in other countries, and generous welfare benefits encourage them to become parents.
5. The easy availability of contraceptives and abortions along with sex education encourages adolescents to have sex and thereby increases the risk of pregnancy.
6. Adolescents lack the maturity to use contraceptives regularly.
7. Unmarried women with children comprise the core of a new, self-perpetuating underclass.

According to Katz (1989), the data demonstrate that the "epidemic" shows some signs of abating, particularly among blacks, and AFDC payments to teen mothers constitute a small percent of the AFDC budget which, including other cash transfers, make up .8 percent of the GNP or 2 percent of the share of GNP spent by the government (p. 216). Americans have high rates of teen births because of nonuse of birth control, not early sex, and most of the people who are very poor do not live in female-headed households, though a disproportionate percentage of female-headed households are poor.

participants have histories they bring with them which contribute to the shaping of their experiences within the program boundaries. Personnel have both their personal and professional experiences. Many of the participants have failed in the standard youth institutions (school), they have become mothers before the "appropriate" time as designated by much of the wider society, and they live on welfare benefits. With these experiences, the participants' sensitivity to and the potential for reading any action as having moral significance is great.

Social service organizations have a strong evaluative component. Symbols, rituals, stories, and interaction patterns that develop communicate messages about who the participants are: what kind of people the personnel think they are and should be. Interactions between personnel and participants may open to challenge the core self of the participants as the personnel instruct the participants about skills and about how they might organize their lives. Moral organizations (Kleinman and Fine 1979, 275) have personnel who "(1) share a moral rhetoric, (2) use this rhetoric to justify social control measures, and (3) actively engage in changing the core self of recruits." It is unnecessary, however, to limit the definition of an organization as a moral organization to the control of the personnel, and it is possible that the participants may interpret the actions of the personnel as attacking their core selves when the personnel use the rhetoric of learning or improving a skill. In this situation, the participants may read more into staffs' activities than purely technical or informational communications. As Kleinman and Fine (1979) note, they are using Becker's view that the morality of an act is determined by audience evaluation, which can be either the personnel or the participants. The participants may read morality when the personnel read instrumental, task-facilitating activities.

It is possible to have an organization in which shared meanings do not develop. One group may regard the performance of a ritual as merely ceremonial; another may regard it as justifying the moral order or as indicating something about the state of the individual. Sometimes actions performed to explain something, to provide information, or to accomplish a specific task can be interpreted as symbolic action, that is, as communicating a message about the social order, about the moral order, or about the individual receiving the information.

The individual may or may not be aware of what he or she is communicating, but unless it is attributed to error or lack of intention, the action may be read as communicating a message to the audience. In a moral organization there is a heightened sensitivity to others' cues and actions. People generally try to demonstrate and dramatize the way they wish to be seen by others and what they would like them to do. Goffman (1959) refers to these expressions or cues as "given" and "given off." There appear to be two elements that differentiate expressions "given" and "given off": the degree of intention attributed to the actor by the audience and whether the action was largely verbal (gives) or communication that occurred when the action was done for some other purpose (gives off).

> The first (gives) involves verbal symbols or their substitutes which he uses admittedly and solely to convey the information that he and the others are known to attach to these symbols. This is communication in the traditional and narrow sense. The second (gives off) involves a wide range of actions that others can treat as symptomatic of the actor, the expectation being that the action was performed for reasons other than the information conveyed in this way. (Goffman 1959, 2)

A third element seems to be implicit in the discussion and blurs the distinction between the two. While both can convey misinformation, "verbal symbols or their substitutes" also means relatively simple actions or material symbols that generally and readily convey a reasonably clear single meaning to those in the interaction; expressions "given off" may require more interpretive work and, given the complexity of the situation, therefore, may be more ambiguous and more open to multiple interpretations and multiple levels of meaning.

Ambiguity encourages multiple interpretations, particularly when actions are appraised in a broad context. While Goffman appears more concerned with the surface meaning that may be regarded as intentional by the audience, the audience may see a second more hidden or deeper meaning when they look at the larger context or the history of the relationship. This hidden meaning may be viewed by the audience as secret and, therefore, unintentionally revealed and more valid. This interpretation may blur Goffman's conceptualization but encourages the examination of the broader context of relationships in addition to the relationship in the context of the immediate situation. It may be that searching for additional meanings may occur in particular contexts, embedded in past experiences and dreams of the future. It is imperative in developing an understanding of social service programs to examine the cues of the actors and the meanings that the others attribute to those actions and cues. There is no necessary agreement between what ones says one meant and how the others interpret the same cues. The audience may give moral meaning to an action that might be, on the surface, solely the provision of information.

The Parameters of the Personnel/Participant Relation

I will argue that the construction of the personnel/participant relationship is critical (Bush 1988; Janowitz 1969; Perlman 1979). It is an asymmetrical relationship: the personnel are hired and paid to teach something to the participants who are voluntarily in the program to get something out of it, whether that is the free day care, a place to stay out of the rain, a GED, or new skills and ideas. These, among other factors, place some limits on the construction of the relationship, but many possible variations in such a relationship exist.

Frequently, studies of schools or social service organizations focus on the curriculum, the skills acquired, the arrangements of classrooms, or variables such as the size of the class or school. However, an analysis of such factors only provides a partial answer to the question about what goes on in a program or classroom. What is critical, particularly in organizations that have the potential for moral evaluations, is the nature of the relationship between personnel and participants (Janowitz 1969). As social actions and arrangements communicate something about actors' relations to one another, they convey meanings. Not only does how personnel attempt to construct that relationship say something about what they think of the participants, it also can influence how the participants evaluate the information that they receive from the personnel.

Not only is the immediate situation important, but the history of the relationship is critical in structuring the meaning of the present. How the relationship has been constructed sets some of the parameters for what can be said both on the side of the subordinate and the superordinate to maintain the routine of the interaction. For example, depending on the type of relationship established, two staff members may say the same thing to the participants and elicit a very different response as the relationship contributes to the construction of the meaning of the interaction. People interpret what others say and do in terms of how they view the established relationship.

Social work has not always focused on the personnel/participant relationship, but there are several different models of the degree of importance of that relationship and what it should be. In the 1960s and 1970s, much of the focus of social work was on the social problems of society and the task of social workers was to ameliorate the problems through organizing poor communities for protests or rent strikes; more recently, the focus has swung back to the individual client and the social worker as therapist.

A continuing dispute exists about the importance of the client/social worker relationship itself. The influential systems theory approach in social work argues that the social worker stands outside of the client's social system and is detached, objective, and interventionist (Hearn 1969). A second method, which uses an ecological systems approach (Germaine and Gitterman 1980), permits closer relations and reciprocity between clients and staff; however, the worker still plays a secondary reactive role in the relationship and is still very much in charge of the client's changes. The model still contains the cause and effect model (what the staff does effects changes in the client) with the worker in charge and in control of the relationship (Petr 1988). The relationship is determined by the roles of the individuals and is stable and unproblematic.

Focus on the importance of the relationship itself has not been significantly emphasized in the social work literature—with some important exceptions (Perlman 1979). According to Perlman (1979, 2) "'relationship' is a catalyst, an enabling dynamism in the support, nurture, and freeing of people's energies and motivations toward problem solving and the use of help." She sees the relationship as a motivator and enabler and as directly affecting what the social worker hopes to accomplish. Moreover, she emphasizes that relationships are a process and are continually evolving. This perspective on the importance of the relationship itself should place the worker and the client within the same framework of inevitable self-determination for the client (Petr 1988). It is the client who has ideas of what is best for her, and power and control rest more with the client (Petr 1988). However, it is incomplete and does not provide a model for what the social worker can or should do with or for the clients.

I will employ three analytical dimensions of social relationships to examine the personnel's relationships with the participants as they continuously interact and redefine that relationship. They are social distance, helping (direction and type of resource flow), and ways of claiming power. While these are analytically separate dimensions, they are often intricately interwoven in daily interaction and experience. Negotiations occur around these dimensions and, while many claims are asserted by personnel and responded to by participants, they are also made by participants and responded to by personnel.

Social Distance as Manipulable

The relative advantages of distance (objectivity and perspective) and closeness (adequate knowledge and understanding) have been debated in the fieldwork literature (Adler and Adler 1987; Horowitz 1986; Jules-Rosette 1978; Lofland and Lofland 1984; Mehan and Wood 1975; Schatzman and Strauss 1973). A number of studies have examined how social distance affects the client/professional relationship, especially its affect on the stability of their interactions (Kadushin 1962). Much research conceptualizes distance as either attitudinal or structural differences (membership in different communities with different role expectations, rates of interaction, separate values, and personal empathy). Indicators of social distance may be diverse and communicate more than one message to the audience. Moreover, most symbols that suggest social distance can be manipulated by playing up or down certain group memberships or linking people together by emphasizing certain symbols or employing others to create or maintain separation. Many characteristics and memberships are manipulable, including social class, age, and educational differences. Even racial and gender differences, in a society where both are crucial and indicate deep social divisions, can be emphasized or downplayed.

There is another dimension to distance which may be implied either directly or indirectly from the actions that imply social distance—the moral implications of the establishment of social distance. Some people behave as "normal-smiths" while others act like "deviant-smiths" (Lofland 1969, 212). "Normal-smiths communicate to him the message that, despite what Actor thinks of himself, despite what normal and deviant others think of him, there lurks within him underneath, after all, essentially a core of being that is normal" (Lofland 1969, 213). Emphasis on symbols that close the difference may be important in convincing a person (here, the participant) she is not trapped in a separate world from us "normal types" (here, the workers) so that her essential nature is not deviant.

On the other hand, it is possible that through communicating symbols of distance and difference, the staff may act as "deviant-smiths." They may begin to convince the participants that workers and participants live in two separate worlds and are different types of people, one deviant and the other conventional. While the attributions may not be totally persuasive, the implications of the personnel's treatment of the participants may impact upon the type of communications the participants may accept and reject. We will show how the mediators try to bridge the gap with the client while the arbiters tend to emphasize the distance between them.

Constructing Helping Relationships

Helping involves a reallocation of resources: money, material goods, information, advice, or emotional support. Help can be very specifically or more ambiguously related to outcome. The situation may be as focused as a doctor telling a patient to take a particular kind of pill on a specific schedule or the more ambiguous situation as when a counselor or social worker instructs the client to reorder her priorities and change the direction of her life. Additionally, a helping relationship is often embedded in other relationships: neighbors, friends, or kin. These relationships tend to continue after help is given and reciprocity occurs. Some is balanced reciprocity when the exchange is relatively rapid and small resources are involved (Sahlins 1972), for example, the exchange of babysitting responsibilities among neighbors. The relationship has the potential to evolve with continuous exchanges into one of friendship where generalized reciprocity, embedded in long-term relationships, may involve significant help without the need to reciprocate immediately.

In a personnel/participant relationship, help is the critical element and is the unique reason for that relation. It generally flows in one direction from the personnel to the client, distributed at her will, and does not necessarily involve reciprocity.[4] In an interaction, it is generally agreed who should benefit and "help" is an uncoerced interaction (Lenrow 1978). While this appears straightforward, there are many ways in which this relationship can be constructed between a professional helper and a client and is typically problematic (Friedson 1989).

Some argue there is inherent sociological ambivalence built into the client role (Merton, Merton, and Barber 1983) and attribute it to the normative structure of the role requirements of the client; for example, the client is dependent on the professional but lives in a culture that promotes the norm of independence and self-reliance or the client needs to reveal very personal facts and thoughts to the professional but has no confidence they will remain private. These ambivalences are based on the supposition that the professional has little

4. Experiments in social psychology have demonstrated that several factors affect the outcome of a situation when help is offered. The outcomes may depend in part on the relationship between the donor and the recipient (high- or low-resource donor) (Fisher and Nadler 1976) and the manner in which the aid is offered (freely or requested aid [Broll, Gross, Piliavin 1974], and positive or negative feedback [Nadler, Altman, Fisher 1979]). These factors were found to affect the mood ratings and self-evaluations of the recipients (Nadler, Altman, Fisher 1979) and whether they engaged in self-help behavior afterwards (Fisher and Nadler 1976). There are a number of theories that predict different relationships among these variables (see Fisher, Nadler and Whictcher-Alagna 1983).

room to maneuver and that relationships are determined by normative arrangements and are not negotiated between the two parties over time (Gergen and Gergen 1984). The professional is victim to her role requirements and is not a creative actor able to construct a relationship that may limit the degree of ambivalence experienced by the client; nor does the client negotiate.

"Help" does not imply a particular process about how help is to occur or what the relationship is between the donor and recipient. While asking for help does create the potential for dependence and the dependent person or group's vulnerability is exposed, the relationship is not necessarily determined by the fixed structure of the "help relationship," but may be emergent; the individuals and the situation mutually determine each other. The helper may communicate a variety of messages; while some may communicate meanings that exacerbate the dependence and vulnerability of the clients, others may help to minimize dependence and increase autonomy. Too often this relation is viewed as determined by the structure of the helping relation rather than negotiated and as static rather than emergent.

It is possible that the relationship could be defined by the personnel as unidirectional with all resources under their control to be distributed according to their own notions of need and fairness. This would fit the model described by Merton, Merton, and Barber (1983). The participants may have little or no say in what they would like or need from the relationship. In other words, there is little negotiation possible. This is the manner in which the arbiters offered their help to the young women of Project GED.

Mediators, however, work to construct a different type of helping relationship with the participation of the participants who communicate what they need to the personnel and together negotiate what is to be given by the personnel. Moreover, it is also possible that resources or information may be exchanged rather than a unidirectional distribution of what the personnel sees as available and necessary. The latter approach recognizes the client as an independent, self-motivated actor and is the model from which the mediators construct a relationship with the young mothers. The individual worker decides the manner in which she offers help.

Interpersonal styles are an important aspect of the "helping" relationship. Classes such as the GED, behavior modification, family life, and job readiness offer help from the personnel to the participants but "help" is communicated through a relationship which gives "help" meaning to the participants. Help is offered in different manners by the arbiters versus the mediators and the young women attribute very different appraisals and evaluations to the help proffered.

Power, Authority, and Persuasion
Problematic in any helping relationship, particularly one constructed by a professional and a client, is how the professional tries to influence the client to go along with what the professional desires, whether it is a very specific action such as cleaning up or a very ambiguous one such as changing the direction of her life. Offering help dramatizes who controls the resources and the degree of asymmetry. There is more than one way to try to get the client to do what the professional wants and the professional cannot be sure that the client will do what she is told or suggested to do.

What and how the helper in her position can say and do are shaped in part by constraints beyond the immediate interaction. Most professional helpers are embedded to some degree within an organization and are also trained and licensed in the profession. Both serve as sources of power and limits on that power. Doctors are constrained by their status as professionals; this occurs indirectly by their education and formal licensing procedures and directly through self-control, that is, "controlling their own behavior conscientiously by virtue of the training and dedication they gained from a long period of schooling" (Friedson 1975, 9). For example, they have traditionally relied on their professional status and license to induce patients to do "what the doctor orders." The doctor has the exclusive license to provide a variety of services, professional authority from all of the training, and also more social status than many of the clients (Friedson 1975) to compel the patient to comply with her wishes. Even doctors' authority has eroded and is more open to challenge by alternative experts and information.

While the welfare worker is largely constrained by her low-level position in a large rule-bound bureaucracy, she has a source of power: she can give and withhold benefits. As the "professional" status of social service providers is unclear—they have varied educational backgrounds and often no license—when they are not backed by bureaucratic authority as is the welfare worker, they may have weaker authority to compel. Just as the controls over them (supervision or social work professional training) are often limited, the sources of authority for the social service providers in this program were also limited. Moreover, unlike workers who decide on benefits and consequences for clients who have no options, the participants in Project GED had other program options.

The personnel have ideas about what they would like to have happen in the program and try to communicate that to the participants; however, it is possible and probable that personnel and participants will often disagree. How can the staff convince the participants that what they say is correct, that their priorities are valid, that the participants should act in particular ways so that their futures will take particular paths?

Under what conditions or in what situations do participants remain unconvinced and resist efforts to get them to go along? Embedded in the personnel/participant *relationship* are issues of power (Weber 1958). Clearly the personnel/participant relation is hierarchical, with the personnel as superordinates and the participants as subordinates. A structure of domination exists (Weber 1958). There is, however, more than one way for the personnel to try to construct such a relationship and each communicates a different message to the participants which may or may not convince them to go along. In face-to-face interaction a superordinate may have to convince the subordinate of her authority as the subordinate is not necessarily a passive recipient. Not everyone submits simply because they do not have the moral and social strength to resist (Horkheimer 1972). People are not necessarily incapable of making decisions, nor do they quiescently obey others' orders. Moreover, they may assess the message separately from the messenger.

While many people worry that authority promotes privatized access to truth and deters rational criticism of existing institutions, most view authority as necessary for establishing social order and collective activities (Lukes 1978; Weber 1958). This may be particularly valid for young people who have yet to become full-fledged members of the larger social world and for those who exist outside or on the periphery of mainstream society, such as the unemployed poor.

Thus, the question arises as to whether there is a particular type of micro-power relationship that may promote the independence and autonomy of subordinates rather than promoting submission to and dependency on authority. Are particular forms of power relations better for helping to develop good citizens who do not uncritically accept the authority of others and who can create a rational path for themselves in the social world in which they must live? Or do relationships embedded in authority necessarily reaffirm and perpetuate superordinate/subordinate relations, dependence, and unquestioning obedience? These questions are developed in the analysis of personnel/participant relations in Project GED.

Some people distinguish between power and authority based on whether or not collective goals, consensus, and cooperation exist. In this view, authority is embedded in collective goals, consensus, and cooperation; that is, subordinates follow without question because they have the same goals and they believe the superordinates have the right to tell them what to do. Power, on the other hand, is embedded in relationships when there are differing subgroup goals and competition, indicating that there will be some resistance by the subordinates (Dahl 1961; Hall 1985; Kemper and Collins 1990; Klockars 1984). While this division leaves open the possibility of evolution from power to authority and authority to power (Hall 1985), it sometimes leads to the argument that authority is merely the pleasant face of raw power. Symbols are used to maintain power by influencing the definition of the situation, which can lead to the voluntary following of the wishes of the superordinate (Hall 1985). Impression management can "disguise manipulation and simulate authority" (Hall 1985, 340). Defined this way, it would be almost impossible to separate the conditions when manipulation leads to consensus and when there is real agreement between the parties so that authority operates rather than power.

On the other hand, the division between power (coercion through negative sanctions) and status (voluntary compliance through rewards, benefits, and acceptance) (Kemper and Collins 1990) points out qualitatively different ways that people construct social relationships. This division views power as distinguishable and in opposition to status, which includes membership in a cultural community—"they share common frames of reference for conditions and emotions" (Kemper and Collins 1990, 34). The idea of membership in a cultural community is useful as one form of social control and motivation.

A more useful conceptualization is that authority is one form of power and persuasion, force, and manipulation are others (Wrong 1988). All are means by which an actor can achieve "an intended effect on another's behavior" (1988, 32). All power is maintained and strengthened through symbols and rituals (Kertzer 1988), as power must be communicated to others. Authority is not an abstraction seen in ritual and ceremony while power is physical, economic, and normative.[5] Authority is a form of power and can be claimed by holding out one's competence as superior, by threatening others, by holding back or giving out resources, or by holding up one's character or

5. "Decisions will be implemented if they are backed by authority and this involves the exercise of power. Authority therefore needs power: physical or economic or normative" (Cohen 1974, 77).

position as superior (Wrong 1988). Obedience to authority means the nonexercise of private judgment. The subordinate does it because she recognizes the public claims of the superordinate and has been instructed by that authority to do something. It is the source, that is, the perceived status, resources, or some personal attributes of the superordinate that enforces compliance (Wrong 1988, 35).

Persuasion, a different form of power, is less dependent on the relationship between the superordinate and subordinate than on the evaluation of the arguments by the listener (Wrong 1988). She follows because, after assessing the content of the communication against other knowledge, it makes sense to her to accept the information or follow through on the requested action. Compliance occurs not because of the source of the information but because of the independent evaluation of the strength and validity of the arguments.

While people may focus on claiming authority or using persuasion, they may go back and forth among different bases of claims of authority and between claims of authority and efforts to persuade. Some claims of authority tend to reinforce hierarchy between the personnel and participants, while persuasive arguments and other claims of authority make few distinctions or dramatizations of the hierarchy of the two groups. The symbols employed do more than work to get others to do what the superordinates want; they also communicate messages to the subordinates about the kind of people they are and their status in the wider society. In Project GED the forms of power claimed and employed varied significantly between the mediators who emphasized persuasion and the establishment of a community and the arbiters who claimed competency and often used manipulation and threats.

Communication of Folk Theories of the Individual and Society

Staff members translate what they see as the goals of the organization into what they do and say to the young women. To some that means training them to do such tasks as filling out a job application and passing the GED, while to others it means reassessing the participants' relationships to their mothers, boyfriends, children, and representatives of the wider society. Most important, in communicating what they hope the participants will learn, staff members communicate how the individual is linked to other social groups, institutions, and individuals. The personnel communicate their views of the social world in which the young women must try to find or make a place: what they view is the nature of the social order and how individuals fit in. While people may not clearly articulate this relationship, they act as though they have such a model which guides them through many complicated social relationships and situations and which observers can see in their social actions. It is not a psychological or attitudinal construct unobservable to outsiders, but through talk and action, others are allowed to appraise and evaluate others' views of how the individual fits into the social world.

A social service program is a unique situation in which to examine peoples' perspectives on the relation of the individual to society as much of what the staff communicates to the participants is what their relationships to the wider society are and should be. These are the staff members' folk theories (Andersen and Moore 1960; Kleinman 1984; Turner 1957) about how individuals do and should interact in the larger social world and how that social world constrains or frees individuals' actions. The staff communicate theories about how the social world operates; they expect others to act in accord with those theories; they evaluate others in terms of their success in that vision of the world; and they attribute moral success or failure based on that model.

What becomes clear from watching people interact and talk about interacting is that they do not all necessarily use the same theory. The different understandings and assumptions that people use when interacting are highlighted when they are attempting to motivate others to change themselves. They are, in fact, teaching a model of what an individual's relationship to the society should be. They talk about social norms and who the individual is in relation to institutions, groups, and other individuals. Through interaction with personnel, participants learn not only how they are supposed to act and what their relationships should be, but what kind of people the personnel think they are.

There were two distinct models of the individual's relation to society that were communicated to the clients. The first is implied in the actions of the arbiters and the second in those of the mediators. Each makes very different assumptions about what constitutes the relationship between the individual and society: what the rules are and who makes them, how rigid those rules are, what the relationship is between rules and action, who the person presented is versus the "real" person, and the ability of actors to create their own paths and relationships in the social world.

As the organizational cultures are only loosely coupled to policy prescription and the proposal, in order to understand what is going on, it is necessary to explore daily life in the program. We must explore the tensions among the organizational cultures that developed and the everyday experiences of the staff and participants. Moreover, it is essential to focus on how the cultures resonate with the participants' and staff's moral judgments, which are derived from their lived experiences, if we are going to understand why some programs appear to reaffirm the subordinate and dependent position of the poor and confirm their status on the periphery while others may provide the basis of independence and equality which contributes to further inclusion in the wider society.

PART TWO

Social Service Providers
and Teen Mothers

CHAPTER THREE

Social Service Providers' Problems of Social Identity

Staff meetings were held every Friday when the participants were allowed to use the day-care facilities but did not attend the program. Some meetings lasted for five hours, but others were shorter. Some were relatively friendly, but, as time passed, emotions became more public and the staff members openly expressed hostility toward each other and the program. Typically, the meeting had two parts: organizational issues and "staffing."

Roberta I don't like these changes in schedules. I don't like to be surprised and I will not be embarrassed in front of others. We have a routine with activities and it should be followed.

Wilma All the programs have an attendance problem. There is always a group who won't attend and another who attend sometimes.

Roberta We have a starting time and they are often late and many of the classes are not on time.

Jenna We have to build up something positive with trips and activities if we are going to do anything with the girls and we must tell the girls that if they are continually late they would get fired.

Roberta If they leave for lunch, they don't come back. That can't be tolerated.

Ivy We need to tell them that it is not a game even if we have to beg them to come back.

Roberta We are being too lax. We can't pamper them too much. This is our last chance to influence them.

The discussion continued with demands for more order within the program, but no one returned to the point of how to make the program more meaningful and interesting to the participants. This conversation is representative of the start of many meetings.

The second part of the meetings consisted of a discussion of several of the participants. One of the participants discussed on this day was Susie, an eighteen-year-old mother of one who had completed the eleventh grade but tested at a seventh-grade level.

> *Jenna* I think one of her strengths is her positive self-image . . . she doesn't seem to socialize with others too much but is independent and thinks for herself.
>
> *Roberta* It isn't too good to be too individualistic or you won't ever fit in well.
>
> *Ivy* Her weakness is that she is shy and stubborn and she doesn't seem to have any goals. [This seemed to disgust Ivy.]
>
> *John* She will have to work hard to pass her GED test because she is so far behind.
>
> *Jenna* That is not her goal—which is to be a good mother now and not to improve her economic situation immediately. She is collecting social security.

Afterwards we talked informally about being middle class and black. Roberta described not being waited on in local department stores when she wanted to purchase something or ask a question and also complained about blacks who were so upper class that they cut themselves off from all other blacks by socializing in exclusive clubs. In the same breath, she denigrated poor blacks who criticize anyone who tries to make it in the middle-class world.

When Jenna said that all blacks had to learn to deal with the problems of being black in a white-dominated society, Roberta replied that she did not like it when whites identified all blacks as being alike. She explained to me, "Some of us work very hard and have more education than whites." Her husband also held a professional position. While she explained that both of her children were unexpected and that she would not have them if she had to do it all over again, she stated on several occasions that she did not want her daughter to be identified with or to socialize with the program participants. She said she did not want her daughter pregnant before college. Jenna, whose daughter was in college, replied that she was proud to be black and that she tried to ignore incidents where she was not treated with respect.

As illustrated in these discussions and throughout the book, the arbiters and the mediators expressed very different ideas about what the program was and should be, what their own roles were and should be inside of the program, and how to make sense of their own life experiences and construct their identities in the wider society. Their interaction patterns with the young mothers were very different; much more was communicated to the young women through their interactions than the rules and skills of how to get a job or GED. Social characteristics, professional experience, and current program organization alone cannot completely "explain" these differences. In order to begin to understand how people in similar positions within one small organization create such different relationships with the participants, we must look not only at existing constraints and incentives but, more importantly, their views on who they are, what the organization should look like, and what social relationships should be like within such an organization.

There were some external constraints on the staff who were hired for this low-wage job. The staff's roles, however, were only minimally constrained by state officials supervision, by professional social work training, and by the mission statements. The arbiters believed that the evaluators, especially my presence, constrained what they did because, at times, some of the arbiters believed there was a chance for the program to continue if they received a positive evaluation. Moreover, the arbiters had to teach skills, which could be more readily measured than any changes which resulted from the mediators' classes about social relationships. With these minimal constraints, the staff had ample opportunity to develop different approaches to their work. While most of the staff had similar backgrounds of limited resources, they identified with different collectivities outside of the program, framed their experiences differently, and viewed their roles and social identities as social service providers distinctly.

Few Constraints or Status Symbols as Social Workers

In this small program the bureaucratic controls were weak and the supervision of staff minimal. While the lack of supervision may be more expected for other types of professionals, those groups tend to have stronger professional controls through licensing and extended educational requirements. Most of the staff members of Project GED had little professional training as social workers and no licenses. All graduated from college but made significantly less working for Project GED than public school teachers. All had worked in the social service or educational field for a substantial period of time.

Some might argue that what the social service providers do in the program is structured largely by their commitments to professionalism or staff role in the organization. While "social service provider" or "teacher" provides some parameters within which they experience the social world and for what they do in the program, the work role provides only that: parameters. While the weak parameters may be understood in part as the lack of specific social service provider education,[1] the profession of social work makes few clear statements about the nature of the work.

Working as a social service provider raises a question: how does one's occupation or job provide the basis or parameters for what one does? Does it constrain how one acts on the job through indicating what one should do or through identification with the occupation? The job of social worker is particularly problematic with its ambiguous definitions of boundaries and content, even to those who consider themselves professionals and who have worked as social workers for many years. Neither the public or social workers[2] agree what the work is or should be and the debate continues both at meetings of the social work association and in the journals (Brieland 1977). Some argue that social work is too diverse and ought to be restricted to casework while others see the future in expanding its boundaries.

1. All staff had similar levels of education and, while several had graduate degrees, none had graduate degrees in social work.

2. At a conference on social work, the proceedings of which were published in *Social Work* (1977), one person argued, "the mission of social work is to help produce effective people" (p. 382), while someone else said, "Perhaps we should move again into examining defects in society as the proper mission of social work" (p. 382). When asked what social workers do, responses ranged from "'Helping' is one of our favorite words, but helping doesn't refer to anything you do. It refers to the outcome . . ." (p. 383), to "[w]hat social work brings that is different is the ability to assess both the individual and the social context and to include immediate intermediate, and long-range planning in terms of mobilizing both the inner resources of clients, their support systems, and the environment. In the process, social workers also have the responsibility for identifying these gaps in the social system" (p. 383).

Others emphasized the wide range of activities done by workers. The conference presentations published in 1981 in *Social Work* again include a range of objectives from "help people enlarge competence" to "influence social and environmental policy" and "facilitate interactions between individuals and others in their environments" (Brieland 1981, 80). They specified areas or institutions in which social workers operated: family, mental health, health, schools, industrial social work, and aging (Brieland 1981, 80–81). During the 1980s, social workers increasingly opened up individual practices, targeting the family rather than the poor for services (Walz and Groze 1991, 502). This trend would tend to relegate jobs working with the poor in a diversified program to the bottom of the profession.

The ambiguity and disagreements on the part of the profession do not make for clear parameters about what social service providers should do.

While "helping" provides a loose frame, there are many ways that work role could be constructed within a program such as the one studied here, particularly as there was little specified by the supervisory staff or the proposal and the staff had little specific training in the field. By comparison, doctors and lawyers have established and generally understood means of further structuring their relationships with clients. They schedule appointments, have private office space, and lower-ranking staff work with them to guard against violations—the social service providers in the project had none of these things. Much of what the staff do and how they do it is up to the individual; these individual choices are framed by past experiences and the immediate situation within the program.

Additionally, social service workers have fewer symbols of established authority and position than many other professionals, and they generally do not have exclusive control over their services. They must develop power to convince others to go along. Moreover, while the doctor or lawyer has generally high social status and class ranking in comparison to many clients, the position of the social worker is significantly lower and may be closer to or identified with their clients. Social workers also may be looked down upon by other professionals. The lack of status makes claiming "professional" status difficult.

The different ways the personnel viewed their relationships as workers in relation to the organization and participants appear as much rooted in their views of themselves outside of the program as it was rooted in their images of themselves as workers. Self-controls developed from a wide variety of educational and personal experiences as men and women, blacks and whites struggling to develop identities that mattered, relationships with participants in the program, and an approach that could make the program work.

Membership in and Identification with Social Units: Class, Race, and Gender

In the United States, membership in and identification with social units is complex and often a highly problematic process (Hewitt 1989). While in some social units membership is clearly defined, in others, membership boundaries are more ambiguous. Moreover, there are many possible degrees of involvement (Hewitt 1989, 139). Identification with a group may also occur whether or not one meets the typical standards of membership, or identification may be weak even if all membership criteria are met. Membership need not be tightly connected to identification.

For those who have a publicly visible feature that identifies them as a member of a social unit that is often discriminated against by those in power, the dilemmas faced are significant. Today, race is such a social unit and a pivotal category (Lofland 1969) of social identity; it tends to dominate all other categories in terms of others' perceptions of those who are categorized as members. The criteria of class membership, however, are more difficult to specify. Not only do sociologists disagree as to those criteria but, for the public, membership criteria are ambiguous and diffuse. People use different sets of criteria to identify others as members of a social class and to identify themselves with a particular class. On the other hand, mothers and women as social units have quite clear membership criteria, yet identification with these social units varies in intensity. For some, the identification is a priority but not for all.

Many of the staff were black. All of them had achieved sufficient levels of education and income to be considered middle class by most others. While economic and some social opportunities have increased for minorities since the passage of the Civil Rights bill, discrimination still exists. As a group, moreover, the black middle class still has a lower income level than the white middle class, is more likely to be clustered in the lower-status white-collar jobs, has less wealth, and is more likely to live in mixed-class neighborhoods (Landry 1987). Being black, and in a relatively marginal economic situation with an ambiguously evaluated profession,[3] affects treatment by others, work opportunities, where one can buy a house, and one's social life. In the social world, the powerful are generally white, male, and rich and, in that world, to be female and black and not have much money does provide a particular experience. Blacks still suffer the indignities of race in public situations. All black staff members talked about experiences in which being black is the pivotal category of the interaction and were self-conscious of being black.

3. Here I mean that social workers are often not only regarded as nonprofessional but are sometimes stigmatized because of their clients (poor people) by members of the middle class who see them as welfare workers. It is generally unclear to many what social workers do that requires special skills.

Some studies show that the image of social workers is improving but that people said they would rarely use social workers as a resource and, instead, choose religious leaders, psychiatrists, and physicians (Condie et al. 1978).

Nevertheless, not everyone appraises and evaluates the experience in a similar fashion or manages it the same way. The relative importance and meaning of the identity attributes of race, class, and gender are developed from reflective, social, and symbolic activities; how the individual defines those interactions and activities and responds to them varies.

Not everyone sees or resolves the dilemmas in their lives in a similar manner. Being both black and middle class today may leave open the question of identification and to some extent, class membership. While sometimes not viewed as middle class by the outside white world and as middle-class traitors by the poor, some people may feel that they must choose between identifying as middle class or black through their associations and presentational styles.

As social service providers, membership in the middle class is minimally assured but still problematic. Much of the public has little knowledge of the field and tends to see social workers as welfare workers or just people who, without special skills or training, help (often ineffectively) others who should be able to help themselves (stigmatized client).[4] Without accountability, it may be difficult to allay the suspicions of the general public (Morris 1977), and there is a possibility of social contagion when the poor are a devalued group. This may be a particular problem working with teen mothers on welfare who are the focus of media attention, especially black teen mothers. These staff members are frequently confronted with situations in which being black cannot be taken for granted. However, identification as black, women, mothers, and middle class is differentially emphasized by the mediators and arbiters. The arbiters in the program emphasized their middle-class membership with both staff and participants, while the mediators tended to emphasize being women and mothers and, in the case of those who were black, being black.

We Identify as Middle Class: The Arbiters

The arbiters were concerned with others' perceptions of their membership in class and racial social units and worked hard to publicly dramatize their middle-class membership in the face of being seen as

---

4. Some people in our individualistic society believe that all are supposed to be able to help themselves, so that anyone who needs some government employee to help out is not defined as a successful individual or part of a responsible network. Social workers work with clients doing things the clients or their families have failed to do; that is, they work with failures who have no one to blame but themselves or their families. Some of that stigma may accrue to them. Interestingly, during the 1980s, there is evidence of a significant change in clientele of social workers from the poor and their problems to the middle class and their different problems (Walz and Groze 1991).

black first and often failing to receive the respect they deserved. Roberta often discussed the failure of clerks to wait on her in stores because of her blackness and complained that she, a middle-class, well-educated person, had to live in a working-class neighborhood full of pickup trucks and men who went to work without ties. She said she would never buy in a neighborhood again if she saw pickup trucks in the driveways. John stated that he lost a number of jobs because he was black, even though he had a graduate degree. Mr. Harrison always emphasized that he had done graduate work and his children were going to college, yet he was laid-off as a teacher. Being treated as black first rather than in terms of educational successes by the white society is a common experience for all the staff members.

The arbiters emphasized their middle-class status but were not fully successful in persuading others of that status, though they worked very hard to acquire and use the local symbols of middle-class status to distance themselves from the poor. They demonstrated great concern over dress. Not only was neatness important but styles should be as similar as possible to the local style of much of the middle class, that is, corduroy slacks with coordinated crew neck sweater for the participants and wrap around or A-line skirts with appliques for the older women. Appropriate dress was a common topic of conversation among the staff and between the arbiters and clients. Additionally, they constantly talked about fixing up their homes so that they would look like the examples in magazines and how important cars were in representing a person in the wider society. Everyone talked about getting a new car and some said that they felt embarrassed about the one they had presently. They made fun of my rusted tiny car. Roberta thought that furniture should be new and matching and was always scheming to get things redone in her home when her husband was away because he did not want to spend the money. Magazines were a source of ideas, but so were invitations to the homes of people they felt were "classy" or successful.

They expressed surprise that my house was not fancier or bigger. In their view, professors had high status and good salaries. Ivy, who lived a few blocks from me said, "You could afford to live bigger." Roberta said, "Your house isn't very big." They found it difficult to understand why I did not make use of more symbols of my class (education was an important indicator of class status to them) and were concerned that I did not use my title with the participants. This was particularly true for Mr. Harrison, who insisted upon the designation "Mr."

Membership in college sororities and fraternities and social clubs provided an important source of socializing and identification with the middle class. Roberta and Mr. Harrison remained active members after graduating from college, and when a community relations officer from the local office of a national firm came to talk to the participants, he and Roberta discussed the importance of their fraternities and sororities, the good times they had had in college, the yearly reunions, and who had become successful from their groups. In class, the arbiters told the participants how important it was to make connections through these types of groups and often discussed well-placed upper middle-class blacks in the local community and how many they knew personally.

High school social clubs were also very important in the worlds of Roberta and Mr. Harrison. Roberta wanted her daughter to join what she considered the classiest group so that she would interact with the "right people" and attend the "correct party" at the end of the year. When Roberta thought that she did not want to join, she was devastated and was very pleased several months later when her daughter was accepted and joined.

Sometimes they expressed the salience of middle-class identification in differentiating themselves both publicly and privately from the clients, both blacks and whites, as poor people. After the participants left, one of the topics concerned Roberta's and Ivy's opinions that the white clients in the program were no better than the blacks; all of them had similar family problems and difficulties in handling their children. On graduation day Roberta explained to the rest of the staff,

> Martha [white] is a power person and wouldn't ask for any-
> thing, which I don't mind, but Samantha [white] feels no
> need for help and is like the twins [black] who are hostile
> and are not agreeable to change. She didn't benefit from any
> of the components but thinks she knows more than anyone
> else. She also fought [like the blacks] two times and comes
> from the same background as the others.

Ivy continued to distance herself from the poor and replied that the poor whites were more prejudiced than anyone else. The arbiters continued to dramatize public symbols of middle-class status in the program to reaffirm their difference from the poor teens. The participants often criticized Ivy and Roberta for putting on airs and failing to understand their lives. The participants told Mr. Harrison they thought he acted as though he was better than they. In the face of these criticisms, the arbiters still emphasized their class differences from the young women in the program. While Roberta and Ivy were women and mothers, they never identified themselves as either in the program. The only time they discussed being wives was when they complained about their husbands. The major identity activities concerned class status for these staff members as they tried to make sense out of their social worlds and construct public identities with which they could feel comfortable.

We Identify as Women and Mothers: Mediators
In contrast, the black mediators said that they generally ignored incidents the arbiters defined as intentional acts of disrespect or saw the offenses as the offender's problem. Both Jenna and Esther lived in largely black urban communities and developed their own styles of presentation of self. None of their external symbols of self emphasized affiliation with a local group. For example, Esther liked to shop for clothes to find bargains in the secondhand shops and to refinish old furniture herself. While Jenna enjoyed a bargain, she dressed very stylishly, but also occasionally wore jeans to work. She and her husband renovated a town house. They do not appear to work to fit in to a particular group.

For those who are black, being black is a major indicator of identity and both Jenna and Esther followed black political leaders, discussed them with the participants, were themselves activists, and encouraged the young women to be politically active. Both became concerned when a problem was portrayed as a black issue in the media. They did not, however, define it as a class problem either. The problem rested with the behavior, rather than the class or race, of the person doing it. They felt that a television show on teen mothers portrayed it as a black problem, whereas they argued that becoming a mother was a problem for any teenager; she is not sufficiently mature or able to support herself and the baby financially.

All, including Amy and Becky, identified themselves publicly as women and mothers first and often talked with the young women and each other about their feelings and the problems they encountered as mothers. The mediators frequently talked about their children and how they work to enable them to make something out of their lives. Nonetheless, it was up to the children to make their own choices and take responsibility for them. They were more open with the participants and with me. After work we frequently talked about politics and our own decisions about careers, marriages, and relationships. We were all women and had some similar experiences despite differences in our backgrounds.

In the different interpretations of their personal situations it is possible to begin to see that the arbiters and mediators have different views of their places in the public world. Dramatization of their social identities embedded in symbols more of class or of gender were linked to their construction of identities and relationships within the program as workers.

As Staff Members

The arbiters and mediators dramatize very different identities in interacting with others, particularly within the program, and interpret situations in a manner consistent with those identities. The mediators' and arbiters' interpretations of the public grumbling of the participants when a man showing them around his company said something which offended the clients was different. The arbiters saw the response as disruptive, as indicating the low status of the participants and reflecting poorly on them (the arbiters). The mediators saw the behavior of the man as inappropriate and the young women's behavior as immature.

Cloak of Professionalism and Efficiency: The Arbiters
The arbiters had their own way of dealing with the ambiguity of their job as "a helping" relationship and as a "professional" occupation by trying to construct a strong "professional" identity and making the program as much like a formal bureaucratic organization as possible. They cloaked their working relations in the program in the language of professionalism and efficiency. Roberta was always talking about efficiency and straightening the file folders with correct forms in the appropriate order. The arbiters made up formal rules whenever possible in order to "make things go smoothly" and make it "like a real job." This statement indicated not only the symbolic work they had to do to make their jobs appear professional but the work involved in making the program site like a job site. They talked about dressing as professionals among themselves and generally arrived and left on schedule. Within the program they worked to define their activities, relationships, and identities as those of professionals.

Sometimes they had to fight to achieve the symbols of professionalism. Professionals have their own office space, and Ivy, Roberta, and John were angry that they had to fight and wait a long time to get partitions set up. They spent enormous amounts of staff meeting time talking about their lack of private office space and worried that they were not being treated like professionals and that they could not do their jobs efficiently without private rooms.

Relationships with the young women had to be defined "professionally"—that is, hierarchically, with significant social and physical distance, and formally. Much of what was defined as professional was defined in terms of what was not. It was important to act in a "professional" manner which, the arbiters explained, meant keeping their distance, not chatting informally, and not going out to lunch with the young women. They told me to stop eating with the young women. They never went across the street to the sandwich shop with the participants but sent the young women to the store to buy things for them, which they ate at the opposite end of the long table. They sat too far away to be overheard or, more typically, they sat behind the partitions. "Professionals do not wander around the streets with clients." I did and was told that I was "unprofessional" in my conduct.

The arbiters rarely identified themselves as social workers, but rather, as teachers, counselors, or job trainers. They taught skills: reading, math, how to fill out an application, and how to look for a job. Roberta always talked about her prior jobs as a GED teacher and her current job as the coordinator and the job prep teacher. Mr. Harrison and John saw themselves as teachers—working as GED instructors was only temporary. Mr. Harrison talked about being a high school teacher in a "real" school with students who "deserved his help." John always emphasized that he had been at a college. Ivy saw herself as a counselor and continually tried to eliminate all tasks she viewed as extending beyond the "counseling" (one-on-one) function, including recruitment and locating day care for the participants.

Efficiency and order was the rhetoric employed for not permitting several of the young women from the first session to continue into the second. They were disruptive, Roberta and Ivy argued, and might influence the new recruits. Students who were too far behind in school to pass the GED were a drain on their resources and, for the purpose of efficiency, should be ignored. When there was no official GED teacher present, organizing the materials so that the young women could work independently and directing them to knock on the door of the partition was efficient and orderly as "we have lots of other work to do," Roberta explained to me. Trips, on the other hand, were "disorderly" and not the most efficient way to inform the young women about different types of jobs. Roberta told the others that along with the fact that the young women embarrassed her, there were more "efficient" means, such as inviting people to speak or filmstrips, to inform them about jobs. With the state representative admonition to enroll forty clients, she was more concerned with whether they registered the forty required participants than with whether or not the enrollees attended. The rhetoric of efficiency and order permitted her to argue that spending time and effort to encourage attendance by making the program more exciting and meaningful or by finding the participants and persuading them to come was not a good use of staff time. They did not have enough staff to work with more than fifteen, forty would create disorder, they claimed.

Despite such vigorous efforts to appear as professionals, they received messages that they were not viewed as professionals by others; their salaries were poor, the status of social worker, as previously discussed, was unclear and often linked with negative associations, the clients failed to treat them with what they viewed as appropriate deference, and the state had insisted that a researcher be present, which they saw as an affront to their independence and professional status.

Rhetoric of Seniority and Community: The Mediators
The mediators dealt with the ambiguity of meaning and lack of work status by defining themselves as older, more experienced women and members of the same community as the young women, not as middle-class professionals. The development of a more egalitarian exchange relation permitted the tough public criticism that the mediators made of the young women's actions. They talked about membership in the same community as that of the young women, and reiterated that as women they had to act together to create a better place to live and to bring up their children. They did not work to distinguish their experiences from those of the participants.

In the mediators' sessions they talked about their own experiences growing up, the types of mistakes they had made, and the challenges they continued to face. They discussed their children, what they expected from them, and their unresolved dilemmas. All were expected to contribute to the topic under discussion and to respect each other. They were all mothers, women, workers, and, most important, they were all the same kind of people. When problems with some of the clients came up at staff meetings, they attributed problems to lack of maturity and the dilemmas faced with the need to be both a teen and a mother. They acknowledged that the young women had to accept more fully the responsibilities of motherhood while also acknowledging their needs as teens to have fun.

The mediators were directly concerned with a positive organizational culture rather than with developing a formal program structure. At staff meetings they talked about generating excitement, creating more symbolic links between the young women and the wider society, and emphasizing the importance of motherhood and responsibility for creating an environment conducive to the raising of children. They wanted more trips to job sites and occasions when children were brought to the program. They organized those few activities that were celebrations and linked the program to the world outside.

The mediators saw their role in the program as facilitators of discussions about new ideas and goals. They saw their jobs as working to broaden the perspectives of the young women by examining their actions and what they said about their future desires. This meant taking them out into the larger community, meeting many new people, and introducing as many new ideas as possible. The young women had to see themselves as members of the wider society under the tutelage of the program in order to expand their horizons.

Emphasizing Differences or Similarities

In establishing a social identity as a professional middle-class person by making claims of membership and identifying with middle-class style and in emphasizing their roles as professionals in the program, the arbiters emphasized difference, distance, and hierarchy. The arbiters constantly used a framework embedded in the role of the professional and in their views of themselves as middle-class persons in constructing their relationship with the clients.

The mediators, on the other hand, established their social identities as mothers and older women, which permitted and encouraged the young women to identify with and become increasingly involved in the wider society. The helping role was embedded in that of experience and seniority and a sense of membership and identification as a community of women developed to confront issues and work them out together. The differing views of the personnel/participant relations and the nature of the program also begin to communicate how the different aspects of one's life should fit together. The mediators and arbiters communicated conflicting views on how social worlds are and should be ordered, in addition to the place of the individual in the social world.

CHAPTER FOUR

Social Distance as a Strategy of Compliance

In the beginning of the second month of the first five-month session, discussions began about the graduation ceremony. One afternoon a spirited dispute erupted among the young women about whether they should wear caps and gowns to make it just like a high school graduation or whether it should be more informal. Several wanted to have a graduation dance, but others wanted to hold a fund-raising "kiddy disco" for children under thirteen to earn money for a band or nice refreshments after the ceremony.

A month later they were still having the same discussion.

> *Rickie* We can do it with cap and gown, ring and pictures. I lost the last three years of my life and I want something special. [She was nineteen and had two children.]
>
> *Ivy* We can borrow church robes but what about speakers?
>
> *Angela* We could try the 76ers and have dinner. [No one followed through on that suggestion.]
>
> *Rachel* May we bring our parents and our boyfriends? [This was later vetoed by Roberta who declared that she did not want a lot of confusion and babies around.]
>
> *Ronda* We need tickets so we don't get a lot of gate crashers. [A highly unlikely possibility.]

A spirited discussion followed about the timing and all agreed that they wanted it to be in the evening and claimed that they would be able to find rides.

> *Rickie* We can all go to the Blue Moon [a night club] afterwards.

August I won't go there.
Rickie We need trophies for things like attendance and GED.
Ronda No trophies.
August I might not pass [GED].
Ivy Who will speak?

Everyone agreed that they would like to ask Dr. James, but he was unable to attend. Several days later, still more than a month prior to the end of the session, Jenna set up committees with the participants and they all wrote down their assignments. With several different participants present, a repeat of the discussion about whether or not to wear gowns ensued, and this time the conclusion was that it should be more informal. The committees did little follow-up and, in the meantime, during the regular Friday staff meeting, Roberta decided that the affair should not be like a graduation. She felt that most would not complete their GEDs or anything else; no one would graduate from anything. It should be an informal affair without family present, without caps and gowns, and during the morning with some light refreshments afterwards. A more elaborate ceremony might be better, claimed Roberta, after the second session when all could be invited back. She did not negotiate or discuss the matter further with the staff or clients and the ceremony after the second session was less elaborate than after the first.

The last week of the first session seemed very difficult for all of the clients. Several complained that they did not know what to do because they did not have jobs and were too young to take the GED test. One said that she would go back to watching the soaps. There was quite a bit of yelling by clients who were usually quiet. The young women appeared very tense.

On the day of the "closing ceremony," all of the young women came dressed in jeans instead of the dresses that Roberta had told them to wear, while all the staff wore dresses. Rickie, a very bright regular participant, called at 9:45 to ask if the ceremony was at 1:00 P.M. Ivy was very annoyed that she called because "I saw Rickie yesterday and told her that the affair was at 10 A.M." Several of the regular participants failed to attend.

Several minutes before 10:00, half of the participants decided to buy sodas at the store across the street. Roberta refused to wait for them to return and Ivy started the ceremony with those few who remained by reading the comments of each of the participants about the program. The others returned to the ceremony at the point when each of the staff members was reciting a few words about how much she liked working with the clients. Roberta then read what each of the participants had told her they would like to do next.

Roberta called each young woman to the podium in the gym and gave her a flower and certificate while I took pictures. Upstairs in the program room, the participants and the directors of the different participating agencies ate cake and drank punch. Two of the state supervisors also attended and took pictures of themselves and the participants.

Though families had not been invited—in fact, the clients had been told *not* to bring any members of their families or friends—Ramona's mother attended, beaming throughout the entire ceremony. Afterwards she told me she had never believed that her daughter would receive a certificate she could frame to hang on the wall.

At 11:30, while all were still laughing and talking, Roberta announced they would be invited back for a real graduation in the fall and the bus was ready to pick up their children in day care and to take all of them home. Roberta immediately began to complain about the clients' failures to dress up and their tardiness when she had explicitly warned them she would start without them.

Through the process of creating this dramatic event which effectively ends their identities as clients, it is possible to see how the arbiters (Roberta, Ivy, John and Mr. Harrison) were able to impose their views of organization and the client role on both the other staff members and the young women; they demanded certain behavior and when they failed to elicit that behavior, they proceeded without negotiation. It is also clear that they were not totally successful in imposing the client role they tried to create on the young women. Most of the participants appeared not to accept fully the "client" identity, even those who received rewards for good performances. The failure to dress as the staff mandated at the closing ceremony dramatized the distance the participants wished to express between themselves and their performances as clients. Not only did the failure to dress dramatize the distance from the clients' identity but also symbolized their respect for those who had no "dress-up" clothes. While the trip to the store emphasized the rejection of the arbiter's authority, it also indicated their fear of not doing well in the future while they desired to do so.

This ceremony was the most dramatic symbol of the collective client identity for both the staff and the participants, yet it occurred only at the end of each session and emphasized more the completion of the program and the arbiters' view of themselves as disciplinary figures than the accomplishment of something which might lead to more training, more education, or a job. Roberta even refused to call it a graduation. To her, they really had not completed anything and most were going nowhere. According to Roberta and Ivy, many had not even been particularly good clients and the first session had been chaotic. For some of the young women, on the other hand, what the staff defined as chaos had been exciting and dramatic during the first part of the first session. They were also afraid and excited about what might happen in the future.

Social service workers often have the difficult job of convincing people what their problem is and to do new complex actions such as making new decisions or handling children in a different manner in order to correct what may be communicated by workers as "deficiencies." Moreover, they have fewer sources of established authority than doctors or lawyers and even welfare workers. In many situations involving professionals, the clientele rarely attempt to diagnose or cure their own problems; they just follow a few commands such as when to take some pills or how to answer certain questions in court. They do not need to know much about the law or medicine, though increasing numbers of clients are demanding to know and understand and will not follow orders unless they fully understand why, much to the dismay of some more traditional doctors and lawyers.

Convincing the clients to take the staff's definition of their problem and their recommendations places great weight on the staff/client relationship. Here we will explore the arbiters' efforts to establish control not only of the program but of the construction of a staff/client relationship through time and space segmentation, expression of competent and bureaucratic authority, and finally threats. The arbiters efforts to establish their authority to compel compliance were not always successful. They and the participants disagreed on the meanings of the symbols that communicated the nature of the staff/client relation to the client and some of the lines of action that being a client required. For the young women to accept the identity as a client meant accepting a demeaning identity, while failure to play the role meant risking being kicked out of the program. This chapter will demonstrate how the young women were able situationally to resolve this dilemma.

From Excitement and Disorder to Last Chance and Routine: The Arbiters Take Control

As the program did not have exclusive rights to the provision of services such as job readiness classes and GED preparations, the clients had alternatives. The staff, consequently, had to convince the clients to join and stay in the program. The approach changed from one of trying to generate excitement, interest, and strong client/staff relationships when Sarah was responsible to one of threatening the "last chance" and a concern for routine and order under Roberta's control.

When the first session began with Sarah directing it, the program was somewhat disorganized and chaotic, but everyone worked to learn something about each other. The staff and clients exchanged personal information at a rapid pace and no one quite knew what was going to happen next. On one of the first days, the participants cut out magazine pictures and constructed collages about who they were and what they would like to be and discussed them with the others. Most cut out pictures of children and talked about their kids and several found pictures of nurses, computer operators, and secretaries and explained that these were the jobs they wanted to do. Several included pictures of nice homes and talked about making a home for their children. The staff talked about their lives—their families, education, and what kinds of work they did. At the end of the day, the new clients chatted excitedly about what they were going to achieve as they left to pick up their children.

After Sarah left and Roberta replaced her, the arbiters explained to the clients that this was their last chance for success; that no alternatives would be available if they failed this time and did not get a GED or succeed sufficiently to get a job. "You are lucky to be getting a second chance. Not everyone is so lucky. We are here to give it to you," explained Roberta on one of her first days as coordinator and job readiness teacher. Whenever a client failed to follow through on the arbiter's instructions, "this is your last chance" was a common response. This became the dominant view espoused by the arbiters as they gained control of the program.

Loose Coupling: Little Supervision by the State
The state and the program were loosely coupled. As the program was new, the proposal lacked specificity and the funding agency and the participating agencies' supervision was minimal, the staff negotiated the construction of the organization, the flow of the movement through the program, the relationship between staff and participants, and the importance of the client role and identity in a hierarchy of roles and identities among themselves and with the participants.

Direct state supervision was limited and they rarely demanded strict accounts, and, if the representatives did, they did not act on them. The first staff meeting included representatives from the state and the four private sponsoring agencies who had written the proposal. It was one of the only meetings with representation from all of the agencies. Sarah had not yet been replaced by Roberta. Discussions concerned the need for good communications among the staff, for all staff to be flexible, and for recruitment to continue until they had forty participants. The heads of the cooperating agencies supported Georgia's statements and encouraged the staff to continue recruiting. Sarah continued until she left, though Ivy kept complaining that it was not in her job description. Roberta did very little even after the program received a letter from the state agency:

> In pre-contract meetings with the staff (of the coordinating agencies), we were repeatedly assured that such clients were already known to them and that finding these clients would be no problem. It is our contractual expectations that recruitment and outreach will be a joint coordinated, ongoing coalition.

Failure to ever have more than twenty-five in attendance, and rarely even that many, was never directly challenged. Most of Georgia's visits to the program started after Roberta arrived and were ritualistic: the event was well staged and thoroughly segmented from a "normal" day. Georgia provided her evaluations of the program to the staff. Roberta prepared the participants well: she told them to dress up, not to swear, and, the day before the event, what they were going to do. She counseled all of them to come except those who were unpredictable. She also developed some of the more successful and interesting activities for those days.

Despite any qualms that Georgia might have had, the program was funded for only one year and Georgia had no strong sanctions that she could have used against the staff except to dock their pay or fire them. She did, however, finally step in and tell the program that they had to fire the teacher, John. That pleased the line staff, who did not believe that they had the authority to fire and were sitting around waiting for someone to tell them what to do about his four-week absence.

The Arbiters Solidify Control: Subterfuge, Recruitment, and Retention
While the state provided boundaries on the activities of the staff, they were not severely limiting. Within the organization, the arbiters, particularly Roberta, gained control of the program and solidified their influence during the break between the two sessions by information

control, setting the schedule, and handling the recruiting. Roberta also discovered that they had the right to get rid of whomever they pleased and to reject any new clients they thought were "unfit" for the program.

The arbiters gained control in part through efforts to discredit the others. During the break between the two sessions, Georgia asked Roberta to have the staff prepare detailed outlines for each of the classes. Roberta and Ivy worked on theirs, but no one told Jenna what Georgia had asked for until the day of the meeting. When Jenna arrived at the meeting with a hastily prepared, overlapping outline, she was taken to task by Georgia for her failure. Jenna later explained that she had not been told and Georgia excused her, but Jenna told me that the incident cooled her to the entire project and she wanted nothing more to do with the other staff members and would just participate a bit at staff meetings and do her sessions. She entered the building, gathered the young women around her, disappeared downstairs with them, and generally left without talking to the arbiters, a change from the first session.

The retreat by the mediators from involvement in the organizational negotiations permitted Roberta and Ivy to control whom they made a client or suspended. At first they felt that their jobs depended on the state's evaluation of their maintenance of enrollments. Roberta wanted to expel several clients from the first session, but felt bound by the commitment to enroll forty. By the end of the second month of the first session, there were forty on the books, but at least fifteen of them had attended no more than two or three times. The daily attendance rarely exceeded twenty. When Georgia told her that any client could be suspended with proper documentation, Roberta began to weed out clients whose behavior did not fit her definition of what was appropriate, but she did so without discussing her decisions with Jenna or the other part-time staff.

During the break between the sessions, Roberta and Ivy recruited and picked only those clients they wished to have participate. They wanted no one with connections to the state agency that dealt with abused and neglected children and relied mostly on fliers they handed out in several public housing projects. Roberta knocked on some doors and handed them fliers. They went to no sources where they could find whites[1] or males. John and Mr. Harrison refused to become involved in recruitment.

They were never successful at achieving the goal of forty partici-

1. There were four white participants in the first session.

pants during the second session, but no one said anything. They had permission to continue clients from the first session who had started the program late and would have substantially increased the number of participants, but Roberta only asked a few to stay. Jenna thought several others would be good candidates for continuation because of their progress and lack of readiness to find work, but they were not asked back. When Jenna demanded to know why one of the young women she had suggested was not asked back, Roberta replied that she must have calculated the client's entry in the program wrong. Yet, Roberta made no attempt to re-enroll her and Jenna told me she felt sufficiently alienated such that it was not worth protesting.

The young women Roberta failed to ask back did not fit her model of the "good" client; they were assertive and tended to be loud. A set of twins, each of whom had a child within two months of each other two years before entering the program and were always together, were not permitted to attend the second session. They were tough, very poor, and had little strong adult support outside of the program. Their academic level of achievement was low, but they were beginning to work very hard to improve. In the beginning of the program neither would volunteer to read aloud, but by the end they often insisted on being first. They also began to contribute to discussions, demanded to be heard, and protested loudly if not called upon. While both had difficulty dealing with their children, they began to realize that what they did had an affect on how the children acted, to see changes in their children during their stays in the day-care facilities, and to want to learn more.

During a lunch between the sessions, Roberta told Ivy and me that she did not want too many from the first session because they might influence the second group with the bad habits of the first group, whom she regarded as being out of control. Roberta also stated that she no longer worried that the state might retract the funding as the second session had begun and she was convinced that it would not continue through another year. Discussions of recruitment after the second session started became largely symbolic as no one actually did much recruitment and attendance dwindled to a regular group of about six or seven by the last two months of the program. Why make an effort to get forty clients and retain difficult ones when there were no negative sanctions for failure or rewards for success?

Roberta increased her control over the orientation of the program when she participated in hiring Mr. Harrison (he insisted on a title), an acquaintance of hers, as the new GED teacher for the second session. Roberta, alone, explained the program to him and disparaged the mediators and their segments of the program even before he met them.

While the arbiters' actions dominated the construction of the organization's cultures, the others did not have to give up their own perspectives in this "loosely coupled" organization of minimal supervision. The mediators ran their classes as they wished. This permitted the arbiters and mediators to organize their relationships with the clients differently and to communicate different messages. The clients developed their own interpretations of staff's actions. The program cultures negotiated were frail, segmented, ambiguous, and often in conflict with each other and with cultures outside of the program.

Establishing a Client Role with the Arbiters

With the few rules created by the state and coordinating agencies and the limited supervision, there were few constraints on the construction of the staff/client relationship apart from the number of participants, the time frame, participant eligibility, and the types of program components. However, the staff were not exclusive gatekeepers to the services provided, and, as they had no licenses and no assured social status, they had few ready-made symbols with which to establish their relationships with the clients. Their authority had to be constructed based on their organizational positions and their competency claims.

There were several ways in which the arbiters attempted to establish a staff/client relationship and to provide the participants with a variety of tasks and symbols for appropriately playing the role they tried to script. This was a substantial change from the start of the program: arbiters attempted to establish social distance by controlling the timing and place of social interaction, they tried to develop competent authority by comparing their own and their friends' successes with the clients' failures, and they used their bureaucratic authority to establish rules and rituals for expected lines of action through the program and disallowed client input. While some of the rules and strategies were practical, it began to appear as though the disciplinary rules had become ends in themselves rather than a means to empowerment and "efficiency" was revealed as a means of establishing distance and authority.

Creating Social Distance: Scheduling and Spatial Divisions

In the first days of the program, classes and days rarely had specific official starts and endings. Sarah explained that they had to "go with the flow" and that things would improve later. When one of the part-time staff arrived, the other class would end. No two days were alike, and there were a number of special activities planned—such as visits to a workplace or a presentation by a special guest. The pace was fast, exhausting both staff and participants.

Roberta, however, wanted to make the program more like a work site. After Esther (a mediator who worked with Jenna) kept a "rap session" going for an extra forty-five minutes, Roberta complained to her that "in all companies you have to work by schedules and you must be on time or you will be docked. If we don't teach them to be on time, how will they get another chance to learn?" She wanted the program to begin at 9:30, with all of the clients ready to start classes, which had official beginnings and endings. She battled with the bus driver to get the clients to the program on time. The days soon settled into a more orderly routine with GED, job readiness, and behavior modification classes held during regular intervals and childcare class scheduled for most of the day on Thursday. The routine was only disrupted when John failed to show up for several weeks so that GED classes had to be reorganized and run by the other staff members. During the second session Roberta made up a poster of the class schedule and hung it up on the wall. The schedule was followed without interruption to the extent that no special trips or events were scheduled during the second session.

When the program first started, most of the classes took place in a large, high-ceiling, bright, undivided room. Ivy, John, and Sarah each had a desk at one end of the room where the telephone and some file drawers were also located. The other end of the room held several long tables that could be organized in a variety of ways, and they had a large movable blackboard. A basement room where Jenna often took her classes was available for use most days as were the gym and library. The long tables in the basement room were organized in a long rectangle so that all faced each other. The library, with its small tables and more comfortable chairs, would have been comfortable for private conversations.

Ivy continually complained in the first weeks of the program about the failure of the host organization to construct partitions around the staffs' desks as she could not counsel the clients without private quarters: "The girls won't tell me anything if they see that I don't have a private office. Everyone will find out what is happening in each other's lives." She reminded the staff of this at every Friday staff meeting until the work was completed about two months into the program. She could have gone downstairs for privacy. The partitions visibly separated the staff from the clients, but did not reach to the very high ceilings of the room and had no real doors. Anyone working quietly in the large room could not only hear voices but, if they tried to listen, could make out much of what was said.

Most important, the erection of the partitions successfully symbolized the asymmetrical relationship and distance that the arbiters desired. Anytime the clients wanted information or needed permission to do something, they were told to knock first and to ask permission to enter the area behind the partition. It made asking for help much more difficult as the helper had almost total control over the situation; only they had access to something that the clients wanted. The staff could and did often refuse a request or delay the delivery of the requested information or resources.

Further Distance: The Separation of the Lunch Period
Lunch tended to get earlier and longer as the year progressed during the second session. Sometimes a young woman hired to cook made hot dogs or some other simple food if the clients signed up in the morning when they came in. Often many of the young women crossed the street to a sandwich shop to buy a sub and soft drink to eat in the program building or, if the weather was nice, on the steps outside.

While the staff generally ate at the same time, they rarely sat or talked informally with the clients. Ivy, Roberta, and Mr. Harrison typically ate behind their partitions and John disappeared. Even when they ate at the long tables, they sat at the end opposite from the clients and talked among themselves. Lunchtime conversations with the participants were almost exclusively requests to go buy the arbiters' sandwiches.

In this way, the arbiters were able to control "program time" as formal and to relate to the clients only as staff members and not on an informal basis during a lunch break. The control and segmentation of time and space created not only the basis of a routine and control of the clients' activities but symbolized the social distance the arbitrators desired for the staff/client relationship. The establishment of social distance created a mystification of similarity of personhood.

Claims of Competent Authority: Invidious Comparisons
As they had few symbols of professional authority and few established symbols of social status, the arbiters had to construct their own symbols of authority. Most of the arbiters frequently attempted to

claim competence by comparing their own successes with the failures of the clients.

To the arbiters, any client setting foot in the program was automatically expected to leave her life outside of the program on the outside. Appropriate demeanor is instrumental in pulling off an acceptable public identity[2] according to the arbiters. The arbiters are particularly concerned with teaching the skills of demeanor and deference appropriate in their eyes for public places in which the public is largely middle class. Demeanor, according to Goffman (1967, 77), is what makes a person a safe interactant and is used to evaluate how well a person handles a position. It indicates through behavior, dress, and expressions in face-to-face situations an individual's discretion, sincerity, modesty, control of language, control over her own emotions, poise under pressure, etc.—that is, what makes her a desirable or less than desirable person.

To establish the notion of a proper public identity, Roberta vociferously compared her successful use of proper clothes to the clients' inability to dress appropriately. She linked the establishment of a proper public identity to her success in the middle-class world and their failure to establish a proper public identity to their failure in the wider society. Roberta always wore clothes that were appropriate to the local middle-class suburban crowd: wraparound or A-line skirts and blouses or cotton jerseys. She told them that they should dress her way while participating in the program and outside of it as well. They were not supposed to wear rubber shoes, blue jeans, or shorts. Several times she came in wearing a suit to tell them how she always impressed people at interviews with her well-chosen attire as opposed to the poor impressions they would make on a job interview. Rubber sandals showed people that they were poor and would permit others to treat them as inferior. She was critical of those who failed to meet her standards but did not differentiate between those who had no other clothes and those who were just sloppy.

Sometimes Roberta singled out those clients whom she thought dressed well. Several of the clients had already adopted "preppie" standards. Val and Matti explained to me that they had first seen "preppie" clothes when they were bussed to junior high school in a predominantly white neighborhood and thought this type of attire very pretty. Moreover, they thought these clothes always looked

2. I am using "public identity" here to distinguish it from Goffman's (1963) social identity. Here public identity indicates that social identity (the identity imputed by others) that is manifest in the world of work and in interaction with public middle-class institutions.

clean and didn't wear out very fast. Val explained, "As soon as I get some money together I'm going to get another one of those nice cloth purses with the wooden handles." They then went on to discuss the relative merits of brand-name baby clothes. Roberta frequently used Val as an example to the others of someone dressing well and would always place her where she could be seen when Roberta expected visitors, especially one time when a reporter was to attend the program to write a story.

More frequently, Roberta would criticize a failure to wear appropriate clothes by comparing it with what she would do. When one of the clients arrived in the afternoon after attending a morning funeral wearing light-colored pants, Roberta reacted by telling the client that her clothes were totally inappropriate. What were people going to think? She said, "*I* always have a black dress just in case I have to go to a funeral and *you* all should go out and buy one." One day a client came in with a safety pin replacing a button, and Roberta told them in a voice full of derision, "I always check my clothes before leaving my house. I don't care what you wear in there but when you go out you must be presentable. I don't want you coming in here like that. You can't wear that to an office or this program." Clothes gave off loud messages according to the arbiters and the arbiters own presentations gave off the correct message.

There were several other attributes necessary to achieving a proper public identity that the arbiters made known by comparing themselves to the clients. Roberta and Ivy delighted in telling the clients how they were never absent like the clients were. They had always been well thought of in their previous jobs. When a friend of Roberta's, who worked for a large corporation, came to speak, Roberta mentioned at least three times that he was a star employee and was never absent "like them." Smoking was not permitted except during breaks when almost all of the clients would light up a cigarette. Anytime someone would walk into a class with a cigarette, Ivy or Roberta would say, "I wouldn't do that." The arbiters constantly held themselves up as models of the correct public style for a client or worker.

Use of Bureaucratic Authority: Rules by Fiat
Within the program, according to the arbiters, a good client follows the rules imposed by the staff. While during the first session there had been several long, loud discussions with the clients about rules of demeanor, during the second session the rules were dramatized by the presentation of a typed booklet to each person.

During the first session, the spirit of collective efforts to develop rules provided some excitement. The lack of specific organization and formal articulation of rules was the basis for negotiations among the clients and between staff and clients. The negotiations were not always calm and dignified and generally took place during a "rap session."

After what Ivy referred to as an "ice-breaker exercise," the discussion turned to the rules.

> *Ivy* We've got to take care of some business. There was a complaint that there wasn't enough work [John had been absent] but we have that solved.
>
> *Ronda* I want to make a phone call [this was an attempt to disrupt the conversation].
>
> *Ivy* Later. We have to discuss some more rules and get your input. The van. . . .
>
> *Ronda* The van shouldn't wait on you.
>
> *August* It does on me.
>
> *Ivy* Swearing . . .
>
> *Val* I don't curse . . . well out on the street when I get real mad . . .
>
> *August* It's just a slip.
>
> *Tammy* My sister swears every other word. I just walk out. It's worse to talk like that as women. . . .
>
> *Jenna* Everyone's an adult and we can't do anything about it but point it out and reinforce that you really shouldn't do it.
>
> *Ivy* Agreed?
>
> *All* Yes.
>
> *Ivy* Roberta said that we would call the cops if you fight.
>
> *Rickie* We're all friends. Why would we fight?
>
> *August* I don't fight.
>
> *Sharon* She just means that it isn't worth it to put your hands on anyone when you have a child to bring up. I'll talk it down. In the next fight I have, I'll kill.
>
> *Ivy* No eating, drinking, or smoking during class. For two weeks of continuous absenteeism, you are dropped.
>
> *Tammy* What about illness . . .

A month later many of these topics were discussed again. One day the bus and coffee rules were the topic of a rather heated discussion. Sharon explained that she was upset by the others' misbehavior on the bus and Kim argued that she didn't know that there were any rules. Then Tina was accused of snitching and everyone began to talk at once. Tina referred to the others as chicks and Ronda yelled that they were not chicks, "I'm Ronda." Then the argument turned to the payment for coffee. Some complained that others were not paying, but instead of discussing the topic, Roberta used her position as co-ordinator to decide on her own to discontinue the availability of coffee.

There was little agreement about the meaning of the heated discussions between staff and clients. After the discussion, the young women ran out to the bus and continued to talk enthusiastically about how they should behave on the bus and that everyone should be ready in the morning. The arbiters, on the other hand, seemed demoralized by the afternoon, and Roberta said that they would have to set up strict rules or the clients would never learn to behave appropriately and that this type of freewheeling discussion was very destructive for the clients. She determined that afternoon to set up and present rules for clients.

The importance of having rules for the clients to follow was dramatized by the arbiters in Friday's staff meetings.

Ivy We have to set rules.

John Lots of them are misfits and we got to deal with that.

Jenna They have to learn to see that their behavior is counterproductive. They are all adults. We have to deal with negative attitudes. [She is arguing against fixed rules and for developing a community of mothers.]

John We have to write some rules.

Ivy About class attendance, class demeanor, leave permission, arrival time, bus behavior . . .

Following the meeting that took place a week after her determination to write up the rules, Roberta asked me what I thought of the meeting and I replied that I thought the young women were doing very well. She became what I interpreted as defensive and said that they needed to learn how to follow rules because they were so "disadvantaged."

This concern for rules by Roberta and Ivy began to shape the program. In the second session, Roberta and Ivy handed out a manual to all of the new participants that the two had done without other input during the three-week break. The start of the second session was orderly and uneventful. Roberta and Ivy made a big poster of the schedule and hung it on the wall. Everyone knew where to go and when though classes scheduled for an hour often would last for forty minutes. The clients, while waiting for the next class or the bus, talked among themselves and would sometimes do more problems in their workbooks. They also played "Hang Man" frequently at the end of the day.

While time and space divisions and paired comparisons contributed to establishing a daily routine, the arbiters, without client participation, established bureaucratic rules and rituals to convince the participants to perform the role of the client well and to set role parameters which, in the view of the arbiters, were a prerequisite to decreasing welfare dependency. When a participant stepped through the door she became a client, and that entailed a change in behavior. There was a dramatic opening to the day. Upon entering the program, the client signed in, first on pieces of paper and then on a formal chart during the second session. Attendance coupled the program to some extent with the state agency and its importance was symbolized by a large attendance chart to sign when the clients arrived and again when they left. Sometimes they signed the chart and sometimes they did not. Attendance did not improve with the more formal procedures. Schedules were mapped out carefully as were the specific places where activities occurred in order to compel the clients to move smoothly through time and space into the program, through the day, and through its five-month duration.

In order to compel attendance during the second session, the arbiters started giving prizes for the best attendance. Ivy permitted the clients to pick out a piece of inexpensive jewelry from a box she had. The clients, during the first session, had discussed attendance and were in favor of some reward for perfect attendance, but had wanted the prize to be a box of "Pampers" or something for their children. The second group received the jewelry prizes but had not participated in deciding what behavior should be rewarded or what the prizes should be. Roberta gave them awards for student of the week and for perfect attendance. Choosing the particular piece of jewelry was always an exciting event and the clients often wore it or gave it to their mothers. When the clients discussed a desired reward, none was forthcoming, yet when no negotiations took place, it was given by administrative fiat.

Much of the authority that the arbiters claimed arose from their role as staff in the organization and they used it to try to construct a strong client role, one central to the young women. The arbiters increasingly took control over the development and application of rules and the distribution and definition of rewards and punishments. The organization of the program provides some of the information about how the participants are to move through the program and what the relationship of clients to the arbiters is supposed to be. In participating in the program, the clients start the day at a specific time and place and follow a routine until the end of the day. There is no necessary moral meaning attached to the staff/client asymmetry; the staff have a legitimate organizational position and assume special competence to impart skills and information.

Coercion Attempts: Owing Deference
Help flowed from the arbiter to the client, and deference was demanded of the clients to the arbiters. Goffman defines deference as "that component of activity which functions as a symbolic means by which appreciation is regularly conveyed *to* a recipient *of* this recipient, or of something of which this recipient is taken as a symbol, extension, or agent" (1967, 56). It implies regard, respect, trust, and affection. The arbiters argued in the staff meetings that it was their right to demand deference from the clients. A good client learns that the public presentation of self includes deferring to those above her.

After a case staffing, a discussion of some problems with the day-care forms, and an argument as to whether Ivy was responsible for all of the forms, the meeting turned to one of the issues that Roberta and Ivy continually worried about, respect. Ivy was very upset and said that she did not like the way things were going.

> *Roberta* I am not going to tolerate disrespect from the girls. Respect is the key and we have to demand it. It isn't fair to us.
> *Ivy* They talk to John any way they want.
> *Roberta* They say they could leave anytime. I won't tolerate their attitudes and we're here to help them.
> *Ivy* We have to set rules we can enforce.
> *Roberta* I'll present rules to Wilma for her approval. They weren't ready to go on a trip. They were writing while someone was talking.
> *Ivy* They were disrespectful to Pat yesterday. They take as much as they can. They shouldn't be eating when lunch is over.
> *John* You shouldn't be shocked.
> *Roberta* We can't baby them.
> *Ivy* They take as much as they can.
> *Roberta* They were looking at pictures in class and it made me angry.

Phrases such as "I'm coordinator so I can kick you out" were common threats elicited by behavior that appeared to demonstrate a lack of respect. But, on most occasions, they were not acted upon, in part, because the arbiters still felt that they had to come fairly close to the state's demand for an enrollment of forty. Roberta explained her first termination at a staff meeting.

> *Roberta* I'm proud to say I made the first termination this week.
>
> *Ivy* She [the client] took over. We said she wouldn't last long because she came for a letter for food stamps.
>
> *Becky* Explain the fight incident.
>
> *Jenna* I had an incident. Her body language showed that she wanted to control. I let her know that she wasn't going to control me and then she behaved. [She negotiated with the client to calm down and listen. I had seen it work very effectively.]
>
> *Roberta* [A bit on the defensive] I had to put her out. She had leadership potential but used it negatively. The students were supportive of my dropping her [I never heard any student say anything supportive of Roberta's action].
>
> *Ivy* Her motive was money [Roberta said after the meeting that they did not believe she was pregnant] because she was the youngest and just turned eighteen so her mother needed the new welfare source.
>
> *Roberta* The staff is documenting two other cases for termination.

Demeanor demonstrating respect was owed to the arbiters. If Roberta did not like how the clients behaved while a guest was present, she would say, "You are making me look bad by falling asleep in class or talking in class." That is, their poor demeanor indicated they were failing to give her the respect she thought that she deserved. She was furious on several occasions when someone failed to sit still or ate during a talk. Once, during a particularly uninteresting and painful talk (the woman's voice was extremely flat and she could barely complete a sentence), Cindy, who was seven months pregnant, fell asleep. The anger directed at the clients was not for failing to measure up or for demonstrating undesirable qualities, but because they had embarrassed Roberta. She was the one who suffered the loss of the visitor's respect because of the clients' behavior. The evaluation is not in the interest of the clients but in the interest of the staff—not for the governed but the governors. It is difficult to get others to go along when the link of "common interest" appears to be that of the superordinate only, for whom the subordinates are "screwing it up." The arbiters felt that they had already earned the symbols necessary for the clients to demonstrate deferential behavior; they did not have to earn it. When they did not receive the respect they expected, they demanded it by threatening the participants.

Client Performance Violations: Real World Exigencies

While the young women rarely violated the obvious parameters of client performance such as polite interaction, signing in, and dressing well, when they violated arguably the most important parameter, attendance, it was often as a response to real world exigencies, not to the role of client or client/staff interaction. The arbiters, however, did not distinguish between rule violations that arose from lack of choice and others that did. For example, many of the clients owned little or inappropriate clothing. Shorts that Roberta thought were too short or old jeans with patches were sometimes the only clean clothes among the few things they owned. Roberta thought that Martha was wearing old jeans just to spite her and complained to her that she should dress better. I went to Martha's house and she did not own anything else; all of her resources went to clothe and feed her daughter (she refused to ask for welfare). This was true for a number of the clients.

There were also many real problems that kept the clients from attending. Babies became ill and needed to be taken to the doctor on days other than Friday. Sometimes the mothers had no one to stay home with a child too sick for day care. On other occasions a sister needed the client to do childcare, or some other family business kept them away from the program, such as court dates and funerals. One young woman's child was placed in a day-care center where one of the aide's children had the same father as her daughter. She felt that she could not leave her daughter with that aide and, when Ivy refused to change the day-care assignment, she left the program.

The arbiters appraised these failures to perform the client role as resulting from welfare dependency and irresponsibility. "Girls are the most difficult group to work with. When I have boys, they always are more motivated and directed." "Welfare makes them irresponsible and they have to want to come." These types of statements were frequent and generally received support by arbiters. The arbiters rarely distinguished between failure to perform the client role because of real world exigencies and active choice. The failure to acknowledge this difference contributed to the young women's rejection of the client identity.

Loosening the Grip of the Client Role: The Clients' Views of Staff/Client Relations

Whereas some identities such as homelessness (Snow and Anderson 1987) have a generally understood moral evaluation as either stigmatized or worthwhile and valuable, such as motherhood, the client role does not necessarily imply a moral evaluation. Before tasklike activities "can become an identity-providing role, these activities must be clothed in a moral performance of some kind" (Goffman 1961, 101). Clients of doctors who go for a yearly physical or clients who go to a lawyer to draw up a will or to settle on a house do not typically experience the relationship as having moral significance. Whether moral judgments are made about clients depends on the situation and particular construction of the relationship in which the client identity is embedded.

The client of a social worker has a greater chance of experiencing the relationship in moral terms as people generally go to social workers when they have failed elsewhere in doing something that others expect them to do in another setting (get an education in the schools) or obtain elsewhere (money through a job or inheritance). Most of the content of the behavior expected from a client by the arbiters has little moral content; however, the clients' interpretation of how the arbiters viewed them as clients had negative moral implications even when they received praise and material rewards for a good performance. It is embedded in the way the arbiters structured the staff/client relationship.

While the arbiters told the clients that the staff/client relationship was instrumental and that they respected the young women, the clients had distinctive views about the meaning of that relationship. The rhetoric of what the arbiters said and what the clients heard differed considerably. The clients talked about the arbiters' views of them as clients in terms of dependency and subordination, that is, unable to think for themselves. This interpretation of the arbiters' actions indicated to the clients that they were unworthy of the arbiters' respect.

For example, while the staff saw the partitions as increasing their sense of order and privacy, the clients saw these partitions differently. When the partitions went up, they hid the staff and the arbiters' desks from the rest of the room. Having to knock on the partition in order to ask permission to speak to the staff and then being asked to wait increases experiences of dependency. One discussion took place during lunch while the clients and I were gathered around one table and Ivy and Roberta were, as usual, eating lunch and talking behind

Roberta's partition. Sharon explained her feelings about Ivy and Roberta: "They're scared of us. They sit at their desks and hide in the corner and eat lunch together. They want us when they want us to go to the store for them." This position was juxtaposed with her interpretation of the young women's relation with Jenna, a mediator, as she then went on to explain why they liked Jenna: "She always asks if we like what we're doing and if we want to do something different. She cares what we think." On another occasion, Ronda again said, "They [Roberta, Ivy, and John] don't think we is good enough to eat with them. We just go to the store for them." It appeared to the clients that they were always in a subordinate and dependent position and had to take orders. Moreover, no matter what their demeanor was, proper or improper, they received no respect from the arbiters.

The subordinate, dependent position that the clients experienced also dramatized that the arbiters did not demonstrate respect for the clients. The clients often extended courtesy to the arbiters. For example, Bobbie always said "good morning" to Mr. Harrison, but he often did not even reply. Once she became very angry and talked about it for the rest of the day. Marge, one of the best clients according to the arbiters, burst into tears after Roberta referred to her as "you girl." The arbiters communicated that they were owed respect because of their position, but that they did not have to return the respect they were paid.

The dilemma between the lack of desire to see oneself as a client (dependent and subordinate) who could not command respect, while continuing to behave in a sufficiently appropriate manner to be allowed to complete the program is dramatized in problematic situations where following the expectations of the arbiters is judged impossible. These situations dramatize the meaning of the staff/client relationship that is communicated to the clients and the clients' rejection of that identity. They publicly challenged the arbiters and made it clear that other roles were more salient. They evaluated these situations as requiring them to resolve the dilemma between the need to follow the behavior and expectations established by arbiters and not wanting to be seen as the type of people who were clients. They did so by establishing that they did not want to be seen as clients and, in doing so, risked the ire of the arbiters and suspension.

Challenges to Staff Authority: Rejection of Client Identity

Most of the time the young women played along, but at times they rejected the subordinate and dependent relationship and challenged the authority of the arbiters. These young women attend voluntarily and do want help in getting on with their lives to find employment to support their children. A core group attended regularly and several would arrive on their own when the bus failed to pick them up. The clients did believe that this was one of the last chances that they would have to succeed and were frightened of not making it—as they were when they ran out to the store when the closing program was to start. Performing a role[3] is different than accepting the evaluations of who one is as a person, which may be communicated in the relationship in which the role is played.

When Competency Is Assessed by Additional Information
Claims of competent authority are not automatically accepted by subordinates. In certain situations competency must be demonstrated and the assessed failure to demonstrate this may lead to questioning the authority claimed. As all information and directives flowed from the arbiters to the clients and the arbiters continually held themselves up as correct and successful compared with the clients as failures, the clients saw themselves as being judged as passive and inferior.

At times they believed this evaluation; however, obtaining knowledge garnered from alternative sources made following the authority of the arbiters questionable and provided an opportunity to challenge the dependent, passive role expected by the arbiters. The clients reversed their positions as inferior and dependent by taking on the position of instructor after Ivy demonstrated her lack of knowledge, par-

3. Failure to accept the personal identity of client when they generally play the role is inconsistent with the role/identity (structural) model (Stryker 1968 and 1980; Weigert et al. 1986) in which identity is created by one's role performance and one's self is created as a result. Identity is composed of internalized positional designations. If participants play the role of client, then the client identity becomes part of the self and one then plays the part of a client to validate one's identity as a client.

The situation explicated here is more consistent with the processual view of Snow and Anderson (1987), in which they argue that the self plays an active role in the creation of identities and that there is a problematic relation between role-based social identities (imputations by others to place actors as social objects) and personal identity (meanings attributed to the self by the actor). If the social identity is positively affirmed by the other, then the personal identity likely will be consistent, but not if the social identity is negatively evaluated; on the other hand, Snow and Anderson (1987) argue that when a role-based social identity is positively evaluated by others, the identity will be accepted as a personal identity. Even those who did well and were rewarded by the staff failed to accept fully the client identity as a personal identity. That is, there appear to be problematic relationships among playing a role and receiving an evaluation of how well that identity has been mastered and accepting it as an identity. The inconsistency between being evaluated highly for playing a role well and then not accepting it as a personal identity can be understood in terms of the meanings of the relationship (the appraisals and evaluations that the person understands that the others in the relationship have given to those who perform that role).

ticularly of the world in which the clients lived, in her presentation about the dangers of drugs. After she showed a rather old movie, Ivy tried to direct a discussion about the film. When she mispronounced the names of several drugs and failed to know any of the street names for them, the clients set about trying to correct her. She also innocently asked whether it was possible to get bad drugs. Several of the young women opened their eyes wide in astonishment and described the problem in detail. But when she tried to revert to the "in control" role and asked them to discuss the film, no one said anything. Ivy then said that she was not aware of the extent that TV commercials encouraged drug usage, but no one volunteered to discuss anything. After Ivy ended the class early, the clients said she seemed very naive and they did not have anything to say to her because she was always so shocked by what they said. Marge said, "She doesn't want to hear it anyway."

Sometimes the clients held up an alternative source of information as more expert. On one occasion Ivy gave them an article on child abuse to read, but they did not read it before class. She interpreted the clients' lack of willingness to do homework as a lack of respect for her and complained bitterly to the other staff. While trying to discuss the issue of abuse, one of the clients said, "Why don't you get Becky [a worker who came occasionally to help out] to talk about abuse? It's her specialty." Again they usurped her authority by indicating that they were not dependent on her knowledge. Ivy proceeded to ask about what we all heard as "fonning" and became angry when no one knew what she was talking about. Finally, I figured out that she was saying "fondling" and Paula exclaimed, "Why didn't you say so?" Ivy then took up another tactic and asked if they had seen "Something about Amelia" (the story concerns incest) on TV. Most had, but she again had a difficult time trying to explain what she wanted them to talk about and they were not particularly cooperative. They finally did discuss how kids could be lured by people and taken advantage of. Several said that they had told their kids not to talk to strangers. The discussion was rather perfunctory and Ivy asked me afterwards whether they said more in Jenna's classes. I told her that they talked about different things. She complained bitterly at a staff meeting that they did homework for Roberta and Dr. James but not for her. She saw their behavior as failing to give her the respect she felt she deserved.

On other occasions, competence was not the issue as much as new information about the arbiters. The clients were confronted by information that indicated to them that some of the staff members were not who they claimed to be. They were not as perfect as they tried to portray themselves. When Roberta and Ivy took off for two days for a training session, they left John in charge of the program. One day John even failed to check in before noon and did nothing when he did arrive. I gave them work and at the end of the day Kim said, "Ruth helped and she doesn't even get paid." All of the clients blamed Roberta for not caring about what happened to them in the program. She always told them she was responsible for the program and had not missed work at her other jobs. When Ivy and Roberta returned and told the clients about the conference they had attended, the clients just stared and finally Rickie said, "You just left us here and we wouldn't have had anything to do if Ruth weren't here." When clients have evidence to the contrary, they tend to reject the authority of arbiters. They refuse to act subserviently toward staff.

When Help Becomes Dependency
When the client must ask for help many times in one day, he or she may experience the necessity of asking politely as demeaning. One day when Rosie was working on a difficult project, she had to knock on Roberta's partition three times. Each time she was told to wait. After she was told to wait the third time she just screamed her question through the walls. While they were supposed to ask permission before making a phone call, if they had to ask permission more than once during the day, they usually just went ahead and dialed.

During the second session, the clients asked questions of Marge, who had already received her GED, or of me before they would knock on the partition to ask for Mr. Harrison or Roberta's help. She gave both Marge and me a lecture about how we were not supposed to help. This rarely stopped the others, but we often could not help because Roberta could hear through the walls. Here again they were not rejecting their need for help but the way it was offered.

The young women tried on several occasions to break the spatial and social barrier to demonstrate not only that they were generous but could play an active contributing role rather than being only the recipient of rules and depending on others for everything. They were usually rebuffed. They offered to share some of their lunches with the arbiters who sometimes even wrinkled up their noses while refusing. By the end of the second session the freeze was so great that the clients often chose to eat outside in the extreme heat rather than in the air-conditioned room. Segmenting time and space were justified by the arbiters by using a rhetoric of efficiency and privacy and needing time away from the clients to relax but were seen by the clients as symbolizing their subordinate position and social distance from the arbiters.

Occasionally, the dependency on the arbiters for information was so demeaning that the staff's actions actually were the basis for fights. Fighting violated one of the most sacred rules and was an extreme challenge to the arbiters' authority. According to the pronouncements by the staff, fighting was immediate cause for dismissal. One fight between a black and a white client started during GED class. Several of the white clients had completed more schooling and had more academic skills than some of the blacks. Instead of dividing the clients into smaller groups or permitting them to work on their own, John lectured to the entire group. He kept calling on Steele (a white participant) to answer all of the questions when no one else responded and Sandy (a black participant) became increasingly annoyed when she did not understand some of the problems. The two young women exchanged fighting words. They started for each other and Steele scratched Sandy before Sandy hit Steele. They were separated after a few minutes.

Choosing the Community over the Program

The young women challenged the boundaries to the external world and the boundaries within the program. The arbiters seemed to feel that they could construct a program in which the outside world did not have to be included in their plans and that it would not affect the participants' actions within the program. This was not in fact the case. Their worlds outside of the program were complex and often problematic. Babies, friends, and money problems do not disappear because of program attendance. Lack of salience of the client identity was frequently the source of client boundary violations but was not understood as such by the arbiters.

While some of the situations that drew the young women out of the program were embedded in situations in which they had little choice, others were real choices. Sandy often invited one of the clients for lunch at her house. Sometimes they would return for the afternoon; however, more frequently, they would disappear for the rest of the day. During lunch we were often regaled with stories of attending parties which made it impossible to get up in time for the bus. Sometimes a young woman would explain that she had to meet her boyfriend and would miss two days. Sometimes they decided to go shopping. One day I was flagged down by Bette, who was carrying several department store bags. She asked for a ride to her home and explained that she had gotten a ride to the mall but had to take the bus back. In these cases they made choices indicating that the client role was less important than girlfriend, shopper, party-goer, etc.

Often the clients' style of challenging the importance of the client role is expressed in a more passive manner: falling asleep in class. Sometimes this behavior is a reflection of admitted failure to get any sleep because they were out partying most of the night rather than staying up with a sick baby. They made a choice between meeting the program expectations and having a good time, and the "social time" took precedence.

Much as the pull and tensions of the outside world created untenable situations and pulled clients away from following the new expectations emphasized by the arbiters, conflicts within also pushed people out. Two cousins, who were both attending the program regularly and sharing an apartment with their three children, argued and fought over the payment of some bills. They felt they could not show up at the program together and began to attend sporadically, about once a week each. Their relationship as alienated cousins was stronger than their wishes to maintain the client identity and complete the program.

The manner in which the arbiters communicated how the young women were to play the role also communicated messages about what kinds of people clients were compared with people who were staff members. Clients were made to feel dependent on the arbiters and subordinate in status to them. It was these messages that the clients and arbiters disagreed about, but the staff failed to acknowledge the difference in meanings. It became clear that the arbiters did not have as much power as they thought to create the client culture, that is, the way performances are appraised and evaluated. In certain situations the clients were able to reject the culture that the arbiters were creating without leaving the program.

Discussion: Routine and Few Client/Client Relations

An intensive program culture did not develop either during the first or second session. No myths or stories developed about the program or staff. The clients rarely discussed the program or staff in their free time, when they talked about boyfriends, childbirth, and children. The young women were united as mothers. The only time that the program or staff was discussed was if someone made a specific complaint. No collective memories were developed and the young women rarely interacted with each other as clients. They interacted as mothers, friends, even students—and sometimes as rivals—but not as clients.

While during the first session there were a few ceremonies that brought the group together—visits to work sites, a Christmas party, and mother-children activities day—there were none during the second session. Moreover, there were few symbols in those ceremonies relating to their status as clients—most had more to do with motherhood and future worker status and were organized by the mediators. The arbiters failed to develop a strong staff/client culture, and performances as clients were given only to remain in the program. While the arbiters tried to establish their authority through dramatizing their "professionalism" and successes in comparison with the lack of success of the clients in order to create the culture and social life of the program, as clients the young women, generally, played along but did not fully accept that culture. They sometimes rejected it and violated the rules of appropriate demeanor. This raises a question which I will try to answer in the next chapter: Is demonstrated competent authority sufficient to override a context of threats and demands for deference to compel certain behaviors?

CHAPTER FIVE

Classroom Failure without Redress

The seventeen students in attendance gathered around two long tables facing John, who was writing fractions on the movable blackboard and mumbling an "explanation" of how to divide them. Steele and Martha had completed the problem and rolled their eyes every time they looked up from their doodles. Martha drew hearts with arrows through them. Some of the students had their eyes fixed on the board, frowning as they tried to understand. Others had given up and talked quietly to each other or drew on scraps of paper.

Finally, after about twenty minutes, Steele said, "This is boring, can't we do something else?" Rickie, staring at her paper and writing and erasing quickly said, "I think I've almost gotten it." Two of the other students started to argue about something that had occurred last night. John gave up and I heard one student whisper to another, "He's been drinking again." They were seated closest to him.

John tried to speak over their voices and mumbled under his breath to no one in particular, "How can I be expected to teach so many with no books." The students and the staff heard this complaint almost every day. Roberta discovered workbooks in the closet the day after John left to be "with his sick son"; they had been there for more than three months.

When it became clear that John would not return soon, Roberta and Becky devised a new system for teaching GED. Roberta said she believed in individual, independent work and set up individual files so each student had assigned work at her own level based on initial test scores. Roberta told the students where they could find their folders and when to begin work but stayed behind her partition for most of the GED period. One day with eleven students present and working industriously in different workbooks, the students resolved typical problems of broken pencils and two who wanted to use the same books among themselves. Randy worked on her math problems but became stymied by a particular fraction. She continued to work on it for a while, but then threw her pencil down in disgust. "You have to go ask Roberta," one of the other students informed her. Roberta sat at her desk behind the partition. Randy proceeded to ask in a loud voice for Roberta to come and help. Roberta did not respond but must have heard as the dividers did not reach to the ceiling and there was no real door. Randy got up and knocked on the wall and Roberta informed her that she would be out soon. About ten minutes later Roberta emerged from behind the partition and explained the problem.

During the second session, Mr. Harrison, the new teacher, had the seven students present gathered around one table where he sat at the head telling everyone to get out pencils and paper for the spelling test. Marge spelled the ten words correctly as she had for the last several weeks and won the dollar provided by Mr. Harrison. After he returned to his desk, Ella complained that no one else except Paula had any chance of winning and that she had never even gotten to be student of the week.

The teacher/student relationship is often considered a relatively straightforward one with a clear demarcation of power and functions: the teacher teaches and the students learn; however, disputes occur over the content of what should be taught and the methodology for doing so. Moreover, students often do not learn and drop out. Blame for not learning is often placed outside of the school: on the community, on the student's class or culture, the family, or peers. This should not be as significant an issue here; the students are in the program voluntarily and want a GED. On the one hand, why, when the students want a GED, do they seem so weakly involved in the learning process? On the other hand, why do they remain and continue studying when the teacher/student relationship appears so problematic in this program? Why and when do students submit to or challenge the teachers? In order to respond to these questions, we must examine the evolution of the teacher/student relationships in the program.

The three scenes described above illustrate a number of the elements present in the attempts to negotiate the teacher/student relationships in the program. While all bring experiences to the program of being teachers or students, that relationship must be negotiated within the particular context. It is a task-directed relationship. These students know from experience that teachers are supposed to explain new knowledge, to give homework, and to correct papers, that is, they expect the teacher to demonstrate technical competence to complete these tasks. The teacher/student relationship is, however, a much more complex relationship involving not only issues of competence but, especially for these students, issues arising from often difficult prior experiences in school and the significant inequality with the help flowing only from teacher to student. Is demonstration of teacher competence sufficient for young women to act as students and to invest themselves in the student role? This chapter will show that the organization of the schooling and the teachers' construction of the relationship conveys much more in the daily enactment of relations than how to spell or complete a math problem; the relation can be constructed to create and reinforce hierarchy, dependence, and competition among the students, which makes commitment to being a student difficult, even for those who receive rewards for their successes.

Societies have largely given over their tutelage of the young to professional teachers who teach in large formal institutions, schools. While criticism about the ability of our schools to educate has increased, as a society we have placed the authority to educate with the schools, and we basically trust the schools to teach our children, with some institutionalized guardians to protect that trust (Shapiro 1987) and ensure competency through processes such as credentialing of teachers, school boards, and evaluation procedures for teachers (observations of classroom techniques, test scores of children, and parental complaints). In this program, as we saw in the last chapter, there were few institutionalized controls over the staff that would work to guarantee the trust granted the teachers in their authority over students. The funding and the coordinating agencies relied on credentials and an assumption of staff professionalism. The evaluation team did plan to use changes in scores to tests given to the students at the beginning and end of each session and the percentage of students who received their GEDs to evaluate the program.

Although teachers may be trusted and granted the authority to teach the youth by the school administrators, boards, and parents, it does not necessarily mean that trust will evolve in the teacher/student relationship. There is more to the relationship and learning than the expressed desire to "get an education" on the part of the student and the teachers' skills to enable the students to obtain their GEDs.

First, this relationship is situated in a nontraditional place (a social service program) and the students are young women who were unable to complete their education in the traditional school. The teachers are paid less than school-based teachers to teach students who have not succeeded and may be defined by some as less capable and stigmatized. Moreover, the GED is often not considered equivalent to a high school diploma.[1] This context makes completing a GED a highly risky task and one's status as a student or a teacher somewhat problematic.

Second, desiring a GED certificate may be an insufficient motivation to doing what is necessary to pass. The teacher/student relation is embedded in a power relationship in which the teachers employ various methods to compel the student to go along with what the teachers want them to do. This relationship takes various forms. Power can be exercised by threats of force in which little negotiation and interpretation is possible, that is, threats of being kicked out of the program. While this did occur in the program, it rarely occurred within the context of the student/teacher relation. Sometimes the teachers attempted to compel the students to do something by manipulating them, but other times they used symbols of competence, positive inducements, claims of legitimacy, or personal exhortations.[2] Most power communications can be interpreted and evaluated as all power must be legitimized (Ben-Yehuda 1990, 49). Control may be achieved through influencing the definition of the situation, but the audience does not have to go along. In the instance of attempts to compel the students to do something, it is possible for the students to assess the credibility of the teachers' statements about their authority. Is it really their "last chance?" Do the staff members really mean what they say? "I will kick you out if . . ." Do the teachers really know what they are doing?

Even when teachers use positive encouragements to legitimize their power to compel students to do things, questions about trust-

---

1. Cameron and Heckman (1993) found that people with a GED did not fair as well on the job market as those with a high school diploma unless they continued their education beyond the high school level.
2. According to the model developed here, all of these are forms of power as categorized by Wrong (1988). The latter two forms, he argues, are types of authority which are symbolically constructed and may be negative or positive. Kemper and Collins (1990) distinguish these from power which "in a social relationship entails conduct by which actors have (or try to gain) the ability to compel other actors to do what they do not wish to do" (p. 34). Compliance is coerced, whether through force, deception, threat, or withdrawal of benefits. They do not distinguish between forms of power that can have different interpretations, which one must believe in, and force. Status, on the other hand, involves willingness, deference and accepting, that is, it is voluntary. This relationship involves trust in the other. Here the distinction is made between positive and negative legitimators.

worthiness arise. Trust permits people to follow because they accept that others know what they are doing and it is the right thing to do. They leave decisions up to others and trust that they will do what they promise. On what is this trust based and how does it develop?

Models of trust are based on different assumptions about social relationships. They vary between models where trust is ensured by values and norms taught during socialization and followed in the enactment of social roles[3] and models of society made up of rational atomized individuals who need formal institutionalized social control agencies to ensure the smooth functioning of relations and trust. These perspectives need some modifications to deal with face-to-face relations where trust is not fixed or assumed in roles but must be negotiated.

A third view (Granovetter 1985) conceptualizes trust as embedded within personal relationships and views personal embeddedness as a necessary if not sufficient precondition for trust in economic relations. Behavior is constrained by ongoing social relations (Granovetter 1985, 482). In this third view, trust is negotiated in face-to-face, reasonably long-term relationships. Like Granovetter, I agree that embeddedness is critical and the degree to which and how it is negotiated is problematic. Students are skeptical of teachers because of many of their previous experiences and do not trust without evidence. How do the teachers act in order to appear trustworthy to the students and how do the students evaluate such actions? Goffman (1967) focuses our attention on what is necessary to maintain ongoing interaction; that is, to appear trustworthy and considerate (Rawls 1990). A person demonstrates trustworthiness according to Goffman (1967) when she works to save the face of others because she is able and does identify with them. While he acknowledges that the more powerful and prestigious the others are, the more consideration people are going to demonstrate toward them, he is less concerned about how the more powerful must demonstrate similar consideration if they want the less powerful to go along voluntarily and enthusiastically.

While trust is sometimes defined as a property of individuals or of emotional content of interpersonal relationships (faith, confidence, reliance, security), trust in economic relations according to Shapiro (1987, 625–26) involves a specific form of organization that does not necessarily involve face-to-face relations but involves a risky investment and one actor or set of actors acting on behalf of others for some unknown future return. Granovetter's definition requires personal

3. This model is based on an oversocialized vision of men and women (Wrong 1961).

embeddedness, while this second does not. While my argument is concerned with trust that must be negotiated in interaction, it is help-ful to focus on risk and unknown future return. To achieve trust, a technically competent role performance and an assumption of loy-alty—in that all partners will place others' interests over their own when acting on their behalf—are necessary (Barber 1983). In the law, fiduciary duty is largely conceptualized as duty of loyalty, that is, the person uses power for the purposes intended and not for personal enrichment. This focuses our attention on the way staff try to com-municate competency and selflessness and on the assessment the stu-dents make of the teachers demonstrations of competency and of placing the interests of the students over their personal interests.

Students do not acquiesce passively to the power of the teachers. While in most high schools students are not asked to publicly evalu-ate the competency or loyalty of teachers, it does not mean they do not question the authority some teachers have to teach. Students can empower the teacher by listening, accepting what they say, working hard, and learning because they desire the goals of learning and trust that the teachers know how to educate them and will put teaching ahead of their own interests. However, if students do not trust the teachers, they may challenge their authority. From the perspective of the student, especially those who have had difficult previous experi-ences, loyalty as a predicate of trust communicates a lot about the kind of people students are from the perspective of the program's teachers.

The students' evaluation of the trustworthiness of their teachers plays a part in the students' interest in, commitment to, and achieve-ments in educational activities. The teacher who is evaluated as fail-ing to demonstrate trust is failing to respect the young women as students and their desire to obtain an education. When teachers say that education is important, but certain people are not educable, then their actions are interpreted as not valuing the person as a student. When teachers say that they respect students, but put their own needs ahead of the students, they are not respecting the students as worthwhile persons. If these are the situations in which trust is open to question, we must focus on the types of strategies used by the students to question the authority of the teachers and, occasionally, to challenge it successfully.

Education as a Publicly Expressed Value

Educational achievements were considered important by the stu-dents, but such "values" or "attitudes" provide little basis for understanding what goes on in the classroom or for predicting whether the work toward the GED would be successful. Neither was the talk about the importance and value of the GED by the staff a very good indicator of what the teachers tried to do. While the students were relatively sensitive to the opinions of others, they were not totally obedient to the dictates of the value of education which they know is supported, at least verbally, by the vast majority of the people they meet (Granovetter 1985; Wrong 1961). Many of the young women expressed their dreams of following careers that required significant years of additional education[4] and, when discussing what they wanted for their children, education was always mentioned as essential. Many expressed regret for failure to complete and others for failure to start high school.

While everyone agreed on the importance of education, the actual educational experience of most of these young women had not been positive. The difficulties many had experienced made this new attempt a very risky undertaking. As with many other teen mothers, getting pregnant and having the baby was associated with problems in school. For some, a history of problems in school culminated in pregnancy and dropping out; for others dropping out was followed by pregnancy[5]; and for a minority, having the child made school attendance too complicated, even though they had done reasonably well before having the baby. No one had totally negative things to say about school, but few were enthusiastic about their experiences.

Many were in trouble for their low grades or had behavioral problems prior to pregnancy. Kim had been suspended for fighting in school before becoming pregnant and Sandy was suspended for drug involvement. Most just drifted away from school and were in the midst of that process when they became pregnant. Paula cut school regularly to be with her boyfriend, and, when she became pregnant, dropped out. A few attempted to return to school after the birth of their babies but dropped out again as they had no one to care for their

4. In their follow-up study of adolescent mothers in later life, Furstenberg, Brooks-Gunn, and Morgan (1987) found that many of the mothers went back to school later and completed high school. They did find, however, that those who dropped out before or early on in their first pregnancies were less likely to graduate eventually (slightly more than half) as "compared to fourth-fifths of the women who remained in school throughout their pregnancy" (p. 27).

5. According to Moore et al. (1978) and Rindfuss, Bumpass, and St. John (1980), one-third to one-half of school-age mothers dropped out of school at least a year before their first pregnancy. Other studies have found that high educational aspirations are correlated with delayed childbearing (Devaney and Hubley 1981; Hogan and Kitagawa 1983) and that those enrolled in college preparatory programs are less likely to give birth early (Moore and Hofferth 1980).

babies on a regular basis. Val, on the track team and a good student, tried returning to high school, but the baby was often sick during his first year, she had no regular sitter, she had no money for day care, and she quit again.

Problems in school were complicated by a particular historical situation. Both black and white students had been affected by the start of busing in junior high school. With busing, some found themselves in middle- and upper middle-class school environments. Steele, a white student who completed the tenth grade, told the other young women that the students in her school were very snobby and made fun of her even though one of her teachers had been very nice and tried to encourage her to stay in school. She started hitching home along the interstate highway almost every morning, right after the school bus dropped her off. Her skill level was close to the last grade she completed. Sharon, a black student who had been placed in the college track, explained that she had told the principal that she would probably flunk and, she said gleefully, "I did." She said that the school was not bad and that the people were pretty nice to her. "But I didn't fit in."

A few of the students were in special classes and had high rates of absenteeism prior to becoming pregnant. Most dropped out a few months after they became pregnant and attended a special educational program for pregnant teens. No rule prohibits continuing in school while pregnant, though many of the young women said they felt as though schools preferred not to have pregnant students. Several said teachers had suggested they should go elsewhere.

The negative experiences with the schools were memorable for some. One young mother's experiences were so poor that when teachers told her that they wanted to test her daughter who was in kindergarten for possible placement in the highest ability grouping, she would not let them. When I asked her if she knew why they wanted to test her daughter, Matti replied that they *said* they thought her daughter was smart. She then explained that she did not feel that it was the true reason.

Taking on the role of the student again with the hope of attaining a specific level of achievement was made more risky by the actual skill levels attained. They were both excited and worried about taking the "locator" exam, a short test giving a general indication about the level of math and verbal skills, and sat nervously awaiting the test results, talking quietly among themselves. Several were dismayed to discover their tested achievement level was substantially below the last grade they had completed. The acquired skills as indicated on an exam to test achievement level ranged from about third grade to eleventh, while most of the students had finished the eighth grade and a few had dropped out in the eleventh. Testing dramatized the risk of failure.

Despite their poor experiences, the young women liked to be treated as students. Both the first and second groups were very excited about being students and, in the beginning, looked forward to classes; several bought dictionaries. The students clustered around and discussed "homework," if anyone thought to give it to them and sometimes demanded to be given homework and talked enthusiastically when given something specific to learn. They argued vehemently with Roberta when she refused to allow them to take home any of the books. How could they possibly do all of the work, they asked, if they could not take books home? The gesture was as much a symbol of their desire to be regarded as students as instrumental for learning. They often did not complete assigned work.

They liked to be asked to do things students are typically asked to do. On several occasions, the students asked whether they should take notes and were pleased that they were told to do so. When Dr. James's assistant, Mrs. Sims, requested that they learn how to spell the names of medical specialists and learn what each of them did, they took and studied their notes, and, when Amy gave the students specific information in the family life classes they could write down, their estimation of the class rose significantly. All of these gestures were dramatic symbols of their student status and emphasized their wish to present that identity both within the program and to others outside.

The GED as Critical
The staff's many discussions of the importance of education and whether obtaining a GED was or should be the major focus of the program was linked to many of the arbiters' desires to be seen and to see themselves as teachers, not as social service workers. Teachers generally have higher status than social workers. Teachers work with "normal" young people, while social workers risk stigmatization or social contagion from their clients. John, Roberta, and Mr. Harrison wanted regular school jobs and said so.

One of the biggest debates over the mission of the program was whether GED was the most critical component of the program. In the first mission statement made by the staff, most of their goals were in support of the GED component, including evaluating the readiness of the participants to take the GED and "to successfully instruct

50 percent of the participants to pass the GED test." Despite this stated goal, the program of four days a week, with five and one-half hours a day, contained only six scheduled hours a week of GED classes for each student.

A discussion erupted during a staff meeting about halfway through the first session over whether or not they were promising people their GEDs, because the original flyer said "GED" instead of "GED Preparation." Finally, even Jenna said that the GED was the most important mission of the organization and all components should work toward that goal. This became the overt public mission of the program. The approaches of the staff members were diverse, and reading and writing skills were only part of what staff communicated to the students. And sometimes those skills were not taught.

Despite the staff's concern about the GED component, no one took responsibility for a formal replacement when John failed to show up for several weeks. John's long excused (by Wilma) absence was the source of great consternation by the other staff. They even accepted him back after an absence with pay of more than three weeks. He was paid for the entire first session. The staff lost its control to the state because they failed to take the initiative before Georgia, the state representative, told the staff to get rid of him.

Additionally, the various staff members could not decide who should be doing what kind of teaching or who was doing it appropriately. During the first session Dr. James announced publicly that no one was teaching GED skills, the only worthwhile activity of the program. This was taken as a direct criticism by John, who was supposed to be teaching GED, but the criticism did not change his actions or his effort.

The GED as Moral Indicator

Simultaneous with John's failure to teach the students anything, Dr. James, a part-time consultant, told them that he "will pay attention only to those who pass . . . You are responsible. You are grown up. I wouldn't decorate a tree or shop. You know how to shop and there shouldn't be classes . . . The GED will change your life . . ." A 45-minute diatribe continued along these lines. A month later Dr. James again explained, "You're all smart, look at all you've done and I see growth. I set a goal for you. Pass the GED. You've lost a friend if you don't get a GED . . . I know that you will pass, then you will like yourself. Many of you will be at a University next year." With this kind of message and very little help on anyone's part to help them achieve this goal, the students became increasingly sensitive to others' imputations about their abilities. A good person should be able to pass the exam.

The "value" and importance given education and, more specifically here, the GED, did little more than vaguely frame the student/teacher relationship and what was taught about skills and what "education" meant. That relationship had to be constructed in the immediate situation within the context set by the teachers and the experiences brought to the program by the participants. Education meant taking the GED exam and passing it, a very risky proposition given the skill levels of many of the young women and their lack of prior success as students.

Using Learning to Dramatize Competition

The culture of competition emphasized the risk of failure and reduced the willingness to invest one's self in a student identity. While both the teachers and students appeared to agree that they were generally pleased with a teacher/student relationship, it did not stop the teachers from questioning the performances the young women tried to enact as students. The construction of the cultural climate of competition made it difficult for some of the young women to maintain their identities as students. In a win or lose situation, someone always loses. The risk of taking on the student identity was very high as most had experienced prior failures as students. Moreover, this culture of competition discouraged consideration of others, both students of each other and teachers of students. Someone always lost face.

> Just as the member of any group is expected to have self-respect, so also is he expected to sustain a standard of considerateness; he is expected to go to certain lengths to save the feelings and face of others present, and he is expected to do this willingly and spontaneously because of emotional identification with the others and with their feelings. (Goffman 1967, 10)

Teachers have power over students and here did not treat them with the same regard as they did social equals. Instead, the teachers seemed more interested in establishing a series of competitive activities that made it particularly difficult for the less-skilled students to achieve. Moreover, they compared all the students' failures with the teachers' successes. If they had encouraged all of the young women to emphasize the student role and demonstrated respect for individual progress, the young women might have become more committed to student activities.

The teachers actively encouraged competition. It took various forms with different arbiters but was clearly an underlying theme. For example, the "best student of the week" prize usually went to the student who had the most skills, not the one who had gained more that week. Mr. Harrison paid a dollar to the winner of the Thursday spelling contest. During both sessions the most advanced students were chosen to read aloud first or answer questions in GED classes, Job Readiness classes, or discussion groups lead by Ivy.

Prizes for winning also served to increase competition and to make those who never won feel demeaned and worthless. Achievement was rewarded, rarely improvement. During the second session, prizes were the norm and the same students received the prizes every week. The student of the week received a piece of inexpensive jewelry, but, more important, the staff posted her name on the bulletin board along with a short biography written by Mr. Harrison and examples of her written work. Several of the students received it more than once, while others who tried but were less skilled never did. Those who won often dragged the others to look at the board. Those who lost generally managed to compliment the winners.

There was, however, little to encourage students who were not rewarded for their skills to remain enthusiastic. Mr. Harrison's Thursday spelling contest was always between Paula and Marge and they loved it. Ella, after trying very hard to study for several weeks, said, "I'll never win unless they are absent and I really did better this week didn't I, Ruth?" Most of the winners made an effort to mitigate the divisions created by the rewards. With their winnings both Marge and Paula bought and shared food.

Winning was important. The excitement and joy on Ella's face when she received the best student award at the closing ceremony should have told everyone that she should have received some acknowledgment sooner. She said that she was going to sleep on the award and then hang it in her room. Ella explained that she had never received an award before and she was going to treasure it forever. Jenna told me that the other staff had agreed because Marge had already left to go into a job training school and all of the other regulars had received some other prize. At the staff meetings the arbiters had little positive to say about Ella.

Even those who were successful and received some recognition had little confidence in their abilities. Martha, who was reading and doing math at an advanced high school level when she entered the program, was convinced she could not pass the GED test and would not consider attending a local junior college when she passed it on the first try. With a year of junior college I believe she would have been ready for university-level work.

A few of those who succeeded under the system appeared to gain confidence, and many of those who did not do well did not stay long enough to improve. For many, the risks appeared too great; often they had failed to achieve in school or anywhere else in the middle-class institutions. What chances did they have for success? The symbols that meant almost sure failure, academic competition, were reemphasized, so why take the risk? With the risks, it was difficult to invest oneself in being a student. The competition generates winners and losers and there is no general demonstration of respect for the young women as students. Moreover, the academic skills contests take on moral qualities from the perspective of the students because in part they have linked their failures as students to failures as people. Moreover, the threat by the teachers of "last chance" educational success in passing the GED was linked to success in getting off welfare and becoming morally acceptable people who can support themselves in the wider society. The culture of competition, while never totally dominating the students, emphasized the risks involved in investing oneself in being a student. It is too easy to lose.

Conflict over the Meaning of Competition
The meanings of the competitive events were not always the same for all of the teachers or the students and were debated. For the teachers, competition was the unquestioned basis for all social relationships in the work world and one must learn to survive in it. For the students, failure to win equaled moral inferiority. While the teachers were empowered to develop the culture of competition, the students continually challenged its appropriateness and some of the better students were more sensitive to the slower students than the teachers.

The most dramatic series of negotiations during the first session concerned the meaning of the division of the students into two groups that were to meet separately for GED and Job Readiness classes. The original program design designated two sections of twenty students each. On most days fewer than twenty attended so the division was not mentioned. During the third month of the program, Ivy and Roberta decided to divide the students into two groups "because some will never pass and they shouldn't have to do too much." In a discussion with John about being sensitive to criticism, I said that I thought we had to be careful about the "A" and "B" group designations, but John replied, "The world is like that. They have to learn that some are better than others." Several days later some were told to go to Job Readiness class and the rest to GED. It was a very slow day and there was no immediate reaction.

At first the staff were successful in generating a culture of competition. The next week several of the students in the "A" group expressed their excitement about their inclusion in that group and explained to each other that they were smarter and knew more than the others. While they were divided based on standardized test scores, they assumed that it was based on motivation: "those who want to learn" was how Rickie explained the division. Dr. James had explained the previous week that they ought to be divided that way. When Mrs. Sims arrived, Dr. James was not with her, so she said the groups would not be divided. Dr. James came in over an hour later. He discussed publicly the different types of students:

> There are two types of students: those who want to learn
> and consequently will learn and those who don't think
> about education and mess up for others. I suggest that they
> walk out. You have never been part of a real educational in-
> stitution with all of you eating potato chips and smoking in
> class. Don't mess up if you want to be part of the educa-
> tional system. You are adults, here to better yourselves. The
> "A" group wants to get an education and the "B" group will
> have to deal with me. You'll never be able to make a success
> out of yourself if you don't attend class every day or go to
> work. Then you wouldn't have any money. In college if you
> come to class every day you pass . . . After sixty years I can
> tell you who will do well . . .

He never got around to dividing the groups. But whether the divisions meant differences in ability or differences in commitment to the program, it was humiliating to the young women to be placed in the lower group.

The arbiters emphasized the need for students to discover that in the real world testing and measurement are common and they should know where they stood. The arbiters did this by rewarding those who measured highest on standard tests and by telling all of them what level they were really achieving at. Whereas Dr. James tried to reward persistence and hard work by saying that those who worked hard and came every day would be in the "A" group, the others just measured testable academic achievement levels and rewarded those who did well in those terms. Dr. James's alternative culture failed to dominate.

Challenges to the Power to Create Competition
The competition was frequently humiliating; nevertheless, the students were sometimes able to challenge the teachers. In the rap session at which Ivy and Jenna were present, the division of the groups was brought up as an issue. Ronda was very upset. She had been placed in the "B" group.

> I got something to say. I don't like what Dr. James is doing with dividing the sections. It's not fair. He said something about those who come and want to learn will be in the "A" group, but I was absent that day. I had an appointment. You know that Ivy. Now all the girls in the "A" group are not coming any more. I don't like the "A" and "B" groups. It's not fair.

Gay told her, "It's not for those who come or want to learn, it is for the smarter girls to be in the 'A' group." Everyone was confused and there was some shouting back and forth about what the groups meant and that "if you were here more often, then everyone would know." Jenna promised to find out what Dr. James meant by his groups as compared with the GED groups. No one spoke to each other while they waited for the bus.

The staff made little effort to mitigate the competition. The next week they became the XX and YY groups. Some days they were divided and on other days no one bothered. Mrs. Sims and Dr. James sometimes used it to tell the two groups to do different activities without specifying who was in which group. Mrs. Sims said to the students the week after the rap session: "Group 'A' must take out and read a book from the library by next week." Rachel was the only one who followed through on the assignment. It was the last they heard of it. Later, in the same class, Mrs. Sims said:

> It's my feeling that some of you move faster than the others. Yes? We were supposed to break up into sections weren't we? I feel that some of you absorb faster and remember more. New people hold you back and so do those who do not attend. We've done a lot of testing and none of you are dumb. You've lots of ability. We've had long discussions about you.

The next week Mrs. Sims tried to split up the group again, but everyone started asking what group they were in, and with the angry voices, shouting, "we are all here, weren't we?" she dropped it. The confusion gave the students power.

The power of the students was limited to the particular teacher. Two days later Roberta announced that GED would be divided and that no one could be excused from the class: "That's what I was told." This created a stir because a job recruiter was coming to one job readiness class and not the other, so those in one group could not attend the recruitment session. Ronda was very upset because she wanted to hear the recruiter and was not in that group. Roberta explained, "This is not like school where you all have to be going at the same rate and the same level. You progress at your own pace here. Erase the 'A' and 'B' idea from your mind." The XX and YY group division lasted about another month until John started not showing up for work. Roberta was then in charge of both. Challenges to Roberta's actions were rarely successful.

Students directly challenged other forms of competition. In classes taught by Roberta, Ivy, John, and later Mr. Harrison, the best reader or math student was always called on first. Roberta gave the students scenes about work to read aloud and discuss. One day, about halfway through the first session, just as Roberta was about to call on one of her regulars to read, Ronda interrupted and said in no uncertain terms that she was going to read first. She did not read well but managed to get through the passage without great difficulty. When she finished, she grinned and then glared at Roberta. After that she took matters into her own hands and regularly demanded to read first but was never asked.

Sometimes the students supported each other against the teacher. During the second session, Ivy gave them scenes to read and discuss. One of the papers was handwritten and poorly xeroxed. One of the less-skilled readers hesitated in the middle of a sentence and said that she could not read it. Ivy, in a very disgusted tone, said, "I'll do that. Why can't you read it?" The students complained that it was illegible. I could not decipher it either.

Some of the better students challenged the lack of encouragement given to the less-skilled students. Like Roberta, Mr. Harrison always chose the best readers to begin the reading and descended in nearly the same order every day. Some days he skipped either Ella and, even more often, Hilda, and began all over again. The students were not unaware of what he was doing and finally Marge asked, "Why don't you let Hilda read? She deserves a chance to learn." Mr. Harrison did not answer but let Hilda read while a look of distaste came over his face. He did not help her but Marge and Paula did. While he did not change his pattern of interaction, they were able to compel him to give into their demands in the immediate situation.

The competition made it difficult for the students to develop the solidarity to create change. Moreover, some inexpert challenges to teacher authority created conflict among the students. Not only did some of the "A" group like being considered the best students, but some of the competitive organization of teaching created a hierarchy that became the basis of aggression. Competition led to fights among the students. One technique that John used was to call students up to the board to do arithmetic problems. Often they were volunteers, typically the best math students (they had completed algebra) who happened to be white. This began to create some tension as the same students were always at the board and could always do the problems (simple fractions). One day Sandy, a black student, was at the board and could not complete a problem. Instead of John going to her aid, she was stuck in front of the class with everyone watching her. For what seemed to be an eternity, no one said anything. Steele, who knew how to do the problem, watched and looked over toward John. He made no move and the tension became greater. Steele, who told me later that she was just trying to get Sandy out of that untenable position, got out of her seat and went to the front of the class. She asked Sandy if she could help and Sandy threw down the chalk and said that the whites think that they know everything. It looked as if they would fight, but Sandy walked out and did not return for several days. Here the organization of teaching was designed to further competition and created the situation where competition encouraged antagonism between blacks and whites.

During the first session, the seating in the GED classes generally reflected this tension, particularly after this incident. The whites sat off to one side. Later this was broken down by Rickie and Rachel who were the best math students among the blacks. One or two of the other more advanced students joined them and then the seating in the room reflected the math skill level of the students. While some segregation existed between the whites and blacks in all classes, it never reached the level as in John's class, nor was the division by level of achievement so clear. Challenges to competition were rarely successful.

Incompetence and Failure of Loyalty: John

John seemed more concerned with his salary and past educational accomplishments as certifying him in the current situation than in maintaining respect or teaching in the program classroom. The only way he attempted to express competence was to talk about his former successes, which everyone began to doubt as the first session progressed. John never appeared to doubt his competency to teach; he always talked about his education and explained to the staff that his failure at his previous college job was a political problem. If anyone offered to help him by taking some of the better or poorest students, he did not accept. Becky, a highly organized and competent volunteer, offered to help him with some grading. He could handle it, he claimed, but never corrected any papers.

Publicly, in front of the students, he emphasized that he had more than one degree and that he had been at an institution of higher learning. The immediate problem with his class he defined in terms of the failure of the books to arrive and the large number of students at many different skill levels. Even the size of the blackboard became a major issue for him. He claimed that he could not teach with one movable board.

Incompetence

The classes were disorganized, his explanations were unclear, and he never taught reading, only math. He was rarely able to explain anything clearly. The students who knew what they were doing did the problems on their own, some tried to learn from him, and others paid little attention after the first fifteen minutes thoroughly confused them.

He could not cover his poor performance in front of the students and the students had several ways to assess John's teaching competency. First, they could compare their ability to understand a problem when he explained it with their comprehension when others tried. In a taped group interview that was conducted by the evaluation team (I was not present), the greatest complaint the students had about the program was John's lack of skill. They knew that it was not they who were at fault: "Ruth explained it to us at lunch and we understood it immediately." The speaker, Rickie, was trying very hard to learn enough to pass the GED and, on her own, had purchased a dictionary and several workbooks. Several months after the program, she passed.

Second, the students also knew people in other programs who seemed to be learning more. Val complained more generally about the education they were getting by comparing it with the program her mother attended, funded out of the same grant. "You can take home books and really learn a lot there. My mother used to know less than me and now she helps me. They got really good teachers there."

Third, the students had evidence that John lacked knowledge of the educational system, especially the requirements for the GED. He failed to find out about the minimum age requirement prior to taking a group to take the GED test. This infuriated three of the four who went but were too young and not permitted to take the test. They yelled at him and did not show up for the rest of the week. He delayed for more than a month finding the information of when and where the test was to be given and was either unaware of or did not care to give a pre-test that would indicate who was ready to take the GED test.

Fourth, they measured their own knowledge against his. In the middle of a family life class with Amy, the students began to talk about a teacher who never knew the answers. This arose in a general class discussion about responses to problems. Amy asked a specific question, "What if you have a problem with a math test, what would you do?" This was not intended as a discussion of John. Several said that they were afraid of failing. Sandy broke in and vehemently stated, "The dumb teacher doesn't teach. He can't explain anything and doesn't know his multiplication tables."[6] Someone else joined in, "He gets confused when he explains. He's not paying attention to what he is trying to explain." There were constant complaints about his inability to teach. Ronnie complained, "I was doing a problem right and he messed it all up." Ronda continued, "We don't get any English because he can't speak it, besides, he's drunk." The evaluation of competence is largely embedded within a task-oriented relationship, but much more is communicated by someone's actions, especially given the last comment about his drinking.

Failure of Loyalty

John's duty to loyalty, that is, to place students' interests over his own when acting on their behalf, was problematic from the perspective of his students. He used his position as a teacher for his personal enrichment rather than for facilitating the academic success of his students. He did not respect them sufficiently to put aside his own needs for theirs. The students noticed his early morning and lunch time drinking before the staff did and talked about it or rolled their eyes when he smelled of liquor by 10:00 A.M.

After the first three weeks, when the excitement of the program had worn off, he would tell them to do a problem and they would not, or he would say that they ought to quiet down because he was the teacher but, again, they would not. His behavior and their evalua-

6. It was also my judgment that he was unable to explain simple math problems.

tion that he did not care increased the tension and made the students increasingly sensitive to any criticisms of them that might be inferred from his actions. When John failed to time the practice test, one of the students screamed at him that no one cared about them at all and they would not be able to pass anything. At one point some of the students confronted him, and I heard Ronda say to him, "You were drinking and don't care anything about us or if we pass the test." Afterwards he came up to me and claimed that he was upset that none of the students talked to him and that he did not approve of strict teachers. He was sensitive enough to notice that I had witnessed the confrontation and felt it necessary to justify himself. However, he did nothing to demonstrate any respect for the students or to improve his performance.

Occasionally, John's lack of demonstrated respect led to a direct conflict. He and Val engaged in an actual physical confrontation after John told her that the form that she was filling out in pencil had to be done in pen. Roberta told me about the fight and said that she blamed John because Val was such a polite, well-mannered girl that his lack of tact must have really offended her. The following day he arrived late and sat behind his desk for the entire morning.

The weeks that he was gone were both positive and negative. On the one hand, the absence confirmed to the students that John's loyalty lay elsewhere. He misused the trust he had been given. He took the job because he wanted the money, not to help them obtain the GED. On the other hand, more work was done after Roberta and Becky set up a new system.

Even without demonstrated competence or loyalty, several of the young women continued to try to learn the skills necessary to pass their GEDs. Why did they keep trying? John's authority was destroyed. He had no legitimacy. Part of the reason they continued to study, if sporadically, was that they were convinced of the importance of obtaining a GED and that practicing in the workbooks would give them what was necessary to succeed. Those who attended regularly were convinced it was their ticket into a "good job" and the American mainstream. John failed totally to construct a trusting relationship and the other arbiters, while performing with competency, failed in their duty to loyalty.

Competence without Loyalty

Both Roberta and Mr. Harrison clearly demonstrated their competence to teach; however, Roberta's expressed desire for them to depend on her and Mr. Harrison's failure to demonstrate that he cared about them and their success made their loyalty to the students appear problematic. With John's absence, Becky helped Roberta rapidly set up a system of files in which each of the students received a form telling her which books she was to use and in which she was to put all her completed work to be corrected. Much of the work was corrected and that pleased the students. "Now we're really getting somewhere," explained Tanya to Randy who had been absent for several weeks. The change in the work habits of the students was enormous. Suddenly, instead of coming into the program and sitting around eating and talking in the morning, they immediately took out their files and went to work. Even at the end of the day they would pull out their work until the van was available to take them home. The excitement generated by her demonstrated skill in organizing the GED work, did not, however, appear to be sufficient to maintain their initial enthusiasm.

Roberta's behavior emphasized to the young women that a dependency relationship existed between teacher and student and that she derived personal benefits from being in power. She was always behind the partition and would only answer questions if approached politely and asked in the appropriate manner. This meant that the students had to get up, go across the room, knock on the partition, and ask whether she had the time to answer the question. She often made them wait. She also made sure she was their only resource for academic help, telling me not to answer questions. She told me they had to learn to do everything without help. When they were told that I was not supposed to help them, they started giving me knowing glances before they approached Roberta's partition. Having to make such an effort to ask a question exacerbates feelings of inadequacy, dependence, and that the other does not care; it allows the provider of knowledge to control the situation.

In the students' view, her personal business appeared to come before their needs. She failed to demonstrate her loyalty to the students over her own needs. Not only was she not free when needed, but she failed to allow them to maintain their self-respect when she told them their real reading and math levels. Two girls cried and three others, looking very depressed, left during lunch.

After several weeks of using the files, the initial enthusiasm wore off and classes began to start later in the morning and attendance dropped again. On several occasions, the students challenged Roberta's rules by either yelling at her when she was behind her partition from the room or by criticizing her to her face. This was in addition to the comments made behind her back about being so "standoffish." It was difficult to criticize or revolt directly because they wanted to pass the test; however, investing too much meant accepting a high risk of failure. A competent performance (ability to explain) by the teacher was insufficient to generate long-term enthusiasm for the hard work necessary to learn enough skills to pass the GED test, especially when they felt demeaned by her actions.

During the second session there was never any question from the students' perspectives concerning Mr. Harrison's competency, but his teaching techniques and what his actions implied about their moral qualities created considerable tension. He wanted to run the GED program as though it were a high school and planned his week so that on certain days they were to study math and on others social studies, grammar, or science. He provided them with some acknowledgment of work completed by posting it on the wall. He graded papers with real grades and often used a recitation-style classroom despite their skill-level disparity.

He demonstrated, however, that he did not put helping the students learn above other things he did. His expectation of deference was similar to that of Roberta; he was the only one besides Dr. James and Mrs. Sims to be called by his last name, and he spent his time when he was not lecturing behind his desk. Seth, a new student, asked the others why everyone called him "Mr. Harrison" when Ivy and the rest were called by their first names and "Ruth has a real title." Ella explained, "You better not call him anything but Mr. Harrison. He really thinks he's something special." The students were always wary about asking him questions and would hesitate before doing so. No shrinking violet, Ella was afraid to ask him for a pencil and asked Ivy instead. "I don't like to bother him while he's reading his paper. He makes you feel like he has better things to do besides help us. He always reads the help wanted section. I guess he's looking for another job," explained Marge to Paula, an excellent student who attended regularly. Marge said, "He doesn't like to explain things and he only comes over if you demand it. If we could do it [pass the test], we wouldn't be here."[7] On another occasion while waiting for the van, Paula explained, "Mr. Harrison doesn't like women and doesn't like to explain things to us." The others reiterated Paula's thoughts and spent several minutes complaining.

From the students' perspective, he gave them no indication that he cared about them or had any respect for their abilities or as people.

7. She was identifying with the others as she had already passed the exam.

Liz claimed, "He thinks we are dumb and gives us stuff that we can't possibly do on our own to show it." That morning he had given them a science reading that was very difficult, boring, and very long.[8] Marge, who was reading at a high-school level, was unable to get through it and answer the questions at the end. Ella read at the sixth-grade level and Hilda was almost illiterate but trying very hard to learn. They saw this type of assignment as attempting to demonstrate both their lack of skills and his lack of caring enough about them to tailor the reading materials to their different needs. He even developed word contests in which he engaged the other staff. They could never answer correctly, so he always won and made it into a big performance.

Instead of working with the students so that all could improve their skills, he wanted to be the sole competent person to provide those skills. He put his own importance over the needs of the students. He also came over and told Marge to stop helping Hilda with another very difficult topic that she could not possibly begin to comprehend. One day several of the students expressed their feelings to me about Mr. Harrison always giving Hilda work that she could not possibly do and then not letting them help her. Marge was sure that it would discourage her from learning and did not see why she could not help because she was not preparing to take a test and it might be useful to see if she could explain things to others. Mr. Harrison failed to demonstrate that he was committed to helping them pass the GED exam and his loyalty to them was seen as questionable.

Discussion: GED as Legitimacy

Passing the GED test became an end in itself, both for the staff and the students. For the teachers, the GED was a symbol of movement toward legitimate citizenship. It gave the young woman a patina of respectability in the world where academic degrees seem to provide status that cannot be erased completely by race. While a GED degree indicates some respectability, it often is insufficient to obtain a job. The students felt betrayed when they were told that it was insufficient for military service: a woman needed to complete high school or obtain several college credits after passing the GED test. Moreover, there was little effort to teach any specific content. Only Jenna discussed current issues such as civil rights, elections, and foreign affairs.

8. I agreed with the students' evaluations.

The students either accepted the goal of the program to pass the GED or dropped out. Those who stayed and were unable to pass, stayed without rewards, respect, or encouragement. Roberta worked with those she viewed as having the academic and behavioral skills to place them in additional programs or get them jobs and ignored the others.

Not only were some of the teachers incompetent, but the performance of the teachers demonstrated to the students that these people placed their own interests above that of the students and did not recognize any of their fears. They did not permit the young women to maintain their self-respect as students. There was little opportunity, however, in the program to protest this indignity or to demand skills that would serve them and respect for trying to achieve where they had failed before. The students tried to express their hurt and dismay over the efforts of staff, but protests had little affect on the arbiters and they could not protest too much or they would risk expulsion. They believed in the importance of the GED and that it might be their last chance. Those students who stayed continued to work toward completing the GED, a testament to their desire to finish. They did not, however, invest much of their selves in that role; it was too risky.

CHAPTER SIX

Sex and Boyfriends: Your Dirty Laundry or Dramatic Dreams

At 6:00 P.M. eight young women, plus Jenna and I, started the short drive to the women's prison. Selma, cheerful when we started, became increasingly quiet as we approached the prison. Arriving on the "campus," she burst into tears and told Jenna she did not want to enter. She started to run toward the gates and Jenna went after her. Not only was one of her aunts institutionalized there, but our arrival on the grounds brought back memories of her own stay in the juvenile facilities on the same "campus." She joined the rest of us as we entered the main building for the "rap session" with some of the women on the inside. The woman in charge took all of our possessions, including our handbags, before she led us down a corridor with cells on both sides filled with women commenting loudly on our appearances, particularly parts of our anatomy. Selma lingered behind when she saw her aunt and spoke with her until the guard told her to join the rest of the group.

A number of women lounged around the bright day room with windows that almost looked like real, normal ones. An inmate called out "Ruth." I turned around to see one of the young women who had been in the program for about two weeks and was awaiting trial on drug charges. She was nearly in tears and asked me to write to her. About eight of the prisoners stayed to talk with our group. All had already spent more than a year in prison except one who anticipated getting out within the year.

We sat in a circle and each of the inmates proceeded to tell her story and to warn the young women that they were capable of doing any of these things if they did not start watching their actions. A young, very attractive, and well-spoken woman got up and told the group that she shot and killed the brother of the father of her three children. He had repeatedly visited her home, made sexual advances over several weeks, and, on the night she shot him, refused to leave her house. She told us that she pointed her gun only in order to threaten him, and she vividly described her three years in prison: seeing her three young children only when they were brought to the prison, missing them very much, and wanting to watch them grow. She started to cry as did several of the young women from Project GED.

One of the women in her mid-thirties who, along with several men, had been involved in a number of drug-related offenses, started looking at and speaking directly to Cindy. She spoke in generalities about not hanging around with men who were using or selling drugs. Then she remarked that she had seen several of them in the shooting galleries and this could only lead to trouble. Cindy, pregnant and usually very quiet, started to tell her off about not implying that they were all using drugs, and they argued back and forth for several minutes. Jenna and I looked at each other but said nothing. She finished and another woman spoke. Cindy, her face usually inexpressive, sat fuming (my interpretation at the time).

Two hours after we entered the prison, the guards ushered us out, but the young women did not respond to the various comments made by the inmates on our way out as they had on the way in. All were very quiet on the drive home.

The following day Jenna spoke with Cindy, who told her that she and the woman in the prison had been seeing the same man and that man was the father of the baby Cindy was expecting. The next session with Jenna was one of the most intense about how men used women. The dramatic event of the prison visit and the discussions about men using women is only one aspect of the relations between the sexes. The young women also try to use the men.

These same young women also can be found drawing hearts with their boyfriends' names in the center or drawing their boyfriends' names with fancy letters. They had a long discussion of "love and romance" with one young woman who had received flowers from a man. When Randy came in wearing a "diamond" ring and told everyone that she was engaged, no one questioned the authenticity of the engagement or the stone but mooned over the possibility that one day they too would be engaged.

As with most teens, life often revolves around the opposite sex:

their desires to be viewed as attractive and to be "in love" with good-looking young men. For many, their relationships with young men started early and proceeded rapidly to sexual involvement and pregnancy, though some in this program had their first pregnancies much earlier than others. While one seventeen-year-old had her third child while in the program and two more rapidly after the program, Cindy, at seventeen, was pregnant with her first. Rachel had two children by the same man and was still with him after five years, whereas Kim's three were each by a different man. Kim stabbed and killed one of her boyfriends in an argument on a street corner a year after she left the program, while Val struggled with her boyfriend to get him off drugs and stayed loyally by his side the entire time. Several years later she was working as an aid in the public school system but had not married the father of her only child.

Some of the most dramatic events of these young women's lives involve their relationships with men: falling in love, sex, violence, intrigue, manipulation, drugs, fast cars, and despair. Their relationships with men are also the most intense subjects of their dreams. However, the relationships of their dreams are very different than daily reality. They dream of love, affection, loyalty, respect, being taken care of, and long-term relationships. Daily life was filled with deception, hurt, chasing men and losing, and getting pregnant without really wanting to. Lunch-time and after-program discussions were filled with dreams of romantic love like the "good girls" who are always loved by or saved from disaster by the "good guys" on the afternoon soap operas. Many explained how the soap operas or "stories" were good models for life and dealt with real problems. They spent many hours discussing the lives and romances of their favorite characters.[1]

The arbiters and mediators had differing views of the extent that sexuality and relations with men ought to be part of the discussion within the program. Moreover, they had different perspectives on what the young women's relationships with young men were, how they should be evaluated, and what they thought they should be. While the mission of the program was intended to get the young women off welfare and working, there was little discussion among the staff of how working might be affected by and effect their relationships with men and having more children. The arbiters and mediators handled the issues differently in the program.

1. Cf. Anderson (1990).

The links between personal (spouse or significant other relation) and work life are problematic: both what they are and should be. For some upper-echelon white-collar jobs it is sometimes considered necessary to include an evaluation of the spouse of the applicant for a new job or promotion. The extent to which this is done or should be done is still debated. The questions and issues raised about the links of spousal relations to work for the marginal worker or unemployed are very different. What effect does a woman working have on a relationship with a boyfriend? Work is considered by some to be necessary for maintaining a long-term family relationship, but usually on the part of the male (Anderson 1990; Liebow 1967; Wilson 1987). Some argue that working provides a strong basis of self-respect for the woman who can then demand respect from her boyfriend, while others see it as threatening. Sometimes, however, among young workers, a boyfriend or girlfriend will pull the other away from work. While the mediators acknowledged links and developed new relationships between working and young men for the young unemployed women, the arbiters treated the two worlds as necessarily separate and without connection. How did the young women interpret the messages sent by the staff about boyfriends and the world of work?

Interactions between staff and participants concerning boyfriends raise issues concerning the "real self" (Turner 1968 and 1976). Avoiding acknowledgment of a particular activity or identity used to construct a person's biography when that activity or identity may be considered a stigma may help to facilitate interaction (Goffman 1963). However, when that activity or side of one's self is a critical identity from which one's real self is constructed, lack of acknowledgment or suggestions that this activity or identity ought to be concealed may be interpreted as casting aspersion, showing lack of respect for that which the person considers commendable and important. The person so challenged, if the self is largely situational, fragile, and adaptive (Cooley 1902; Goffman 1959; Strauss 1959) will readily incorporate this new evaluation into the self. To avoid deviant labels, the individual learns impression management. The self derives from performance and its evaluation. If, however, the self is a more enduring social object (Schwalbe 1988; Turner 1968) with changes derived from a continual editing process rather than sharp shifts, then the person may fight at least some of the moral implications of the stigmatization. In the latter view, the "real me" is shaped not only by performance and others' evaluations of that performance but also by what the person would like to be or is trying to do (Turner 1968, 97), that is, it is shaped by values and efforts and "what I am like at my best moments" (Turner 1968, 1976) and here, "what I could be like"—a future orientation.[2] Should the latter model be valid, it may be possible to assuage or challenge some of the implications of stigma.

Should a separation exist between performance evaluation and the real self, then it may be possible, by acknowledging this separation, to challenge a performance without morally criticizing a person. This process may be initiated by challenging the people to increase their perspective-taking[3] ability (accuracy, range, and depth) and their propensity to do so (Schwalbe 1988). This means that staff can avoid attacks on the real self of the participants by increasing the young women's accuracy on how the young men perceive them and by increasing the range of perspectives on work and relationships by showing how work rather than manipulation can be used to demand respect in male-female relations. In so doing, it may be possible to develop a more critical self.[4]

Discussion of Sexuality: Staff Politics

Relations with men were the basis for some of the most dramatic incidents in the lives of the young women and were often linked to problems they had in other spheres of their lives—with their mothers, with their children, with school, and with jobs. The arbiters, however, did not think it necessary to discuss these linkages. During the first session, the staff rarely discussed the young women's relations with men at meetings when they presented individual cases or at the end of the day. At case conferences they talked about program demeanor and educational accomplishments, but once, Roberta mentioned that Steele always took care of her boyfriend's problems: bailing him out of jail, finding him a lawyer, and dealing with his boss. The arbiters felt that this indicated she was a responsible person, but then Roberta said to the others that Steele's relationship to her boy-

2. This "future self" has been referred to as "possible selves" (Nurius 1991) which serves not only as a social product but a social force. It is what one could become and may serve as "one critical determinant of actual goal achievement" (Nurius 1991, 243).

3. "A perspective comprises a perceiving subject with a definite spatiotemporal standpoint and a consentient set of objects . . . Entering the perspective of the other requires that we share the imagery that attaches to the other's perceptual field" (Schwalbe 1988, 415).

4. That is, learn to take a critical attitude toward oneself by weaving "one's action into a collective act or to place oneself in the perspective of 'the generalized other' . . ." (Shalin 1986, 17). A critical self implies social control without conformity.

friend was as poor as the others and she was also a troubling a case. No one ever took Steele aside to talk to her about her relationship.[5]

The arbiters and mediators disagreed as to whether or not the young women should always be held to adult standards. In discussing the maturity of the relationships of the young women, Jenna said, "They are all still children both socially and emotionally . . . They need time to party. They have to go through the same stages of development as everyone." But Ivy responded, "They don't feel guilty when they go out on weekends. They have a double standard. They say they want the best for their children and go out with every Tom, Dick and Harry." Ivy felt that they had no right to act as children as they had responsibilities. Jenna responded that even though they had responsibilities, they were still very young and it was natural that they act that way on occasion. Their job as staff members was to increase the young women's decision-making skills so they could better decide when and how "to party" responsibly and when their responsibilities to their children needed to take precedence. In discussions of individuals at staff meetings, Jenna focused on their decision-making skills: those who were able to make clear decisions were more likely to succeed.

Sexuality did not become a program issue until the transition period between the two sessions. During the first session, Jenna and the people with whom she worked talked about whatever they wanted without reporting anything to Roberta. Sexuality became the issue that not only involved the state monitor, Georgia, but widened the rift between the arbiters and mediators. This resulted when Roberta failed to tell Jenna about Georgia's request for course outlines so that the overlap between Ivy's outline and Jenna's hastily prepared outline involved discussions of birth control and sexual relations, along with drugs and fighting. Georgia told them to divide the tasks but they never got together after the meeting. Behind Jenna's back, Ivy claimed that it should be her job to discuss sexual relations in "group counseling" and that it was not fair for Jenna to do so. They ignored each other and taught what each wanted.

The Importance of Boyfriends: Vivid Dreams and Action

Whether at lunch or waiting for the bus, one of the topics most fervently discussed was "men." On many days stories of wild parties,

5. This may be defined as gossip because there was no point in mentioning Steele's relationship since no one intended to or did say anything to her.

fights over men, sneaking out of their family homes to see boyfriends, stealing another's man, and the attention received by a desirable man dominated the conversation. Everyone had good stories that excited the others' interests and created an intense and dramatic atmosphere. They described details of some of the fights that they had seen or participated in over males, including the damage inflicted on both sides and the circumstances that led up to the conflict. All eyes were on the speaker and someone else was always ready to jump in to describe a bigger or more interesting fight. They laughed heartily at others who fought and were manipulated. Each participant had an exciting story about sneaking out of the family's house and nearly being caught or getting caught and being beaten. While some of the facts seemed to change slightly with each telling of an event, they represented the drama that made life exciting and linked the young women together. As they told the stories, they were always in control of the situation and it was always the other person who was being manipulated. The events were dramatized as rituals of what they viewed themselves as capable of achieving or becoming, which, most often, was not indicative of their actual performance: In the storytelling, the young woman telling the story was never manipulated but was always the manipulator.

Dreams, on the other hand, are more difficult to talk about and leave a person vulnerable to attributions of failure or lack of complete success. They are the ideal. Romance, falling in love, respect, and the security of long-term relationships were at the core of the dreams of most of the young women, but they were not encouraged to talk about those dreams except in a few of the discussions with Jenna. Their most fully articulated dreams involved falling in love with a wonderful man who would respect and protect them from the harsh reality of the world. Their dreams were like those of all the teen romance stories. The desire for respect was central. One young woman, after returning from an all-night bar-hopping party in another town, sighed as she told the others that the boys in that town really respected girls and did not expect them to go immediately to bed like the local guys did. Rickie added that she wanted to join the armed forces because soldiers really respected women.

In their dreams, people get married and stay married forever. Rachel's long-term relationship (five years) with the father of her children was the closest to a dream relationship and one which the others admired and envied. No manipulation of each other was ever involved in discussions of dreams when real feelings developed for each other and the men respected them. The men protected and married the women just like the "good women" on the soaps who always get the nice men in the end.

The Reality and Drama of Manipulation and Being Manipulated
While romantic dreams of authentic love predominate the "wishes," manipulating men and being manipulated by them is the reality the young women live with everyday. Manipulation provides the dramatic talk among friends. While they often laughed at both the perpetrators and victims of manipulation, they both manipulated and were the victims of manipulation by others. Indirectly, they criticized themselves by making fun of others' performances.

They often made fun of the women who actively (publicly) pursued men. One day during lunch, Selma described a scene she had witnessed the previous Saturday night. A woman had chased a man down the street in front of a large crowd of people. He got away and returned later to make fun of her publicly by talking about the chase and laughing along with the crowd. The participants all laughed with her as she added that she had heard that the woman had told the man that her kids were not his. Ella thought the woman made a fool of herself and she, Ella, would never do anything like that.

Despite the humor they found in others' manipulations, many had become manipulators in their own right and worked very hard to entice men and play one off against the other. Most of the time manipulation involved small efforts to make their boyfriends feel indebted to them. Discussions of buying presents for boyfriends often revolved around making them thankful. These presents often cost much more than they could afford and had to be bought "on layaway." They closely monitored the movement of their boyfriends and expected them to be in certain places at specific times.

Sometimes manipulation involved going after someone else's boyfriend. One late afternoon, Steele asked Martha who had given her "hickeys" and Martha replied that it was her ex-boyfriend. Steele said it was not and that the guy who had, had a girlfriend.

> *Martha* No, I wasn't with him.
> *Steele* Yes, you were. I saw you dancing with him. Where did you go afterwards?
> *Martha* Just down to Jan's basement.
> *Steele* You shouldn't.
> *Martha* He had an argument with her and she left with someone else so it was all right.

Other times manipulation meant playing off one boyfriend against another. Ronda and her twin sister were having an argument about their boyfriends and Ronda said that she was going to make her present boyfriend jealous when her other boyfriend got out of jail. There was more discussion about getting two different groups of guys to come over that weekend and how to keep them apart or get rid of one before the other group showed up. A few days later a discussion developed about not trusting girls as friends because they may try to steal your boyfriends. While they become furious with others for going after their boyfriends, they sometimes chased others' boyfriends.

Despite their bravura, they were at least as likely to be the victim of a manipulator as the manipulator. These stories were not the gist of raucous discussion but were the experiences they did not like to discuss. They often waited in vain for their boyfriends to arrive at an appointed time and place. Everyone had a story of sending the father of her children to the store with money to buy "Pampers" and cigarettes and his failure to return either with the money or the "Pampers." On one occasion, Paula asked me and two others to accompany her to a sub shop about five blocks from the program where her boyfriend was supposed to meet her with some money for their children. He never showed up and after laughing and teasing each other for at least forty-five minutes, we returned to the program. Paula cried quietly on the way back and the others pretended not to notice. Too often they found their boyfriends with someone else, and too often they discovered that he already had a child with someone else after discovering they were pregnant. Two young women in the program found out that their boyfriends had gotten both of them and a third woman pregnant in the same month. Involvement in a relationship provided excitement and thoughts of achieving one's dreams but was often short-term and emotionally difficult.

Real-life relationships appear to involve continual manipulation and impression management. Gifts bring promises of love and affection, but, from the perspective of the young women, things do not always work out as planned and many of them were no longer with the father of their children. During one lunch-time discussion about men and sex, everyone agreed with Ginny when she said, "Men do what they want. They tell you one thing and do another . . . You say yes to keep them off your back. . . ." Marge cried as she told me that her boyfriend had not showed up or even called all weekend when he had promised to take her and their son to the beach. Several had been burned more than once and had children by more than one man.

Romantic Dreams of Relationships

Nonetheless, they always hoped to attain that dream of romantic love they saw on the soaps, with a man who respected them, supported them financially, and gave them all of the affection they desired. This dream of a romantic relationship provided a prism through which they could obscure manipulation and experience the relationship as "being in love." They saw the relationship and its future through the dream—it became their reality for the moment. That is, behavior is problematically connected to the real person, and the real me is distinguishable from my behavior (Turner 1968). The real me involves future possibilities: a loving, long-term relationship of respect and security. Boyfriends are a central relationship for these young women just as for most teens. Their relationships have been more consequential and evaluated as questionable by many in the wider society. These young women were very sensitive to any indications of others that might be critical of them as girlfriends, yet were aware that their performances and experiences were often distant from their dreams for the future and how they would like to see themselves.

The Arbiters: A Public Self Does Not Include Boyfriends

The arbiters were concerned with public performance and held a narrow view of the parameters of the public social life. Strategies that the arbiters used to deal with issues of sexuality and boyfriends communicated that these activities belonged to the private realm and should never enter the public sphere of the workplace. The program was equivalent to the work-world so the arbiters rarely mentioned their own family lives and failed to bridge their private world with that of the young women. Instead, the arbiters failure to mention their own families further emphasized differences and inequality. The power of Roberta to define much of the program as "work" and to compel the young women to use their impression management skills in her work-world was significant; however, she was not completely successful in stigmatizing or repressing the young women's sense of who they were and would like to be. While largely interacting in order to please the arbiters, the young women did, on occasion, challenge the demands of some of the arbiters.

There were several strategies that the young women used to manage their interaction with the arbiters concerning their relationships with boyfriends: failing to discuss male/female relationships and sexuality during the few classes when the arbiters did want to discuss them, using their impression management skills in accord with the wishes of the staff so as not to reveal anything personal, telling untrue or exaggerated stories just to get the staff excited, taking control of the topic of discussion, and failing to sign up for individual counseling.

A Narrow View of Public Self: Roberta
Sometimes the lack of mention of an important relationship can communicate that it is stigmatized. Roberta never dealt with the issues of boyfriends or sexuality; they came under the heading of things that one should not talk about publicly, particularly at work, because she claimed, "No one is interested," and "They do not care." She would often follow this type of statement with "This program is like a job and you ought to act in the program as if it were a job." They were in training and "Behavior that is unacceptable on the job is not acceptable here" was an often-heard expression, but her favorite expression was "No one wants to hear your personal business."

Roberta strongly communicated that sex and boyfriends, the world of drama, of parties, and of social life were not to enter the program, certainly not in front of her. In this she was largely successful. She rarely discussed or even mentioned her husband or family. Her daughter, the same age as many of the participants, came once to deliver something but left before anyone realized who she was (I asked Ivy at the end of the day). Roberta reemphasized the exclusion of family from the workplace when she made sure boyfriends were not included in the graduation ceremony and moved the ceremony to the morning, partly to exclude guests. The young women had originally planned to hold an evening ceremony, but she set the time and place and decided who was to be invited (the state representatives and the heads of various agencies who put the program together). All the time that the "young ladies" sat around talking about the event was unconnected to the actual production of the event. Performances that are defined in the young women's community as public are defined by the arbiters as private performances which should never become public. What is public is narrowly defined.

When Roberta defined the situation as "work-related," the young women did not discuss their "personal business" there, but her cultural power to define what was work-related action only extended to sessions organized by the arbiters; however, it was strong enough so that when Ivy tried to hold discussions about family life, the participants would not open up. Most intimate talk took place when the arbiters were not present.

Failure to Create a Bridge: Consequences for Ivy
Roberta successfully communicated that discussions of family and social life were off limits on the job and in the program. Ivy publicly
interacted with Roberta and spent time behind the partitions with
her, which contributed to the identification of Ivy with Roberta's position. Moreover, she never worked to establish a closer relationship
with the participants by connecting her more private experience with
the young women's, such as how she handled any personal issues,
her family, her relationships with men, or any problems that she
might have had. Not only does discussion of one's own experiences
help to bridge the gap between the social worlds of the staff and clients, but "real life" had more meaning to the young women than
printed matter.

The young women saw knowledge that arose from experience as
more valid or truthful than that from books. Things read in books
needed to be measured against lived experience. Ivy, however, generally tried to initiate discussions by using examples from the media—TV shows, advice columns, or prepared scenarios. None arose
from "real life." It always astounded the young women if I said something about children that made sense to them, as they knew that I
had no children. One day during lunch Val asked me in front of the
others: "How come you know so much about kids when you don't
have any?" They were satisfied with my response that I had many
friends with kids and I watched them interact. Ronda responded that
she knew I couldn't get all that from books.[6]

Lived experience was extended to include television on occasions
when the shows were judged to be consistent with experience. Many
of the soap operas, the young women argued, really indicated what
relationships were like: manipulative, people stabbing each other in
the back, and others doing almost anything to get what they wanted.
Women had babies prior to marriage, people moved in and out of
relationships, women were hurt by men, and almost everyone suffered. Against all odds, the "good women" got their men. This was
consistent with their dreams. The Cosby show was a "fairy tale" because no black family in their experience acted like that, explained
Ronda.

Additionally, Ivy communicated that she had limited understanding of and empathy for their experiences. The examples she used to
initiate discussions involved middle-class people and social experiences from a world foreign to their own. She implied that the other

6. The young women are making a similar point to that of Collins (1990)—any social
theory that cannot speak to or validate experience is invalid.

world, her world, was better. The young women decided that Ivy's world was similar to Roberta's, where public and personal experiences are totally separate.

During the second session, Ivy held a weekly session on a topic of her choice, which often concerned male-female relationships. These sessions were very difficult for Ivy and she explained to Amy, who volunteered once a week, that Amy could not attend a rape film she was showing because it might get "too personal." This probably indicated her own lack of comfort, not that of the young women. Ivy's discussions rarely became personal; most of the time she could not get them to talk. The film generated little discussion that day.

Not only did the young women often refuse to discuss the topic broached by Ivy, but her authority was so limited that the young women were able to take control of the discussions, thus rejecting her claims. They took charge by changing the topic to talk about a tangential or unrelated issue. In one session, Ivy tried to talk about "sexual pressures on them," but they refused to discuss the proposed topic. She started out by asking: "What are your sexual values?" No one responded and then she asked, "Do you like your body?" They replied, "Yes." Ginny said that you "do it sometimes to keep the men off your back." A minute of discussion followed but then stopped. Ivy tried again and proceeded to read an advice column about a woman who was seeing, but did not love, a man who was twenty years older than she and wanted sex all of the time. Instead of discussing the issue of sex and relationships, the young women turned it into a discussion of age. Several had examples of couples with substantial age differences which they told in mocking tones. Then Ivy tried to discuss what the young mothers tell their children about their fathers. Most said that the kids knew their fathers and that the fathers brought them gifts. Marge said that she would not go out with a guy if he did not like her son. The others agreed, but the discussion stopped there. They were capable of impression management skills.

Ivy appeared to lack the skill to take the perspective of the young women. Not only did she sometimes appear astounded by their behavior, but she also compared them to more middle-class youth. Once she used an example of a problem relationship between a boy and girl who attended a private school: "This story is by a student from a *good* school and kids from *good* backgrounds." The young women interpreted it as though kids from *good* backgrounds were basically good kids, but *they* were from *bad* families so that nothing was expected from them. Bobbie, a thoughtful young woman, asked me just before they boarded the bus, "Ruth, are we really different from the rich girls?"

Ivy did not appear to be aware of how little she was seeing of the lives of the young women. Even on the occasions when they talked in Ivy's classes, the discussions were limited. In a conversation about the optimal number of children to have and whether they thought that there was a problem with a man who had children by three different women within a year, most said that they wanted one to three children and also claimed that they wished they had waited until after they had finished school. In a questionnaire that Ivy had them fill out in the beginning of the period, the eight in attendance replied "yes" to the statement "I do believe that young people should wait until they are much older before they have sex, then they will understand their emotions better and how to deal with them." While this seemed to be a revelation to Ivy, when we talked about the discussion after class, the young women had talked about the topic previously with Jenna in greater depth and had been much more open about expressing their doubts about having had children so early.

The young women had a difficult time trying to reject some of the implications of the arbiters' performances. Most responses were indirect. Sometimes the young women withheld information or kept quiet when staff wanted a discussion, or they changed the direction of the discussion. They were rarely able to directly challenge or confront the arbiters, particularly Roberta, who threatened that this was their "last chance." Ivy's appearance of little knowledge and confidence provided them with some opportunities. The young women worked to protect their selves but limited their "rejection" responses to remain in the program.

Attacks on Moral Character: Consequences for the Young Women

Placing one's identity as a girlfriend and all of the associated activities in the private realm was more problematic than concealing welfare use, a social choice the arbiters also espoused. The young women appreciated that welfare use is often viewed as unacceptable by the wider society and it was something on which they did not wish to rely. Relationships with men, however, will always be important and are not generally considered deviant. In response to Ivy's questionnaire, four answered "yes" and four "no" to the statement "People who work and pay taxes dislike people on welfare and free food stamps," and seven answered "yes" and one "no" to "Females are only on welfare until they can get a well paying job." But all responded "yes" to the statement "A young girl of 16 years really should not have a baby at this age, but some can make good mothers" and they vociferously changed *some* to *most*. The relationship between men and women is critical to these young women, and if public interaction, where people must try to live up to "ideals," does not include some discussion of their social life, it indicates to the young women that their behavior does not measure up to others' standards. They perceive that others talk about their social relations on the job and that talk is not deviant, so that the arbiters must believe that the young women have a flaw in their moral character and should not reveal anything about their personal lives. Many of the dramatic events that make up the basis for claiming the real self (Turner 1968) are relegated to a separate social world that is to remain strictly bounded from the legitimate public world of the program and work. Their most important relationships belonged with their private dirty laundry.

As a group with little power, the young women were skillful at working to understand the perspective of the staff. They often searched beyond the face-value of the arbiters statements.[7] The mystification created by the attempts to maintain social distance through strictly separating the boyfriends and social life from the world of work and the program was penetrated by the young women. The young women were able to discern correctly that the arbiters, despite their claims of respect and rules that talking about personal lives was inappropriate at work, gossiped behind their backs, particularly about their relationships with men.

While these staff members always said to the young women, "We respect you," the young women suspected otherwise. The arbiters' actions communicated alternative meanings. The staff spent too much time in their private space behind their partitions talking while the young women were working in their workbooks or eating lunch. The participants asked each other what the arbiters could be constantly talking about and what did they write down in the files that were supposed to be kept under lock and key but were sometimes in public view? They knew that it was "personal" information because they had been emphatically told not to touch any of the personal papers on the desk when they used the telephone. Someone read one of the files because some of the private information about sexual activity became public. It did not concern them that the staff collected

7. Turner (1968, 103) offers three levels at which people interpret the communications of others: (1) face value (no search for hidden meanings), (2) empathetic (regarded as concealing true feelings), and (3) diagnostic (at variance with face value and of which alter is unaware). Here the young women use other actions to help them discover what they view as true feelings.

private information because they were never worried about me taking notes openly in many of the classes. What concerned them was others' negative evaluations of their private lives.

They assumed that the staff was continually gossiping about them and gossip generally has an element of negative evaluation in it. No one gossips about positive characteristics, just those that are juicy, sexy, or embarrassing. There were too many hushed conversations behind the partitions not to be suspicious; in fact, they were correct. These staff members often did talk about the details of the participants' lives and often not in the context of trying to solve some of their dilemmas. After the bus left to take the young women to pick up their children, Roberta and Ivy and, during the second session, Mr. Harrison, often sat around talking about the participants. The conversations often consisted of statements such as, "You wouldn't believe what X told me today." While discussions of how to advise the young women about relationships were scarce, the arbiters "told tales" of the young women's sex lives in gossip sessions at the end of the day. Ivy was full of tales from her counseling sessions. She went into a detailed description, with her eyes wide open, about one of the participants who became pregnant three months after the birth of her first baby and was not sure who the father was. What increased Ivy's shock was that the young man suspected of being the father was, in her words, "such a nice young man." Ivy doubted he was the father. Ivy frequently appeared shocked by the sexual activity of the young women.

The young women responded to the arbiters' gossiping. In an effort to tease the arbiters, the participants sometimes told them false or exaggerated stories. Several of the young women were aware that Ivy got excited by "different" sexual attitudes and they enjoyed feeding her imagination. Irma told Ivy that she wanted to become a prostitute and that it was a good life. While Irma talked calmly of the life she envisioned as a prostitute, Ivy's jaw dropped. She did not respond to Irma's tale. The story produced the desired result; that afternoon Ivy could not wait to tell the rest of the staff of this revelation and breathlessly informed them how terrible it was. Irma and the other young women laughed during lunch about the story.

The Young Women's Acceptance of the Program Self
There was little to be gained and much risk involved in openly criticizing the staff, so most of the young women used the impression management skills that the arbiters were trying so hard to teach. They could read the message that the arbiters were not interested in and

did not respect their relationships with men, but sometimes they used these skills in a way that the arbiters may not have envisioned. The young women rarely informed the staff members of court appearances and fights were never mentioned with any of the staff present. During lunch one young woman told us about her case in Superior Court on assault charges stemming from a fight over a man and several others mentioned serious fights they had had. On Monday morning someone would often have a story about a weekend fight. They never mentioned them in front of any staff.

The young women knew who their audiences were. Most successfully concealed important aspects of their lives from the staff. They hid much more from the arbiters than the mediators. One of the young women who was evaluated by the arbiters as one of the best-behaved and as one who would succeed in the middle-class world was one of the wildest on the street. She was one of the only participants in the program who had been in juvenile detention for delinquent behavior, she knew all of the drug pushers and street people in the neighborhood, and got into several fights even while pregnant. In the program she was well-behaved, was more advanced scholastically than many of the others, and said "yes ma'am" to the staff. Her impression management skills were excellent and she was able to segment her life successfully.

The young women were so convinced that the arbiters disrespected their private lives and did not want to hear about them, they did not respond truthfully when asked by the arbiters to discuss their private lives. They did not want to be stared at, criticized, or gossiped about and frequently distorted the truth. The arbiters, however, never questioned them and either did not realize that what they were hearing was distorted or untrue or did not care. In one discussion, Ivy attempted to talk about the young women's relationships with the fathers of their children, but they all claimed that they got on quite well and the fathers often brought their children presents. This was not true for most of them. During lunch the young women constantly complained that the fathers infrequently thought of their children and often showed up without even a box of diapers. One young woman cried as she told a group of us during lunch about her son's father's failure to show up for their son's second birthday party. He did not even call. The young women had very complex feelings about these men, but they would not talk about them in front of the arbiters. They frequently failed to share with these staff members those aspects of their lives they thought would be disapproved of and gossiped about.

The young women became increasingly concerned with guarding their family lives. By the third month of the first session, fewer requested private counseling sessions with Ivy even though it meant that they could be excused from one of their least favorite classes. By the end of that month, one Tuesday passed when no one signed up, and during the second session, almost no one ever did. During the break Ivy decided to hold regular classes, otherwise she would have had little to do except find day care for their children.

Being told not to talk with anyone on the job about their relationships with their boyfriends or the parties they attended and their awareness that the arbiters gossiped about their "private" lives indicated to the young women that there was something wrong with their particular relations. They knew not to gossip with a boss. The young women talked about the "soaps" as instructive about "real life." On the soap operas, everyone seemed to talk about scandals, disastrous relationships, who slept with whom, babies born outside of marriage, and whose boyfriend or girlfriend ran off. People had engagement parties and baby showers at work and discussed their lives at lunch. If an entire show talks about such things, one of the young women reasoned, "Why can't we talk about our relationships? What's wrong with ours?"

Their "Success": Arbiters' Interpretations
The arbiters were split in their interpretations of the young women's actions, such as the failure to sign up for counseling. Roberta approved more of the participants in the second group who were so much better, she claimed, at keeping their "dirty laundry" at home and away from the program than the first group, who had always gossiped and talked publicly about their problems.

She had little desire to understand how her actions were viewed by the young women. She was successful from her perspective at developing a positive program culture; a social and cultural order that separated the program from community social life. Ivy, however, felt that she was losing her importance in the program but did not see how her actions were judged when she tried to get the young women to talk in her discussion groups. She was less convinced of the program's success when she had to recreate her job for the second session.

The arbiters were, despite their rhetoric of describing their job as teaching the young women the skills to follow the rules of appropriate demeanor on the job, moral agents. By communicating that all social life should remain private, and by failing to demonstrate respect by gossiping, they implied that something is morally wrong with the young women's actions as girlfriends. They use their theory of public behavior to invalidate the clients' experience, considered deviant compared with their own model lives, which totally separate work and family life. The arbiters implied that there was not, and should not, be any relationship between the world of work and social life; it was clear that to succeed in the world of work one needed impression management skills to hide one's sordid identity as a girlfriend. This lack of importance given to their social relationships with men affected the young women, but they were also able, to some extent, to ward off these evaluations by controlling the arbiters' access to information.

The Mediators: Sexuality Is Natural and Important

Both the message and the manner in which sexuality, relationships, and work were discussed by the mediators were different from that of the arbiters. The message read by the young women from the actions of the mediators was that not only is sexuality natural, but it is an important aspect of relationships, and relationships with men are important and linked to work. The mediators, talking among themselves, claimed that sexuality and male-female relationships were critical areas that had to be confronted directly as they were such important aspects of the young women's lives. Unless they learned to deal differently with their relationships, the young women would never gain the control they desired over their own lives and become more socially independent and economically self-supporting. The mediators were able to communicate that a strong connection exists between work and social life and that work improves the chances of obtaining dream relationships.

Instead of trying to tell them how they should behave, the mediators attempted to renegotiate the links between performance and dreams of love. The new links involved different ways of critically examining their performances and ideal relationships and, the mediators reasoned, would permit the young women to more readily obtain their dreams of a secure, long-lasting relationship with a man and independence for themselves. In discussions about social relationships, sex was discussed as natural, but it was emphasized that it should be linked to good health and love, not to manipulation. Love should not be a "blinder" that obscures manipulation and links sex to obtaining a dream of security and a long-term relationship. Respect and independence in this model must come before love and sex. There was much to be learned about feelings, love, sex, self-control, and responsibility.

Most of the discussions used the provision of new information (persuasion) to broaden the range of available perspectives and used the examination of their actions through the eyes of others to increase the importance of accuracy in perspective taking. The mediators employed these techniques to persuade the young women to make new choices through seeing themselves and their performances differently and provided them with alternative means or ideas about managing their relationships.

The mediators looked for ways to help the young women develop their skills and propensity to take the perspective of the other in order to make choices that would increase the possibility of obtaining the world of their dreams. Working to understand and showing respect for the perspective of the young women permitted the mediators to criticize and insist upon the young women making more critical self-assessments of relationships with men. However, before the mediators took a critical stance, they constructed a relationship with the young women which permitted them to identify each other as the same kind of people: all were women who had to face similar situations with regard to their relationships with men.

Developing a Shared Perspective: Closing the Social Distance
with the Young Women
It is not easy to discuss relationships and sexuality with a group of teen mothers who are sensitive to others' attributions that they have violated the norms of the wider society by becoming pregnant as single teens. These young women are often reminded of their stigma in interaction with welfare workers, in the checkout lines with their food stamps in the supermarkets, while waiting on the special lines in the bank to cash their welfare checks, and by a blank space in the newspaper announcement of their child's birth where the father's name generally appears. The social life which the arbiters relegated to the private sphere is often made public by situations constructed by strangers.

The mediators tried to develop a shared perspective. Jenna, Esther, Lena, Rita, and Jean are examples of staff members who used their own experiences to make points and to create symbols that would dramatize that they all were the same kind of people so that the young women would listen to what they have to say. While the "help" flowed largely in one direction from the staff to the young people, by the helpers revealing that they have all had similar problems and needed help in the past, they were revealing their own vulnerability. As one needs to abandon to some extent the notion of self-sufficiency and grant others the license to interfere to accept help (Merton, Merton, and Barber 1983), knowing that the helper has needed and accepted help in the past makes the relationship more palatable. It leaves open the possibility that those who accept help may help others in the future.

It is not unidirectional communication where the client reveals all and the staff member then tries to show where the problem is and how to deal with it. Personal revelations occur in both directions so that on the symbolic level the relationship is one that more closely resembles balanced reciprocity (Sahlins 1972). Everyone was encouraged to voice opinions both to praise and to be critical of others, including the staff. All women in the drama presented by the staff were faced with the same dilemmas, making the good women/bad women division false. In this way, they were able to establish relationships with the young women as the "same kind of people" for whom male-female relations and sexuality are important and difficult for all. Being a woman becomes a basis for solidarity.

Esther, for example, in a very long afternoon session, talked about her children and how she expected them to behave. She explained how she set some rules for her young son as well as her daughter. She told the young women her son knew that if he got a girl pregnant, he would have to support her and the baby until the baby went to college. When Esther told them that he had a curfew, they gasped and started to argue that while it was appropriate for girls to have curfew, even though they all violated it, that for boys, it was not. Arguing with them about the issue, she tried to show them something about the consequences of the double standard. She related the freedom of the boys and the supervision of girls to the lack of responsibility of the fathers and their own total responsibility for their children's welfare. This active critical discussion with Esther was different than the lack of discussion which followed filling out Ivy's questionnaire. Five responded "yes," two "no," and one "not sure" to the statement "Males are not as responsible as females are for producing and caring for babies." This split was consistent with the views expressed in Esther's discussion but the young women would not talk about their experiences with Ivy. The double standard was also supported by the majority in the six out of eight positive responses to the statement, "It is okay for a man to be seen drunk, but it is ugly to see a woman in this shape." Again, Ivy was unable to elicit much discussion and they would only talk about other drunk women but not their own conduct.

Jenna, when trying to emphasize the importance of planning for the future, talked about her own experiences when her child was born and how she did not have enough education to get the type of job that she desired and did not wish to marry the father of her child. He was "not about anything." Only after she had a baby did she start to plan to obtain the skills she needed. Again, she continually emphasized that they were not unique and she too had been in similar situations. Everyone can do something constructive with their lives. "It may not be easy, but others have succeeded" and "you can too" was the mode she used to get her message across.

When Jean, a white public health nurse, did several sessions on sexuality and birth control during the first session, she used personal stories in order to show that everyone goes through similar experiences and must make the same kinds of decisions. She let them know that everyone does not do it right all the time and she talked about her own thinking about birth control, which she told them she did after her first baby, not before. She had three children and was divorced. She also used her own experiences in choosing a birth control device to talk about decision making and to allow them to see that everyone has to make such decisions and can discuss those decisions publicly in class. They talked and asked many questions.

The technique of the mediators openly discussing their personal lives allowed the young women to see that these women with good jobs were no different from them—the personnel/participant relationship becomes more of an equal relationship as everyone entrusts each other with intimate information. By including their own mistakes and decision making, the mediators were linking what the arbiters refer to as private lives with the young women. They are the same kind of people; they are all women and have struggled with similar issues. If the young women know that the criticisms are aimed not at them as people but at some of their performances, they are more willing to listen. Exchange of information and acknowledgment of vulnerability enabled the mediators to develop a relationship embedded in respect in which they could be critical of the actions of the young women and still treat the self with proper care (Goffman 1967).

After developing a shared perspective by linking private lives, the mediators were able to assess the validity of performances and challenge the statements or actions without attacking the young women themselves. None of these staff members allowed the young women to get away with saying things that they did not think were valid. In a discussion with Jenna and Ivy concerning who the young women could trust and turn to, Ivy tried and was successful only with Ronda. She attempted to get August to talk who replied, "I don't have nobody." Ivy hesitated and the room was silent. Jenna looked directly at August, "Ms. dramatics, why don't you go on stage?" August looked at her and went on to talk about her friend. Jenna closed the session with some encouraging comments: "That was fun. We shared a bit of ourselves today. I'm glad that everyone participated and helped one another." She was going against the arbiters by encouraging the public sharing of personal information.

Broadening the Range of Perspectives: Others' Views and New Information
Criticism can be less direct by indicating how the performance may be viewed by others and providing new information that provides a basis for reinterpretation of a situation or issue. During Jenna's first class of the second session, she watched the participants carefully. When Jenna asked how they proposed to get off welfare Laura smirked, but Jenna saw her and asked why she reacted as she did. "I don't get welfare." Jenna replied, "There's plenty to learn and all have to participate to get anything out of the material." Later, Lisa shouted that she had to go to the bathroom (to break up the class) and Jenna responded, "It is disgusting to ask in that manner, particularly that way (shouted), and you just came back from lunch. Check yourself out. How would people see you at work?" Lisa sat quietly after that response. Jenna emphasized how one's presentation of self was interpreted by other people. She never said, "You have to act this way," but tried to show how others might interpret those actions and then would ask "look at yourself . . . how would you *want* to present yourself to others? Is that what you want others to see?" They were trying to broaden the perspectives of the young women so that they would be better able to take the perspective of the other. By providing information on how others might view their performances, the mediators are using a form of persuasion: You check out how others may see your actions.

Sometimes the mediators directly challenged the young women's justifications for their actions by looking at the actions from the perspectives of significant others and questioning whether they were taking responsibility for their actions, which they claim portray them as their real selves.

> *Jenna* Ok, put aside the personal stuff, what was the truth about you and that woman? [This conversation took place the day after the prison visit and concerned the confrontation between the prisoner and Cindy.]

Cindy Three years ago when I was young [about fourteen or fifteen], I didn't know what I was doing. I was hanging around with him a lot.

Jenna If I were your mother [important alternative perspective], I would have broken your neck. You've got no business hanging around with junkies.

Cindy I never held the bag.

Jenna You must take responsibility for your actions [don't excuse behavior which you claim is your real self]. You must know what you are about. You know it's a bad world out there and you have to protect yourself and your kids [an important alternative perspective]. You got a kid on the way to bring up. No one is going to do it for you. You have to learn from your mistakes. There is too much information out there today for you to be innocent. You must read the papers, watch the news on TV [broaden your perspective]. As mothers it is important to know a lot to protect your children . . . Anybody can end up in jail. Remember the school teacher? She got into trouble because of her boyfriend.

Jenna and Rita, women who often gave talks to young people about birth control, conducted their discussions of sexuality and birth control as though they assumed that everyone was a sexual person and that all of the young women were going to continue to be involved in sexual activities. They made no moral assessments of the young women's sexual activities: they were natural. Jenna introduced Rita to the class, "Rita and I are going to talk with you today about your needs as a sexual person, your relationships with men. We have a lot of information and a lot of ideas about services for you." Rita continued with a series of choices. "There are lots of other birth control devices besides the pill. I'm not the type of person who says use birth control because you are on AFDC . . . but because of your own health. It's bad for your body to get pregnant too close together . . . You shouldn't wait until you are sick to see a doctor. Blacks die from uterine cancer at a much higher rate than others and you should be checked." She presents information and arguments and leaves it up to the young women to assess what she has told them. Moreover, she equates use of birth control with a health rather than a moral issue.

Increasing Accuracy in Perspective Taking: Using Love to Mystify Male Sexual Desire

None of these women implied that sex was wrong or that the young women were immoral for engaging in sexual activities. The message was clear; many were using sex improperly by using it to try to hold onto their boyfriends and they had to see clearly how the young men viewed them and their actions. Moreover, the mediators argued that sex was not an isolated activity without links to other aspects of one's life. They sent a message that sex was not equivalent to love and that a young woman must be able to *choose* when to engage in sexual relations. Love should not blind one to manipulation. The young women need to use their skills to see beneath the surface meaning. Men are too often manipulative; they say they are "in love" and ask for sex all in one breath and "You believe them." Using their understanding of the world of the young women, these staff members were able to point out new resolutions to the dilemmas and contradictions experienced by the young women in their relationships with men.

> *Louise* He hit me and then he says he loves me and we have sex . . . Maybe he wants me for my body [she seemed about to cry].
>
> *Selma* Everyone will say that girl's dumb to put up with that. People will talk and you shouldn't put up with that.
>
> *Jenna* All those marks over that pretty face shouldn't be there. You stay and have sex with him because he says he loves you afterward. Ask yourself whether that is really love.

In a discussion in the first session with Jenna and Lena, they had a long talk about the kind of relationships in which most of the young women participated.

> *Lena* Love is not the same as sex, but a lot of people think that it is. [All the young women shook their heads in affirmation.] After they have sex they just up and leave.
>
> *Val* When we were younger we did.
>
> *Ronda* Sex is pleasure. We did it because we thought that we were supposed to. If you said no, then they don't want you.
>
> *Sharon* They don't ever give up and they hit on you and say they love you.
>
> *Jenna* All guys think that they got to have sex and they do anything to get it . . . You're the ones who have to be in control.

Again, this was very different from Ivy's inability to initiate a discussion after all of the young women replied "No" to the statement "Sex and love is basically the same thing." They know "correct" answers but have a difficult time dealing with situations in the real world. "Falling in love" often blinds them to the actions of many of their boyfriends.

Love, according to the mediators, had to be embedded in a relationship of trust, responsibility, and mutual respect. The difficulty of trusting men was another topic that held the interest of the young women. They were not sure it was possible to trust the men they knew, though they dreamed of doing so. They often talked of pursuing their boyfriends and fighting the women they feared were after their boyfriends, though they were critical both of those who chased their boyfriends and those who let their boyfriends get away with such behavior. It appeared that a woman could not win.

Using Dreams as Perspective Taking: Being about Something
Jenna tried to link trust and love together with planning for the future. She argued that hanging around with those who want nothing will make you want nothing and then "You will do what everyone else is doing . . . running after each others' partners so that no one can trust the next person." She tried to link working toward an employment goal to relationships with men.

Being "about something" was linked to respect. Many of the young women worried about receiving the respect they thought they deserved from their boyfriends. Often, when pressed, they admitted that their boyfriends did not respect them and talked about the places where they thought that men respected women. Esther argued in one session that self-respect was necessary before a man would respect you and self-respect is linked to independence. "You shouldn't get married too young . . . you must get started on a career first and decide what you want to do. You must demand things of men, they won't change if you aren't working towards some goal in the future." She said this in the context of discussing her own relationship with her husband.

In one of Jenna's classes, when she was being assisted by Lena, a woman with three children who had put herself through college, they talked of the relationship of their dreams.

> *Rachel* You got to talk.
> *Sharon* I need someone to help and respect me.
> *June* He's got to be there when you need him and to be in love with you. But you don't need him all the time.
> *Ronnie* He's got to treat me nice and help my son. [In a tentative voice] . . . He could see others.

> *Sharon* They are dudes and they can do what they want
> with you and you can't do anything.
> *Val* They sneak around you.
> *Randy* I want respect. He should be able to pick you up
> when you is down and respect your kids.
> *Sarah* Respect and help me.
> *Lena* What do you mean by respect?
> *Val* They should introduce you to their friends. They have
> to let me breathe too.
> *Ronda* They got to respect me in front of other women and
> give me an explanation for their behavior.
> *Sarah* Got to get things for the kids that fit. [She was an-
> noyed when the previous weekend the father of her
> daughter brought their daughter an outfit that did not fit.
> To her it represented that he did not care enough about
> their daughter to know how big she was.]

Everyone began to talk at once and added to their list of what they
wanted; things such as receiving roses and candy and other presents,
having a good job, and looking nice. They did not seem to be convinced that gaining and maintaining the respect that they desired was
a realistic possibility.

Respect and trust only come with self-control, responsibility, and
independence was the message sent to the young women. They debated what independence meant; for some it meant being able to go
out with two men simultaneously or being able to get high while leaving the baby with someone else and for others it meant being self-
supporting. Seth was seeing Ella's brother while she was going out
with another man who gave her some of his paycheck and often took
her out. She said that she could never make him mad no matter what
she did. Ella and Seth laughed about the games they played. Paula
and Bobbie, more convinced by earlier talks, responded between
bites of lunch that they would never go out with two men at the same
time but wanted to be self-supporting. For Bobbie, this new perspective differed from the one she accepted at the start of the session.

Jenna firmly argued that "games" would never lead to respect. Being about something was clearly related to independence gained
through having a job. This conversation occurred toward the end of
the first session.

> *Val and Sarah* You've got to be independent and you can't
> lean on any man.
> *Val* You got to be able not to owe him anything.

Jenna Will you need a job so you don't have to depend on
  him?
Ronda I want one [job] so my kids can have a nice house and
  clothes.
Sarah You don't need to be asking for money at the end of
  the month.
Val You can't depend on no man. I got to get me a job.
Jenna It's important to be financially independent—then you
  can be proud and choose who is right for you. But you
  can't be giving out your check to him when he talks nice
  to you and your kids in the beginning of the month.
Matti Yeah, you see all the guys in the beginning of the
  month with their kids and sweet talking all the girls
  downtown. [General, knowing laughter.]
April Not mine, I don't give nothing away.
Jane Sure. [Jane laughed and others rolled their eyes. Most
  have been in the situation.]
Jenna It's something we should all be thinking about. Independence has to be on both sides. You shouldn't use them
  or be used.

Esther linked responsibility with sex in her discussion of what she
told her teenage children, and on another day she began by saying
that sex without independence and responsibility leaves one feeling
used and abused when you are not sure who you are: "You have to
decide what you want from the situation especially when you're
lonely. There is tension between relationships and a career. [Several
nodded.] But responsibility is not just money . . . You can't let some
man walk over you just because he talks nice. You have to be independent enough to decide whether he is just jiving you or you have
a real relationship." Then she talked about their responsibility as
mothers not to invite a man in until they were sure he really liked the
children and was not after their check or sex.

Sharing Power: You Make Your Own Decisions
The mediators rarely told others how to run their lives, that is, increasing dependency as passive recipients of help. To further help
self-determinacy, they encouraged the young women to set the
agenda for discussion. Not only did Esther talk about her family, but
she also asked them what they would like to discuss, that is, she
encouraged them to take active control of the situation. When she
asked the young women of the first group on the occasion of her third

visit if they had a particular topic they wanted to discuss, they said "relationships." She always asked them about themselves and listened intently to the answers before deciding what to say. The young women sat talking and listening carefully for more than two hours. Esther described what her life had been like growing up and how she had gotten to where she is today. Even Bette, always the first to disrupt class, sat listening and asking questions. Esther spent time talking about getting what they wanted out of life and toward the end of the meeting, in no uncertain terms, was very critical of some of their relationships with the fathers of their children. She told them that they let the fathers of their children get away with not helping out often enough and that it made it difficult for their children. If the young women slept with these men every time they bought something for the children, the young women were not encouraging the fathers to be responsible for the children. They were buying things in exchange for sex. Everyone continued to listen without squirming or protesting. I noticed two young women biting their lips.

Emotions as More Public
In the mediators' classes the young women participated readily in discussions and rarely fell asleep or talked back to the staff as they did in Ivy's classes. Moreover, they were much more likely to admit confusion over their lives, whether it had to do with their boyfriends or their future careers. They would argue with each other and the mediators, encouraged to do so by the mediators. In the discussion classes with the arbiters, they would give all of the "correct" answers about attendance and what constituted a legitimate absence from work; however, in classes with the mediators they admitted that they were unsure how to respond when their boyfriends wanted to be in control and not permit them to go out or attend school. When they were "in love," many felt that they had to give in to their boyfriends' requests. That was how they experienced their lives. Jenna was very aware of that pull and felt it was necessary to confront this reality by linking their experiences to their dreams of love, security, and respect for sex. She did this by trying to show that first a woman had to be "about something"—able to support herself, which would give her independence and self-respect so she could demand the same from her boyfriend.

Emotions such as feeling hurt, confused, stigmatized, or lonely were much more readily expressed in these classes. Rarely did someone say, "this is boring" or "we heard about this in another class." They discussed feeling lonely, used, and wanting to be loved. Emotions were public.

This does not mean that there were no limits to what they talked about or that they were never bored or that they never fell asleep. They often failed to mention activities that they knew would be criticized. They rarely talked about the wild parties attended on weekends. Some of the problems with their boyfriends were never mentioned in class. Marge was miserable when her boyfriend promised two weekends in a row to take her on a trip—the second weekend he did not even call her until Sunday night. She cried over lunch while talking to me and Bobbie but would not say anything in class, even when probed by Jenna about her "long face." Ella had to go to Superior Court on assault charges for fighting with another woman over a man but never said anything to the staff. When the topic of violence was broached by Arnie and Jenna on another occasion, the young women did not want to talk about it and denied fighting now that they were mothers. While Jenna knew differently, they did not want to talk with the mediators, though they discussed fights during lunch. There was much less of a staged performance with the mediators. Because the mediators viewed them as good persons, real feelings and events could be publicly discussed without stigmatizing and hurting the self, that is, the mediators' "theory" was consistent with the experiences of the young women.

In discussing the classes of the mediators, the young women used expressions such as "straight up" and "the kind you can talk to." These staff appeared to be "real people" who listen without judging moral character even when they are critical of performances. "They make you think about things," one young woman explained. At the end of one of Jenna's classes Bobbie broke into the discussion: "I want to say something. Before I started the program, I was really shy and didn't want to say anything. Now I talk more and dare to do things more than before." About Ivy, on the other hand, Val explained, "She thinks she's smart." Another turned to me and explained, "Ruth, we don't mean intelligent, we mean [she thinks she] knows better than us."

Critical Self and Moral Organization

Developing a "critical self" is not an easy task, but the mediators worked hard to try to encourage the young women to critically examine their own actions and to enable them to see those actions from a variety of new perspectives. A self which can act critically toward social experience and social relationships can begin to make changes in the world in which the individual lives, such a person can begin to create a new path.

Jenna explained the idea of a strong critical self during a discussion of the session they had had with the inmates of the women's correctional facility:

> If they [the prisoners] had known who they were, then they would have been able to say no to those men who got them into trouble . . . We all have to work to develop a strong one [self]. We need to know who we are as strong black women. We can't let others tell us what to do.

To develop a more critical self, the mediators worked to increase both the skills and the propensity to take the perspective of the other, so that the young women could and would take more control of their social relationships by reexamining their actions in order to try to achieve the dreams they articulated. The mediators tried, through talking about experiences, to persuade the young women to see and make more choices instead of giving in to manipulative behavior, that is, to view their own behavior critically in terms of what they would like to achieve. Specifically, the mediators tried to persuade the young women in the program through self-revelation, criticism, and by expanding their perspectives that independence through achievement was linked to self-respect, and with that self-respect would come expectations for respect from boyfriends. Love could not truly develop without respect and never within a context of manipulation. If a woman wants to achieve her dreams of love, security, respect, and a long-term relationship, she "has to be about something" and demand that the man must "be about something" also.

This "critical self" means making some changes in the important social relationships in which the young women's lives are currently embedded. It does not mean conforming. The mediators never denied the importance of the male/female relationship and the young women's sexuality but tried to embed "loving" relationships in a context of respect and independence rather than manipulation and sex. The mediators successfully talked about actions critical to change and engaged the young women in confronting but never invalidating their experiences.

The young women responded differently to the arbiters. They rarely talked in class and when they did, it was not revealing. The arbiters communicated very different messages to the young women; their boyfriends were part of their "dirty laundry," to remain permanently in the private region. While the arbiters claimed they were not moralizing but teaching impression management skills necessary for the work world, moral failure was the message that they managed to communicate. It was public performances that counted and by demanding that the young women not discuss their relationships, while gossiping behind their backs, the participants read the message that something was wrong with their particular relationships. This interpretation was strengthened by the young women's views of the wider society from watching the soap operas. In these "stories" everyone's love life is public and discussed at work so why should theirs be different?

The staff's differing views of self impact not only on the different relationships they developed with the young women but in the contradictory messages they communicate about the young women's relationships with young men and what the connection between those relations and the world of work should be. On the one hand, the relationship that the young women view as essential to their sense of self is viewed as dirty laundry and as belonging to the private world by the arbiters, who tell them what the rules of the work game are and how relationships with men are to be totally segmented from that world. On the other hand, the mediators strive to communicate that a strong link between the world of work and relationships exists and that to obtain their dreams the link must exist.

CHAPTER SEVEN

Motherhood: Authenticity and
the Context of Suspicion

During the first session the parenting class staff decided to set aside a day for planned activities: arts and crafts, drawing silhouettes of the children, songs and stories, and other games. The stated purpose was to provide new ideas about what the mothers could do with their children at home. At 9:30 the buses brought fifteen mothers and eighteen children. Several of the children ran around the room and others clung to their mothers. Some mothers shouted at their kids to behave, while others spoke calmly to them. Toni continued to tease her two-and-one-half-year-old son who became increasingly active, running around in circles and shouting. Val and Martha tried very hard not to get too excited and, sitting at one of the long tables, had their children on the floor next to them.

Amy, an inexperienced white volunteer and leader of the parenting class, divided the mothers and their children into five groups. Each was to participate in a different activity and rotate as the morning wore on. Several of the mothers liked the craft table. It was difficult to tell whether they were making things for themselves or their children. Mimi and Sharon worked hard constructing some necklaces and ignored what their children were doing. Another young woman made an Indian headband with a feather for her son. She smiled very brightly when he ran off to show it to the others. By noon everyone seemed tired but happy. Most of the children were slightly calmer and pleased to have made something to take home. For several days, the mothers talked about the activities and commented about the developmental skills of each other's children.

At Christmas, the entire staff and the young mothers planned a party for themselves and the children. The event was a success, according to the participants. Everyone wanted photos to record the celebration in their albums. In planning the party the mothers had discussed holding a drawing to choose someone for whom to buy a small gift. The young women stated that they would probably not get anything for Christmas and they planned to spend all of their money on presents for their children. The exchange of gifts never occurred.

The children arrived in their party outfits and sat wide-eyed on Santa's lap and received a small gift the program provided. Staff members had had to force John into the Santa suit as he had had no desire to participate. The previous day Ivy took several of the young women to the grocery store to buy chicken and ham to cook for the luncheon, while Jenna, with others, made decorations from scraps of material and paper they had found around the building. All of the participants cooperated with the cooking and ate the food with their children.

These were considered special days during the first session about which stories were told. They were never matched during the second session. The staff never met the children in the second session and took no pictures, even of graduation. The arbiters expressed the opinion that activities with the children were disorderly and worthless. The weekly parenting classes during the first and second sessions were much less exciting than these special events, and, during the first session, the young women did not relate well to the family life staff. This changed in the second session.

Amy, after two months, still did not know all of the names of the first session participants:

> *Randy* What are we going to do today?
> *August* Let's get going so we can get it over with.
> *Amy* I work for a parenting group, a group which deals with child abuse. What is abuse?
> *Tammy* Physical.
> *Amy* What constitutes abuse? . . . Does slapping equal abuse? [They responded that it depends on what the child does and that it could often be just punishment.]
> *Amy* If you hit and hit? [Then she starts reading from a book which she has pulled off the shelf behind her.]
> *Randy* Why are you shaking?
> *Amy* I'm leaning on my elbow. . . . What does giving birth feel like?
> *Tammy* With my first I was happy.

Ramona I was always hungry. [Randy walks out of the room in front of everyone.]

Amy What do you do with your child that your parents did to you?

Ramona She rolls her eyes like me and she's so bad nothing stops her, just like me.

Tammy I yell just like my mother did to me.

August Even if you try you can't bring up kids like you used to.

Matti They listen more to their grandmother than to me.

Tammy You tell him what to do and he says that "I'll tell my mama [grandmother]."

Amy Do you feel like a parent?

August Yes. I tell her that it's my daughter but it doesn't work.

There was more talk of punishing kids and that they smacked to punish, not to abuse. It was the intent that counted. Some of the young women remained engaged, while others began to do something else or to talk to each other. Several took out baby pictures and passed them around the room commenting upon them while Amy was trying to talk. Afterwards they told each other that they did not like to be called child abusers and several did not return after lunch. The program organization made absence easy as one entire day was dedicated to parenting classes. Only a few attended on that day after the first two months.

The second session classes were better. The young women listened and tried out some of the suggestions. Amy picked narrower and less evaluative topics to discuss, introduced her daughter to the young women, and carefully learned all of their names. But none of the discussions in these classes ever matched the excitement or detail of lunchtime gossip of pregnancy, childbirth, and their struggles as mothers of young children.

The arbiters, the mediators, Amy, and the young mothers all had differing views of teen motherhood, its place in the program and in the outside world. Moreover, the staff's relationship with the young women affected what the staff could say without a revolt. For the arbiters, teen motherhood was just one of the two eligibility factors (the other was school dropout) for this program; they ignored motherhood. For the young women, it was what made them creative adults, what gave them a purpose and meaning to life. The mediators with their established relationships with the young mothers were able to criticize their parenting skills as well as their relationships with boyfriends and occasional irresponsibility without denying the importance and the creative role of parenting. Amy understood the importance of motherhood to them but not how to communicate that she understood. She might have become more effective as a mediator if she had been able to develop a better understanding of the young women's lives. During the first session she lost control of the class, but during the second, she was able to begin to use the strategies of the mediators.

Awareness Contexts and Risk to Authentic Self

A question arises today about where the authentic self can be located. According to Turner (1976) the expression of the real self is located predominately in impulse (such as undisciplined desire and the wish to make intimate revelations to others), whereas, traditionally, it was located in institutions ("in feelings and actions of an institutional and volitional nature, such as ambition, morality and altruism" [p. 989]).[1] While the impulsive self may predominate today, does everyone have an equal choice and are there limits to the choices?

For some, the consequences of a particular choice may be greater than for others, and those possible consequences may be experienced as limiting choices. Not everyone can choose where to locate their real selves without substantial risk of losing what they desire in other areas of their lives or of interference by others in running their lives. It may be that some can less afford to locate self in impulse, especially those who experience the sting of failure to meet the middle-class "standards," such as young single mothers living on welfare.

For those whose actions are subject to official supervision of the state, embedding one's real self in impulse is a significant risk. When an individual is living on the edge with few resources, choosing a self embedded in impulse may create substantial risk for the stigmatization of self and, additionally, may result in the loss of financial resources when those resources are controlled by others and are dependent on others' assessments of one's actions. It may be very consequential to risk public revelation of frailties as a mother because

1. According to Hochschild (1983, 192), "It is the corporate use of guile and the organized training to sustain it. The more the heart is managed, the more we value the unmanaged heart." This is what leads to the present-day value of authentic and natural feeling that the American middle class often searches for in therapies. One searches for authentic self in the private world away from the corporation, politics, and work site where the managed self prevails.

of the close monitoring by agents of the welfare system. An impulsive self works to discover a real self over time, but those who rely on the state or on low-wage jobs may not have the time or resources to discover their true selves. Additionally, if they permit the "winds of circumstances" (Allport 1955, 50, as quoted in Turner 1976, 993) of the impulsive self to determine their sense of real self, they may increase the risk of losing their children to the state. The state workers may view such behavior as harmful to children, particularly if that means leaving a child "too often."

Moreover, present-time orientation characterizes the person of impulse (Turner 1976), but the poor are blamed for failing because they do not plan for the future and are told by the welfare workers who have power over them that, unless they plan for the future, there may be important consequences. While individualism, a characteristic of impulsiveness, may protect the young women from peer pressures, any rejection of conventional standards would mean a substantial risk for them, given so many "officials" poking into their lives.

Following impulse may lead the young women into situations they sometimes wish they had avoided when they look back—pursuing the "wrong" man, pregnancy, fights, and trouble with the law. Reflecting on their actions, permitting the "winds of circumstance" to rule their lives sometimes had severe and undesired outcomes. Most did not intend to become pregnant and pregnancy has contributed to many of the problems in which they currently find themselves; however, the irony is that motherhood itself is where the young women have been able to locate their authentic selves.

If expressions of authentic self fall largely in the private sphere (mothering), expressions are not evaluated except by those closest to the self, either family or persons freely chosen in that closeness. However, for these young women, outsiders enter or try to enter into the most private aspects of their lives; moreover, the situation is public. Entry into the very private arena of other's lives gives that stranger enormous emotional and, in this situation, financial and social power to evaluate the young mothers' actions, which could result ultimately in loss of their income or, worse yet, their children.

Because the stakes are so high in revealing information about mothering, there is an additional emphasis on questioning the sincerity[2] of the staff in their dealings with "mothering." Do the staff

2. According to Goffman, sincerity is defined by the actor: "individuals who believe in the impression fostered by their own performance" (1959, 18), while for Trilling (1972) sincerity has more objective qualities. For him sincerity is the congruence between avowal and actual feeling or the absence of feigning. Here we are more con-

really mean it when they say they are trying to help? What do their actions really mean? Can anyone be sure that they will not turn reports over to the state? The skepticism toward the sincerity of staff creates an awareness context[3] of suspicion on the part of the young mothers, and they are more likely to work to make it a closed-awareness context if the sincerity of the staff member is in doubt.

Unlike "falling in love," which can blind the young women to careful examination of their boyfriends' actions, a context of suspicion is the starting point of all relationships with the staff. On the one hand, the young women are not sure what the staff know or think of them as mothers. On the other hand, some of the staff have little idea of what the clients think of them or what their behavior means to the young women. The young women suspect that some of the staff wish to find fault with their actions as mothers and turn them over to the state.

The arbiters framed their actions concerning motherhood in terms of equating the program with a work site. The young women, however, were suspicious of the absence of information about the arbiters' children and interpreted their actions as regarding motherhood as deviant. Amy was faced with a situation that she did not fully understand. She liked the young women but at first was unable to understand the young women's lives or how they viewed her actions. She existed in a closed-awareness context. While she worked hard to create a more open-awareness context, she and the others were never completely successful because of the young women's suspicions that these staff were not entirely sincere in what they said and did.

From Fortuity to Authentic Self: Pregnancy to Motherhood

Some people attribute intentionality (desire for welfare, wanting to keep their boyfriends, someone to love, everyone else has one) to the teens becoming mothers, while others claim that the young do not intend to become pregnant (lack of knowledge of sex or birth control,

---

cerned with the audiences' views of the congruence between what others might say, do, and feel and what they may "really" think.

3. An awareness context is "the total combination of what each interactant in a situation knows about the identity of the other and his own identity in the eyes of the other" (Glaser and Strauss 1964, 669). For the most part, they tend to focus on "surface" identities that may be more easily knowable, such as "spy" or "dying" if you have the correct information. Here, in part, we are discussing a more ambiguous situation about assessing what the others think about them as mothers—their qualities as mothers.

or lack of accessibility of birth control, boyfriend does not want to use birth control) and cannot or do not want to obtain abortions. Intentionality is a complex process of negotiation and renegotiation during talk among the local social networks made up of female peers and family, both young and mature. Accounts of intention and lack of intention are closely related to the young women's position in the social structure and their own efforts to develop their authenticity as people in the world that they know and in which they feel comfortable. Without an understanding of the young women's notions of authenticity and its relationship to motherhood, staff could not communicate effectively with them.

The creative experiences of pregnancy and motherhood are also the experiences that unite participants as women. These are the topics they talked about most and which drew them together. Rarely did the participants discuss the program, clothes or makeup (they had no money to buy them), or possible employment. Before classes started, at lunch, or while waiting for the bus, they often discussed pregnancy, the birth experience, and sometimes how "spoilt" their children were. This was always said with some degree of pride but also inferred that the child was difficult to handle. They all enjoyed discussing their experiences when pregnant, particularly how everyone catered to them; how their mother, grandmother, or sister would go out in the middle of the night to buy them some delicacy. The birth of the child was often described in a very positive light despite the pain and, for several, dangerous medical complications. Typically, several female relatives attended the births and lavished attention on the young mothers. They did, however, receive many messages from the society around them that they had become mothers too early and without the necessary marriage. They are all acutely aware that much of society does not approve of their motherhood.

Lack of Intention: Getting Pregnant
In talk it appears that the majority of pregnancies were unintended. Most of the discussions concerning pregnancy occurred when no staff were present, such as during lunch or while waiting for the bus. Val told me she had just started her period and thought she could not get pregnant yet. June, now pregnant with her second, said she wished she had not gotten pregnant again and had been on the pill and, when she stopped taking it, had immediately gotten pregnant again. Sharon, pregnant now, said she had not meant to and did not want the responsibility. In a discussion on responsibility and bringing a

child into the world with David, whose presence was sponsored by Jenna, Kim said she was on the pill when she unintentionally became pregnant with her third baby. Darleen, who was eight months pregnant with her second baby, said she had not even wanted to be pregnant the first time. She was using the pill after her first, but it was making her sick. When the doctor would not change it, she stopped taking it and got pregnant. She said her mother would not let her get an abortion. The other young women concurred with these accounts and never challenged accounts of lack of intention to become pregnant.

Developing Intention: Being Pregnant
Denying the possibility of abortion or adoption begins the transformation from fortuity to intention. When pregnant, it is time to begin to take responsibility for your actions. Their mothers were not pleased when they discovered that their daughters were pregnant, but, according to the young women, many were opposed to abortion. One mother told her daughter that she could only have an abortion if the daughter paid for it herself. At fourteen she could not get a job and the state would not pay, so she was forced to have the child. None accepted the appropriateness of giving a baby up for adoption and all were critical of one young mother, known by several of the participants, who had considered it seriously. If you were grown up enough to get pregnant, they explained, you should be responsible for the baby. This, they claimed, was also what their mothers told them. In one conversation, Gay asked, "Why get pregnant if you are going to give up the baby? That's stupid. If you don't want a baby you shouldn't get pregnant." Marian added that "no one could get as close to an adopted baby as you would your own." While most expressed lack of intention to get pregnant, they were instructed by peers and mothers that they were expected to "intend" to become mothers.

The shift from lack of intention in becoming pregnant to intending to become a mother often occurred within the context of a redefinition of the mother-daughter relationship and the strengthening of the ties with other young mothers. A common bond of experience developed during pregnancy. For many of the young women, pregnancy created a very significant shift in their relationships with their mothers and was also a time when they were the center of attention. Many of their mothers had been teen parents themselves and several were in their early thirties at the time of the birth of their first grandchild.

Martha's situation was atypical. While her mother threw her out when Martha became pregnant, most mothers and daughters appeared to resolve their differences fairly rapidly and mothers began to treat their teenage daughters more as equals. Ramona told the others that her mother began to allow her to play cards with her mother's friends and to hear all of the interesting gossip. Several reported that their mothers did not care as much when they came in, so they were freer to do what they wanted. Not only did mothers begin to include them in adult activities and supervise them less, but often catered to their eating desires. Favorite stories involved midnight trips to the store for fruits, cookies, and shrimp when they had a craving for such goodies. Relationships, though rocky at times, appeared to improve for many of them as the pregnancy continued.

The new stage in the mother/daughter relationship during pregnancy was not without tension. During one discussion with Lena, Sandy told the group that after getting pregnant her mother allowed her to have guys over and said that they were more like sisters now. However, she did admit that her mother would not let her go out at night and she left using the fire escape. Later that day at lunch Sara said that she wanted to do things differently than her mother, but her mother was always telling her what to do and undermining her authority. Her mother liked to slap her around and wrestle, and now they were friends and "kind of like we growed up together."

Some took the "intention" of motherhood less seriously than others. A few during pregnancy remained embedded in the impulsive self and had not taken much care of themselves through the pregnancy, continuing to smoke and drink. For some, this resulted in elevated blood pressure exacerbated by consumption of too much salt from a constant diet of potato chips, fried food, and too few vitamins. Most actively changed their behavior, which demonstrated their intention to become good mothers. They ate well, stopped smoking and drinking, and had relatively easy births. Most started smoking again after the birth and smoked rather constantly in the program. One of the participants who was pregnant and smoking was criticized by several others.

The birth was the culmination in the creation of another life and involved the participation of a number of female relatives. Only a few of the fathers of the babies attended. It was a women's celebration and a sister, an aunt, and/or her mother accompanied the young woman to the hospital. For most of the young mothers, looking back on it later, the birth was an exciting and wonderful event, despite all of the problems and pain. As the young women progressed in their pregnancies with the help of their friends and relatives, they began to talk about the births of their babies as planned and desirable. They meant to have the baby, even if they did not intend to get pregnant.

Intention: Being a Mother
Intention is necessary if one is going to claim that motherhood is an expression of one's authentic self. To be authentic infers choice, yet motherhood is an expected and often normatively required role for women. Motherhood, however, when achieved as a teenager and outside of the bonds of matrimony is often regarded as problematic by outsiders. These young women stepped outside of the expectations for their age and marital status and, according to their own accounts, *chose* to do something they were not supposed to. However, the stigma is somewhat mitigated because it is expected and approved for most women—at least when they are older and married. Having made an independent decision to become a mother over the objections of their own mothers and the wider society, they are able to claim that motherhood is a reflection of their authentic selves and, as an approved status for women, it is only deviant because of their age and marital status. As Lofland (1969, 110) argues, the lure of deviance "is all the stronger when prohibition is not against the activity per se but against engagement in it by particular categories of persons." Sex and motherhood are valued activities and only prohibited for the underaged and unmarried.

The young mothers were aware that representatives of the wider society thought they had become mothers too early and that they were deviant because they were unmarried. These mothers attempted to justify these categorical deviations. They were able to develop a rationale that attempted to resolve the dilemma of doing something that one knew was approved of for women during a certain stage of their lives, yet was disapproved of for them. They said, "I will be able to grow up with my children." This expression was heard over and over in different contexts and served as an explanation for moving back and forth between the demands of adulthood and the pleasures of youth. Several argued that if they had not had children now, they would never have had any.

Motherhood continually posed dilemmas for these young mothers. It was a positive creative act but it also constrained their behavior. Often they said they wished they had waited. Motherhood has an element of permanence: it cannot be taken away, yet there is always a terrifying risk that social workers may take away the child. Motherhood linked the young women to other women in the wider society, yet they were aware that others condemned them for having children as teenagers. With motherhood came financial independence from their own mothers but financial dependence on the welfare system and frequent social and emotional reliance on their mothers, from whom they wished to be independent. With independence came great responsibility and the end of the freedom to come and go as desired. Real tension exists between self-sacrifice to children (institutional locus) and giving in to the desire to hang out on the street or in a bar with friends and with inhibitions lowered (impulse locus) (Turner 1976).

Moreover, relationships with their own mothers are not without conflict. While that relationship changes as they are both mothers now, it is often the case that the children call their grandmothers "mother" and that the young women are called by their names and leave their children with their mothers, who sometimes resent that they have to begin again with the raising of babies while they are still raising their own.[4] Selma said her mother claimed that she was mother to both Selma and her son.

Childraising as a Natural Process: Mothering

Being a mother is viewed as a natural phenomenon that all "normal" women have the skills to do successfully with help from those with more experience—grandmothers or mothers. It is possible to do the job reasonably flawlessly and not reveal human frailties (Turner 1976). Mothering is not viewed the same as being a student or worker, where one is subject to many rules and regulations and technical training is necessary and failure is easy. Mothers and grandmothers have no special training for motherhood and do well, so none is necessary beyond advice from the experienced.

Advice about childrearing is sometimes partially summarized by frequently used phrases such as "she be grown," "she's spoilt," "that girl looks ugly," "she be smart," "he be bad," and "I got an attitude." On a number of occasions when asked about their relationships with their children, the young women responded, "I spoilt her, she won't go to any one else," which is often modified by saying that the child will go to her grandmother too. It appears the young mothers feel children need to be disciplined from a very early age, but they have failed to do enough of it. They believe their children have been

---

4. This has been documented elsewhere (Anderson 1990).

permitted to do whatever they want when visiting a father's family or another relative and worry that fathers spoil their daughters. Most of the time these young women were talking about children under the age of three.

Some believe that their children understand more than they probably do and argue that the way to achieve discipline is to "bust his butt." This is different than abuse, which has no goal but to hurt the child. Kim explained that she was toilet training her two-year-old. He sat on the pot for a half hour, but a few minutes after he got up, he "shit in his pants, so I hit him. He knew what he was supposed to do and he disobeyed me." Most explained that it was all right to slap their wrists or hit them on the rear but not to hit on the face.

Being a mother is viewed as natural and one does not need schooling or book learning to be one. Life experiences are generally considered necessary for knowledge. Their mothers never had lessons and they turned out all right. For example, Cindy, who was pregnant with her first child, finally admitted she was afraid about the delivery and had no idea of what labor would be like. Liz responded, "How would you know? You've never had a baby." Amy tried to describe the process, but the young women, all of whom had had at least one child, were not convinced that anyone could adequately describe the experience. One had to actually deliver the baby. As experience is viewed as the best teacher, it places enormous difficulties on someone who is trying to teach, in a formal manner, the young women to do things differently than they do currently.

Childrearing as Responsibility
Regardless of the age of the child or with whom a child lives, that son or daughter belongs to the mother and is her responsibility. A child is one's future and no one can say that child is not of the mother. All the young women believe this and talk about the responsibility that they have for the welfare and upbringing of their babies. They know that they are held accountable for their children and think they should already know how to bring them up. Their mothers said that they must be held accountable for their pregnancies and then they must take care of their own children and give up much of the desirable partying. Many of them see themselves as making sacrifices for their children.

Being a woman is not the same as having kids but having kids is taking responsibility, argued Rachel in response to David's question "What is a woman?" David replied, "The key word is responsibility.

Raising the baby you must stand alone and take responsibility, that is the responsible job as a parent."

> *Kim* We had too much [responsibility].
> *David* I'm not talking about biology. I'm not expressing my views on women's lib but responsibility of a woman to her kids. They only have you to look up to.
> *Kim* My kids look up to me.
> *David* You got to select good role models—not drug addicts or pimps.
> *Ramona* My son models me. He always rolls his eyes like me.
> *David* You got to look toward the future. I ended up with my daughter and am raising her alone.
> *Ramona* I can raise my child better than those bums out there—I got a bad attitude sometimes.

Despite their discussions of the importance of responsibility and intending to become a mother, when they talked during lunch, they were more ambivalent about whether they wanted or could adequately meet the responsibilities that motherhood entailed. Sharon, after talking about trying to return to school after the birth of her baby and failing to find a sitter on a regular basis, said that her mother wanted her in school because she had never returned to school after she had had Sharon at fourteen. Sharon said that she is still a kid and likes to run around outside and does not want to be a mother. "I don't want any responsibilities . . . I want my freedom."

Childrearing: The Dream of Independence, the Reality of Dependence on Others
Not all remain equally dependent on family members. Some live entirely on their own. This puts a very heavy burden on the young mothers who have no one to help them out, even in an emergency. Judy, at eighteen, had two children under three. She was living alone when she caught a very bad throat infection from her baby. She was alone with the two sick babies for over a week with only one friend, who had two of her own, to help her.

Most are not unaware of their dependence on others and often try to fight it. While not all rely on older family members, some rely heavily on their mothers and a few on their grandmothers. A frequent topic of informal discussion among the young mothers was leaving children with grandmothers, telling them that they (the mothers) are just going to buy something at the corner store but disappearing for several hours. Although the young women were often upset when their boyfriends did the same to them, they often did not see their own behavior in the same light. On other occasions they left children with a family member to "party" all night, just as other family members did to them. Some took greater responsibility, rarely leaving their children with others.

They often worried about who had authority at home and some saw that their own mothers had taken most of it. Sarah said she wanted to do things differently than her mother did, but her mother was always telling her what to do and undermining what she told her child. Another worried that her mother was too harsh with her child, but felt she could not do anything about it. Few sat down and discussed responsibility and authority with their mothers, though they did discuss it in the program.

Resolutions to the dilemma faced between the dream and desire for independence and responsibility and the everyday reality of dependence and irresponsibility are difficult but possible. There are a number of accounts used. First, the expression "me and my mom are like sisters now" is used to indicate that each takes some responsibility and justifies the help the young women receive without experiencing too much dependence. This is not an individual resolution as it was discussed among the young mothers informally and in classes and existed prior to the program. Second, some of the young mothers expressed their independence from others through the names they gave their children. One young woman chose the name of a French perfume but spelled it the way she heard it. Another chose a name because she liked the sound it made. Several expressed real pleasure that they had created these names independently.

While the image they try to maintain of themselves is one of sole responsibility for their children—they are entirely accountable morally, legally, and mentally—they must depend on the state to provide economic resources and are subject to the state's rules and regulations. Moreover, their mothers help out and interfere. In a discussion with Jenna and Lena about what they wanted for themselves and their children, they argued about whether they should turn in the names of the fathers of their babies to the welfare system. When Lena asked what welfare meant, Sara responded, "The baby is supporting you." Lena reemphasized the point, "Parents are living on their children." Moreover, most place some of the burden on their mothers. In reality they are partially dependent on the state and their mothers.

While the young women developed means to partially resolve their dilemmas, they often found they faced a reality they did not particularly like and over which they felt they had little control. Their mothers treated them as children; their children did not obey them and were sometimes out of control; no one was around to help them on occasions when they thought that they needed it; and welfare workers appeared to threaten them with taking away their children or publicly embarrassing them. This was the experience of their daily lives. The young women discovered that they often had to work hard and they did not always like the fact that motherhood frequently conflicted with what they wanted to do. Nevertheless, motherhood still revealed to them their most authentic side: something they could accomplish well.

Distance from the Unsuccessful: The Dilemma of Naturalism and Failure to Take Responsibility

If mothering is a natural skill, how can mothers fail? They often saw, however, expressions of disapproval of their mothering by the people who controlled the resources and appeared to the young women as having status in society. Many of the young women were terrified that representatives of the wider society would turn them in as "bad mothers" and take away their children. Being a bad mother to them did not imply lack of skill; all should have the skills naturally. It means she does not care enough and may be of poor moral character.

The young women worked very hard to distance themselves from those whom they saw as bad mothers. In their discussions they separated the good mothers from the bad ones and worried about what others would say about them. Dressing the child nicely was critical to being seen as a good mother. One of the most vehement discussions in the family life class with Amy concerned what to do if your child wanted to dress herself and put on something that did not match. Randy said that she would try to bribe the kid not to go out like that. Shawn said she would be embarrassed that others might see a child like that. Ronda was adamant that the child should not leave the house prior to changing her clothes because of what other people would think. Ronda exclaimed, "Others would think that the mother doesn't care." Shawn added, "People would blame you." Most of the participants agreed with her and only a few saw the answer that Amy wanted: the merits of praising a child for doing something on her own—dressing herself.

They frequently brought up examples of bad mothers. Poor mothers included those who did not get their children dressed until noon because they were too lazy, those who never had clean clothes for their kids, those who did not change diapers often enough, and abusers. They discussed articles from the newspapers about women who abused their children. During a lunch break several became very upset while discussing one particular case of a local mother leaving her newborn baby at a bus stop in the middle of the winter. They could not understand her cruelty and lack of feeling for her baby. Two participants cried. Another news story that concerned them deeply was of a mother who killed her four children. Several argued that she should get the electric chair. It was incomprehensible that some women do not appear to love their children and, in extreme cases, either abandon or kill them. Marge was very upset when the local newspaper reported that an eight-year-old was raped and could describe the perpetrator perfectly. She was convinced that it was the mother's boyfriend and that the mother was covering up for him. Marge talked about nothing else for several days. According to the newspaper several days later, she was correct; the boyfriend was charged. The mother had violated everything that a mother was supposed to be by jeopardizing the welfare of her child. All of the others agreed strongly with Marge. Some of the longest discussions occurred over these events and they were unyielding in their negative evaluations of these women. There were no acceptable excuses for these mothers.

A moral stigma is attached to interaction with the agency in charge of protecting children, which has the right to initiate termination of parental rights. Not only is anyone who is being served by it considered a bad mother, but the young women fear this agency, as it is the one that can legally evaluate their success at mothering and has the power to jeopardize the permanency of motherhood. While a program that provides supplemental food for pregnant mothers and young children can be regarded as merely providing additional resources to someone without sufficient money, the child agency is regarded as questioning the mother's moral qualities should it become involved with the family. Such a thought strikes terror into the hearts of these young women, though they joked about the mothers who had workers. Perhaps that is why they joked.

The fear is so great that a few were afraid to take their children to the emergency room or to a doctor because they had heard that they would be turned over immediately to the children's agency. Ronda's son fell down and, while afraid that he had done something to his ankle, she did not take him to the hospital because she said she might be blamed for the injury. The validity of this fear was confirmed by others' stories. This real fear of the authorities limited the choices that the young mothers felt they could make. By embedding their authentic selves in fulfilling the role of mother, not only were they finding meaning in this role, they were also protecting themselves from the authorities. However, they were extremely sensitive to any comments that they were not fulfilling that role in an approved manner.

The Arbiters: Closed Awareness by Ignoring Motherhood

These staff members largely chose to ignore the young women's status as mothers. Motherhood was rarely mentioned by Roberta and Ivy, and neither John nor Mr. Harrison ever mentioned parenthood. All had children. Ivy, in her discussions with the group, dealt more with their relations with their boyfriends than with motherhood. The participants learned very little about the arbiters' children, only that Roberta thought her high school aged daughter was immature and that Ivy's youngest went to day care at a very early age when she returned to work. On occasions when the arbiters did mention their children, they were sometimes not very complimentary. Roberta announced proudly to the job readiness class that her seventeen-year-old daughter had not made her a grandmother yet. She explained that her daughter was immature and into clothes and herself. The participants stared at the table while she declared this and at lunch Marge asked the others how you could say that about your own daughter. Others commented that you never knew when you were going to become a grandmother. When I asked one of the young women whether she had friends or relatives who did not have children, she replied after a while that she had one cousin who was twenty-two and did not have any children. I asked why she thought this was the case. She explained, "She had two miscarriages." When asked, the group could think of only a few of their friends and relatives who did not have babies; many of them were only fourteen or fifteen. In their circles, it seemed that almost all of the young women had children, and they thought that it was just a matter of time before Roberta's daughter became pregnant. They worried about the moral implications communicated by the arbiters about the young women's actions by largely ignoring their motherhood and making what the young mothers understood as derogatory comments about their own children.

According to the arbiters, children should not interfere with one's life outside of the home. Neither sick children nor day care problems were appropriate excuses for absence, as one needed to anticipate problems that interfere with work life. They always said that a child at work was inappropriate and paid little attention to any child brought to the program. The participants, on the other hand, always helped each other out when someone brought a child to class by taking turns holding her, feeding him, and changing diapers. The arbiters and participants viewed children's relation to work differently. The arbiters saw the program as a work site and any child's presence as inappropriate, and the young mothers viewed the absence of information on children and the staff's ignoring of children as criticizing their motherhood.

To some extent it was an open-awareness context; the staff were content to play their roles as staff members and to never reveal their experiences as parents, the aspect of themselves that the young mothers felt was probably the most authentic self. The young women knew that motherhood was of secondary importance to the arbiters who did not want to see the young women as mothers, and the arbiters were aware that the young women knew this. The arbiters were not completely aware of what this lack of concern and expression meant to the young women. Ignoring something that others obviously think is important at best expresses indifference. It indicates that the relationship is not serious or important. When the others take this aspect of who they are seriously, the indifference is experienced even more acutely as failure to care. In a deeper sense, it was a closed-awareness context.

Failure of the arbiters to acknowledge what the young women saw as expressing their authentic selves increased the participants' suspicions of the arbiters' claims that they respected the participants. They believed that any mother included some discussion of her children and would not say anything bad about them; moreover, any mother would help out others. The young mothers, on another level, viewed the arbiters' exclusion of motherhood as communicating their failure to respect motherhood. The relatively closed-awareness context about motherhood bled into other contexts; it increased suspicion in all interactions.

The arbiters used silence on the topic of motherhood and their own families to maintain some control over the culture of their classes, mostly without challenge. The young women suspected that the arbiters did not respect their mothering skills or them as mothers and were afraid of the arbiters' criticisms and that the arbiters might report their failures to the state. Because of these fears and because they wanted GED's, the young women never wanted to transform the context to open awareness. The young women also suspected that sincerity was not a good trait to have in the world of one's public life outside of the community. The arbiters' form of control depended on holding themselves up as role models within a rigid set of norms. Any personal revelation might expose a fault or flaw. As the clients saw themselves as potential targets of derision, they participated in maintaining these boundaries.

Family Life Session 1: Strong Context of Suspicion

Precisely because social relations often tend to be manipulative and because the management of self is emphasized within the program as the core of success in the wider society, assessment of what others say and what they really mean is crucial when the topic of discussion is that relationship in which authenticity is embedded and the risk of serious consequences of a negative assessment is so high. Interacting with the young women as mothers who need some "corrective" action heightens the possibility of and sensitivity to their seeing others' actions as criticizing their ability to mother. They saw the situation as risking more than identity; they perceived a risk of state interference in their lives. The young women paid close attention to signals that might indicate what the staff really thought about them as mothers. From the perspective of the young mothers, a context of suspicion was generally maintained with the family life volunteers, which limited what was discussed. Sometimes the classes in the first session evolved into a closed-awareness context on both the staff's and the participants' sides.

A context of suspicion remains as long as the staff are judged as lacking sincerity (whether the participants believe that the staff really feel what they claim to feel). Those assessments are embedded in the larger context of interaction: in the young women's assessments of the workers' knowledge of the social world of the young mothers, in the degree to which the staff appear to care about what happens to the young mothers, and in the degree to which criticism could be assessed as personal. That is, the assessments are based on characteristics of the interaction patterns of the staff, where the criticism appears to be directed, and the relationship constructed between the staff and young women. The provision of information takes place within a relationship, a relationship that has some history. It is human beings who carry meanings, not abstractions (Janowitz 1969). The mediators can criticize directly because of their established relationship, in which the young women think the mediators say what they mean and are on their side. They also revealed their own mistakes, communicating that, while mistakes should be avoided, they are not automatically tantamount to one's failure as a mother or person.

Knowledge from Experience versus Books and Failure to Understand
In a system where knowledge comes from experience and authority is embedded in differential access to experience in addition to judgments about a powerful individual's truthfulness, ignorance (by those who claim authority) of a person's life and experience disallows authority claims and efforts to claim sincerity are suspect. Amy and some of the resource people she brought in had limited knowledge of the young women's experiences, and their actions demonstrated this lack of understanding. Moreover, some dramatized their experiences of working with abusers or the mentally limited, which increased the young mothers' suspicions. The risks of revealing a problem or frailty seemed great.

Knowledge of childrearing, as we discussed above, was based largely on the young women's experiences and that of older relatives and friends. Authority is embedded in experience. A grandmother with many children is worth more than all of the "experts" who have written books. Linda declared at the beginning of a parenting class, "I've been a parent for two years. I don't need to learn." When something would come up that contradicted what they thought, the most common response was, "My grandma said . . ." Grandmothers had valued opinions and information on many subjects from the very important, such as diet, developmental skills, and teaching morals, to what many would consider "old wives' tales," such as why a pregnant woman had itches (the baby's hair was growing), and why hanging up clothes while pregnant was bad (it puts a cord around the baby's neck). They had extensive experience and good practical advice.

Amy, on the other hand, told them about her attendance at parenting classes to improve her skills. The young mothers thought this strange and asked each other after class why anyone who had children would do this. They also complained that Amy's knowledge was useless because she used her older kids as examples; she had forgotten what younger children were like. It was, however, her lack of understanding of their lives that made them suspicious.

Despite revealing problems with their own children, when the staff demonstrated a lack of understanding of the experiences of these young women, it increased the context of suspicion. While Amy was discussing the experiences of families today, she explained that no one lives near relatives and grandmothers rarely have a chance to see their grandchildren.[5] She talked about the mobile society and about going away to school. The young women sat staring blankly as most had many relatives living within a few blocks of their home and some had relatives living in the South whom they visited regularly. Relatives were an important part of their lives.

Continual Revolt of the Young Mothers: Suspicion
The young mothers expressed their suspicions and resentment of these classes in a number of subtle and not so subtle ways. Reactions included changing the topic, sitting without responding to questions, not responding with truthful statements, failure to attend on family life days, and outright hostility directed toward the staff member in the classroom.

With her actions susceptible to multiple interpretations, it was difficult to trust Amy with information that could be judged as indicating failure to be a good mother. What the young women said in class was not always consistent with what they said to each other or some of the mediators. In one discussion in Amy's class they argued about whether a young child should be given liquor. All said no and had stories about women who often gave their children liquor and got them drunk and others who blew smoke (marijuana) in the babies' faces. However, at lunch with no staff members present, some of the participants said that they sometimes put liquor in the bottle to make the baby sleep. While in the family life classes, the young women made it sound as though they were in charge of their babies, in private or during mediator-led discussions, it was clear that the teens and their mothers had frequent conflicts and in some cases the teens' grandmothers were in charge. This never came out in the parenting classes.

Sometimes the way in which Amy approached an issue communicated to the young women that they might reveal something they preferred to hide. Some of the participants' reactions were relatively mild, like changing the topic of discussion, but some were hostile. Amy tried to discuss who a "problem belonged to": the child, you, or there was no problem. No one responded to her questions and Bette talked to everyone about nothing. Gay told Bette to be quiet.

5. Amy is making the assumption, as do many people, that the nuclear family is the norm; consequently, the extended black family is regarded as deviant or dysfunctional (Collins 1990).

Amy You have to learn to help out and communicate when someone has a problem. Let's try to role play. [They paid no attention.]

Sandy I'm hungry.

Amy Listening skills are important. Kim, your baby is over-due. Are you worried?

Kim No, I'm ok. I'm just tired of waiting. [No one was listening. Steele was reading a book on jobs and Marion was reading *Executioner's Song.*]

Bette You shouldn't have gotten pregnant again. [She looked at Kim.]

Amy That isn't being very helpful. She's already pregnant. What if you had a problem with a math test? [They began a long shouting match about John's inability to explain anything and his lack of knowledge.]

Amy had no control over the discussion and the participants said whatever they wanted. Her lack of control permitted the young women to maintain a closed-awareness context where Amy had little idea about what they were really thinking or doing.

They tended not to respond to general questions, suspicious as to what Amy could be looking for. When they responded, it was not what Amy expected.

Amy What did we do last time?

Val [A long silence before she responded.] Talked about Kim's kid.

Amy We listed feelings. We have to learn to listen to others' problems.

Val You can't solve problems when you're angry.

Amy Feelings are roadblocks. Can a two-year-old solve a problem?

Rachel Yes, he can get a chair and climb up to get something.

In order to mitigate the hostility and suspicions, Amy began to talk about practical things. She used examples like putting the good glasses where the child cannot reach them. They had a difficult time, however, relating to such things as they did not have any good glasses. She then turned on a tape of a nine-year-old who would not go to school. Any issue that Amy broached as a problem, the young women deflected away from them and their children.

Amy What's the problem?
Gay The teacher.
Tammy The girl wants to be more independent.
Amy Trust is an issue. Is it important to be honest always?
[No response.]
Amy Let's do a role play. [Silence.]
Val Yes.

Bette, June, and Tanya walked out. A later discussion on kids and activity produced more discussion, but the young mothers did not propose many ideas on what to do on rainy days except watch TV and sleep. Someone suggested dance. Suspicions still remained.

One day Amy attempted to discuss the difference between behavior and evaluation. She asked them to write down five acceptable and five unacceptable behaviors of their children and tried to show how and why the children responded as they did. The participants acted as if they could not relate this to what they were doing with their children. After watching a film later in the day on child abuse with an all white middle-class cast, no one had anything to say. When I talked to them later, they said that the man who had been released from jail after abusing his wife and child, and then remarried, never should have been let out of jail. They often distanced themselves from abusers by criticizing abusers who they knew or the abusers the media described. They were not, however, convinced of what Amy really wanted.

Linking mothering to mental health was as problematic as abuse for the young mothers. One day, when the program was about two months old, the group was divided into two sections; one attended "mental health," while the other saw a movie with Amy. There was some objection to "mental health workers" because, the young women explained, "We don't need mental health." After lunch Amy invited the other group to come down with her to see the movie. All hell broke loose.

Bette You [the other participants] all are just trying to cut out. [She was about halfway out the door at the time.]
Randy It's not fair with all the work we have. We don't need no mental health. [No one was moving toward the downstairs, even the participants who always participated in everything without question.]
Steele It's all so boring. I want to do GED.
June The movie is better than those two fat ladies from mental health.

There were several shouts of "too boring" and "we got to sit too much." Tanya finally moved to the stairs and several others followed her. Several came back up after twenty minutes, and everyone was finally seated in the library, yet the upheaval did not stop there. Someone shouted, "We don't want to hear the prenatal stuff again. We already had our kids. We know about it and don't plan to have any more kids." The shouting continued.

> *Amy* I can try to help you if you calm down and tell me
>   what you want.
> *Bette* You talk about kids but never about them the age of
>   my kid. I'm not interested in others.
> *Martha* I'm not going to have another.
> *Amy* I'm sick and tired of you not listening. [Randy let out
>   with some very nasty language.]
> *Karen to Randy* You shouldn't be so rude. [Amy walked out
>   after threatening to do so.]
> *Ronni* [pointing at me]: Can't she do something?
> *Karen* No she can't. Ruth's not a teacher here.

Several seemed worried that they had gone too far. Amy came back several minutes later and showed the movie, which was about a very middle-class white mother who wanted to be young, could not handle kids, did not communicate at all with her children, and had an interfering mother. They were fairly quiet during the film, but no one wanted to talk about it afterwards.

Most of the reactions to family life classes were unique to them. Sometimes one of the young women would get up and walk out, they made faces at each other, and, on one occasion, Bette walked across the room in front of Amy and started braiding someone's hair. Their displeasure was not always expressed so overtly. The week after the above-described incident, they were all grumpy. Everyone appeared disinterested by the class and would not respond to Amy's questions. She asked them what was fun and Ronda replied that she wanted to read a handout. Amy sounded very annoyed when she replied, "no," but no one looked up.

Less Suspicion: The Provision of Information and Activities
Relationships improved when Amy taught children's activities or how to do projects with children, since these were things which did not communicate an evaluation of them as mothers. One morning when no one would respond to her questions, Amy decided that discussions were not useful and showed everyone her box of what she

called household junk: bits of paper, ribbon, spools, cloth, and other odds and ends. The participants seemed very skeptical at first, but she showed them how to make little toys and craft items for their children. One by one they began to dig items out of the box. They kept asking for help and approval of their work. The morning was interrupted by a fight between Di and a new participant, but other staff members broke it up. It had something to do with someone's brother putting the other's boyfriend in jail. After the new participant left (she never returned), the others went back to work and several of them stayed downstairs through part of their lunch hour to complete their projects.

The young women could not believe that Amy was completely sincere in her efforts on their behalf when they saw that she had little understanding of their lives. They felt they never understood what she was looking for and remained suspicious. Even using her experiences with her children, after failing to establish that she had empathy for their lives, did not succeed. Having failed to establish her sincerity, a context of suspicion remained on the side of the young women. Moreover, they worked hard at times to establish a closed-awareness context. They did what she asked only when it was task-oriented and did not appear risky.

Family Life Session 2: Developing a Partly Shared Perspective and Less Suspicion

While she still made it clear that she was from an agency dealing with abuse, during the second session Amy made an effort to give more specifically skill-oriented classes and to get to know the participants immediately. Taking cues from the mediators, she also talked more informally about her children and personal experiences so that participants could understand who she was—a mother. After the first few weeks, the attendance decreased in the program as a whole and the young women who attended regularly were generally a co-operative group. They did not fight among themselves and took work more seriously than the first group. Few revolts developed during this session and several of the young women tried to utilize some of the skills Amy taught. By developing a stronger relationship with the class first, the communication increased and the awareness context, from the perspective of the young women, became less suspicious. Amy was able, as was Becky, another volunteer, to suggest new ways of handling the children without seeming to criticize. This was possible for Becky, in part, because she revealed more about herself and where she had acquired her knowledge, because of the way she handled the information she provided, and because she understood more about them.

Some suspicion continued and several tried to test Amy's authority, but no one disrupted the class discussion and most listened and responded when asked specific questions. On several occasions, a few slept and, in the beginning of the session, they objected to participating in a class that would neither help them get a GED nor give them grades. They were not really interested in grades, as Jenna also explained that she would not give out grades and no one objected.

Despite the improvements in her classes, Amy still demonstrated that she did not have a good understanding of their social worlds outside of the program, which sustained their suspicions.

> *Amy* Is there something different about being a parent?
> *Tiger* You got to get a job.

Amy again lectured them on how the extended family did not exist and how difficult it was to live without one.

> *Sarah* My mother is always there when I need her.
> *Tiger* Mother helps out with everything.

This lack of understanding did lead to some protests. Before the next class, Sarah said to the others, "She's [Amy] weird" and Lisa responded, "I've been a parent for two and a half years, I don't need to learn." During the class Amy tried to get them to discuss the compositions they had written about their families the week before. No one would respond after she read Cindy's aloud. When she asked who was in charge in their home, all of them responded, "me," which was not the answer they gave in discussions with Jenna or during lunch. After a direct confrontation in the afternoon, things settled down and began to improve.

> *Lisa* I'm going to the bathroom.
> *Amy* You just had your break.
> *Lisa* I have to go. [She gets up from the table and starts to walk toward the door. Amy tries to block her way but backs off and says in a barely controlled voice . . .]
> *Amy* Get a pass from Roberta if you want to come back.
> *Lisa* I'm leaving for the day. [She walked the long way around the table in order to exit.]

Someone said again, "She be growed up," which is the same expression that they use for their children when they misbehave by being too independent. The conversation that followed was calm as they talked about their families. Sharon described growing up with an aunt.

> *Selma* My mom has six and my mother and father make decisions or me when I feel like it. I was the pet and the youngest and cried when I was going to be hit.
> *Andy* My mom and dad made decisions but I was closest to my grandmother and dad.
> *Tiger* I only knew my father when I was thirteen and then he took me on walks.
> *Andrea* At sixteen I was out on my own and didn't get along with my parents.

Several of the others questioned Andrea about being on her own at sixteen, but she held her ground and said that she stayed with friends. She said that she lived with her son and her sister now and had the freedom to do as she wanted. Selma added, "It's great, you don't have to do anything that others tell you to do." Lisa came back with her excuse, "You satisfied?" Then Amy asked them about how they were punished, which allowed them to either differentiate themselves from or claim allegiance with their families.

> *Tiger* I was hit. I would rather punish by sending my son to his room. I hate to hit.
> *Selma* Kids are smarter today. They just don't answer you. I have a problem with a bad attitude and I don't want my son to have it.
> *Tiger* My grandmother, mother and me all have kids at fifteen. It goes down the line.
> *Selma* You got to discipline kids because you can't have negative attitudes.

They made family trees before lunch. The young women began to be less suspicious and were more open in revealing what they felt.

A Shared Perspective
When she became more aware of their suspicions of her, Amy tried to develop a relationship with them as mothers and spent much more time asking about their lives and children and remembering the information. She often talked about what she did with her children. When she brought her daughter, who was a few years younger than most of the participants, the participants were very polite, talked extensively with her, and all of them worked together on sewing projects. At the end of the afternoon, Ella thanked Amy's daughter for her

help. They began to see that Amy might be sincere in her efforts to help them; they were all women and mothers.

New Skills without Criticism
The students were particularly pleased with classes when Amy began to discuss concrete topics, such as toys and the ways specific toys related to the social, physical, and intellectual development of children. Several took notes. Amy also used filmstrips to talk about the different developmental stages. She did not start with problem areas and interested the mothers in trying "time out" with their children at night. If a child misbehaved he or she was asked to sit still for a specified period of time. Marge proudly told them of successfully using "time out" with her five-year-old son and suggested that the others try it as well.

Amy continued with a non-problem-oriented approach and talked about what children can and cannot do at various stages of development. From the "tests" they filled out in the beginning of the class, it appeared that most had a pretty good idea about the order in which children developed certain skills. However, they sometimes thought that their children understood much more than they probably did and imputed intention in their children's behavior when Amy argued that there was none. For example, one of the mothers described how she punished her two-year-old son who had "intentionally" grabbed a glass of juice and knocked it to the floor. In this context, Amy explained that small motor skills typically do not develop sufficiently by age two to permit the child to hold the glass well. The mother listened, but I was not convinced that she was persuaded. She could not measure that information successfully against other experiences. Amy also worked on the need to praise children and how that makes them feel good by discussing how good all of us feel when others praise what we do.

Despite the decrease in suspicion and the improvement in relations, Amy often had a difficult time getting them to talk. One day at the end of the third month of the second session, Amy tried to discuss stress, but no one co-operated. She asked them whom they liked to talk to and Liz responded that she was bored today. Marge and Paula, who sometimes took leadership positions during this session and often were able to change the group dynamics, did not help Amy on this occasion.

Paula Did you see that lady in the prison?
Amy Did you like the trip?
Paula and Marge We were scared.

> *Marge* My son cries a lot since he started day care and he
> gets on my nerves.
> *Amy* Is that your problem or his? Who owns the problem?
> [There was some discussion that followed.]

Becky, who took over for Amy for several weeks, was aware of
their suspicions. She used the approach of providing new information that they were free to use or not and explained the origin of her
knowledge as she was not a mother; she had worked with children
for a long time and hoped to learn more from them. Becky was better
able to persuade the young women to talk, in part, because of the
specificity of her questions and points. She asked, "When do you
spank your kids?" After they listed several types of occasions, she
asked them at what age they stopped spanking and received answers
ranging from fourteen to eighteen. She then asked specifically if there
were other ways to control their children.

> *Marge* Talk or take something away.
> *Becky* If they are one year old will they understand? [They
> all shook their heads no.]
> *Becky* If they make a mess?
> *Seth* They're just curious.
> *Becky* Then you can use a simple no and remove them from
> the situation.
> *Marge* Tell me more about "time out." Do they have to stay
> in one spot?
> *Bobbie* Should it last two to three minutes?
> *Becky* It doesn't start until they are quiet.
> *Marge* My mother interferes.
> *Becky* You have to find a quiet place and praise them when
> they do it right. Tell them that you don't like their behav-
> ior. It's not good to call them names. Choose a couple of
> basic rules and use time out when they break them. If you
> scream at them, they tune out. If I screamed at you, you
> would.
> *Marge* You got to start early?
> *Becky* Yes. You've got to turn off the TV when you talk and
> focus on them.

Marge warned that it was break time and arrived back within the
allotted time. The talk continued about praising children. Marge
asked about the appropriateness of giving cookies as praise and several participated in the discussion. The next week Becky talked about

small and large motor-skill development. Most listened and responded when a question was very specific, but only Marge, Bobbie, and Paula really seemed involved.

Becky was successful in creating a reasonably open context because she immediately explained how she arrived at her knowledge and presented ideas and materials as informed suggestions about which they should make judgments; she used persuasion. She was so successful that when Ivy tried to talk about child sexual abuse, they suggested to Ivy that Becky talk about it because she was an expert. While this was in part an effort to put down Ivy, it also indicated that the young women perceived that talking to Becky was not a risk.

By the middle of the second session, the class was calm and those who remained in the program were dedicated to it and attended regularly, though few in number. While they were not excited about the class, they listened and were very pleased that Amy thought enough of them to introduce her daughter to them; that is, she saw them as worthy of meeting family. Even though they did not always understand what she was saying or its importance, they listened, and, because they judged her to be a more sincere person, suspicions decreased and the discussion became freer.

Discussion: Choice of Locating Self

Those who start from the bottom of the socioeconomic hierarchy and want to stop receiving welfare and join the world of work do not have much choice between an institutional or impulsive locus of real or authentic self. The typically private world of mothering for the welfare recipient is not private but open to prying eyes: eyes with power. Those agents ultimately can take away not only sources of economic support but a child. The impulsive self increases risk of the involvement of powerful and frightening people. Regardless of self location, suspicions remain when such high stakes are involved.

Some of the very poor locate themselves in the impulsive self or dramatic self, at least in part, because they do not experience their lives as being in their control or as having options in the wider society. Developing a "dramatic self" (Rainwater 1970, 380–81) involves an emphasis on qualities and what people express by their actions. They seek to validate this identity in front of an audience of peers. The dramatic self is more prevalent among the men than the women, who can invest themselves in being mothers even if they cannot get a decent job (Rainwater 1970). Choice is always to some degree available but is more of a luxury to some than others. People may have the same number of options, but numbers do not determine the choices one makes. One has to imagine them as choices before they can become choices about which decisions can be made. Lack of experience or poor experiences in the role of student or worker, where self-expression is limited and the "good life" is a distant dream, limits the viability of the choice to invest the self in institutions and roles considered legitimate in the wider society.

The middle class can invest themselves in meaningful jobs and organizations or employ impression management skills at work and seek situations in which they can express their real selves in impulse outside of that sphere. While investing more in an impulsive sphere may limit success in the workplace, they can separate spheres so that it is still possible to earn a reasonable living with less risk of losing their livelihood.

Here, the parenting staff entered the world of the family, generally considered a private world in this society, though the state has increased the occasions in which it can and does interfere. Motherhood was the locus where the young women were trying to develop an authentic self. It was through acting and feeling as a mother that the young women expressed themselves. Motherhood is something achieved and creative, and they wanted to be mothers even if they became pregnant fortuitously. They were mothers because it was right and good for women. Being a mother meant self-sacrifice and hard work to live up to standards and make an error-free performance. Making an error-free performance when an audience of officials appeared to be waiting for failure was very difficult. The risks of failure were enormous—mothers interfered and social workers stepped on their toes and threatened to take away their children.

It was these same children who made them sensitive to criticisms from the staff and who gave them the strength to work toward a better future. Every move of the staff was carefully interpreted and evaluated. It was imperative under the conditions of minimal power to assess carefully the actions of the staff. Were their intentions to help the young mothers toward better futures as mothers as they said or were they inspecting, evaluating, and initiating sanctions? Investing one's self in success as a mother was a risky proposition when so many groups appeared to have a right to interfere. Some of the young mothers invested more of themselves than others in working at becoming a good mother, and several kept a foot in the impulsive self, coveting the freedom and spontaneity often found in the streets and bars.

A context of suspicion never became an open-awareness context because the young women were not able to believe fully that the family life staff were completely sincere in their desires to help. While the family life staff began to use some of the strategies of the mediators, such as trying to reveal their personal lives, they still publicly dramatized their affiliation with an agency that dealt with abuse and demonstrated (particularly Amy) that they still did not entirely understand the world of the young women. The suspicion became much weaker during the second session when Amy demonstrated that she thought enough of them as people to bring in her daughter and began to organize some of the classes more in terms of learning skills.

Despite these improvements on the part of the family life staff, the context of suspicion and lack of understanding mitigated moving to an open awareness context. The young mothers remained on their guard. They were all too familiar with the state agencies that handled abuse cases and, although most of these young women had no personal experiences with this agency, they had friends who had. The lines between what was defined as abuse and convention were too ambiguous to permit them to take risks to reveal information about themselves to these staff members. Moreover, the risk of being criticized for one's lack of skill as a mother, when that identity was so central to one's sense of self, was too great. Only if staff were judged as truly saying what they meant would there be sufficient trust to tell them all about problems with their families, particularly their children, that is, to transform the relationship into an open-awareness context.

The young women were not entirely correct in their suspicions of these staff members. During the first session, Amy was afraid of the young mothers and inexperienced. She told me, "All they need is some love." She wanted to help them and would not have turned in information to the state. During the second session, Amy liked them and would never have done anything to hurt them. However, one needs to convince others of one's sincerity, that is, one's actions must be viewed as expressing what one really thinks.

The arbiters generally mandated the awareness context. Impression management was critical, and to some extent this was a pretense-awareness context; each knew that the other was managing her front. However, on a deeper level it was a very closed-awareness context, in that each group knew little about the other and what they thought. On other occasions, what the arbiters thought was an open awareness was really one of suspicion on the part of the young mothers, particularly on the occasions when the arbiters were thought to be gossiping behind the backs of the young women.

Only among the mediators was a more open-awareness context

possible, because they claimed to be and were seen by the young women as the same kind of people who have problems, make wrong decisions, and respect others for their accomplishments. This did not mean that the context was always completely open or open to the same degree for each young woman. They did not necessarily tell the mediators everything despite the fact that the mediators were largely aware of undisclosed aspects of their lives. In the world of poverty and interference from the state officials, there may be an element of suspicion in almost all social relationships. The participants maintained a degree of self-protection.

CHAPTER EIGHT

Changing Welfare from Stigma
to Scholarship: The Arbiters
versus the Mediators

The young women enthusiastically anticipated the trip to the local phone company. Steele's mother had worked for the company several years earlier, so Steele explained what she knew about the job. All fifteen of us piled into the van and the station wagon for the short ride to the central office. Several knew the location because they paid their back bills there to reconnect their phones. Sarah drove while everyone screamed excitedly about her lack of expertise in handling a large station wagon on the narrow streets and with anticipation of the visit. The guides divided the young women into three groups and, at the end of the tour, each group had the opportunity to talk with an operator about her work. They were very impressed with the number and speed of the tasks and asked many questions concerning how long the operators had been with the phone company, the policies about attendance and vacations, and the necessary qualifications for obtaining such work. The operators politely answered the barrage of questions and the participants responded with more questions. We stayed longer than anticipated and returned after the official end of the school day. Everyone talked about the complexity of the job and the longevity of the operators' careers. They were very impressed that one operator had not missed a day of work in ten years.

Before the enthusiastically anticipated trip to the car assembly plant everyone was noisy. The excited young women discussed people they knew who had a car assembled or who had worked at the plant. When one young woman jokingly asked if they gave away free samples, everyone laughed. It was one of the few occasions when the whites and blacks interacted freely and no one stayed with their old friends. Everyone was well behaved and listened carefully to the tour guides.

The level of excitement remained high during trips until there was an incident at a local company when the guide's behavior upset the participants. The man worked in data processing and repeatedly said that he felt rich and would rather play golf, but that everyone had to keep working. He kept referring to the "gals" and was talking down to them. His comments appeared to assess their unemployment: they were lazy. As they became increasingly restless, he pointed to a messenger and said, "See that big black man? He's been working in our mailroom for many years. We have several of them." Finally, Ronda demanded to know why he was talking down to them and explained afterwards that she would have done something violent if all of us had not been there. Several of the others just stopped listening and either doodled on paper or tried to fill out the applications they had received. This trip was planned prior to Roberta's arrival as the Job Readiness coordinator. It was one of her first days on the job and she did not know any names. She was mortified by what she viewed as their inappropriate behavior and told them afterwards that they had embarrassed her and were not ready to be taken out in public. I noted at the time that I was furious with the man and thought that they behaved well under the circumstances. On a trip several weeks later, Roberta expelled one of the participants for failure to behave appropriately. That was the last trip outside of the program for the first group, and there were no job trips for the second group.

The job site visits created high spirits among the participants and contributed to their connection with the wider society. As welfare recipients, the major ceremonial connection with the wider society was the special check cashing line at the bank and the lines at the welfare office. At the work sites they had a glimpse of a possible working future and every job seemed interesting and possible. Moreover, it was one of the only collective activities where no one came out ahead of anyone else; they were all exploring together, all of them were nervous, but all of them had the others for support.

Without these ceremonies during the second session, the participants were less enthusiastic and fewer and fewer attended regularly. Days began to drag and "hang man" became a regular activity to fill empty hours. The job visits had served the first group as a means of experiencing how they could possibly be seen as respectable. Trips provided the drama of connections with the world outside of the family, block, and local neighborhood. They dramatized the options that were potentially available in the world of work. This opportunity was missed by the second group, who listened to speakers brought into the program.

Arguably, one's involvement in the market place today as both consumer and producer (Wuthnow 1987) is of critical importance in establishing one's moral worth. These public activities are appraised and evaluated by a general audience. Some people are marginal both as consumers and producers and are stigmatized for their marginality. Among this group are welfare recipients who neither "work" for their incomes nor have the money to become active consumers. It was part of the charter of this program to move these young people into the job market.

Both staff and participants declared that they should work; however, there was little consensus among the staff or between the staff and participants as to when or how they should make the transition, and to what type of employment. This chapter focuses largely on the construction of a "future worker" identity and the meaning of welfare receipt, but not on the local availability of employment, a critical element and one often missing.[1]

Developing an identity for the future that will substitute for a presently held stigmatized identity as a welfare recipient is problematic, particularly when there are few culturally defined parameters, no matter how vague, for the preparatory identity. Some preparatory identities like mother- or father-to-be involve elaborate dramatic symbols, rituals, and ceremonies to validate that transitional status, such as baby showers, special clothing, child birth classes, and countless myths and stories. Performed rituals and elaborate myths provide a basis for declaring and evaluating an achieved identity by self and others. There are no such rituals to dramatize a "worker-to-be" identity. The arbiters eliminated ceremonies such as the work site visits that served to validate that identity after the first six weeks of the first session.

Identities are typically situated in particular activities, places, times, and relationships. A worker may validate that identity at a work site, but these young women were housed in a social service program with few "work" activities and were not in school, which generally does and is supposed to predate work. An apprenticeship is a "prework" stage where one can participate in specific tasks and

---

1. There was little effort made to discover what types of jobs (Sullivan 1989) were locally available and could be reached by public transportation. Roberta always pushed "food service" and nurses' aide work at homes for the elderly. No matter how "ready" people are to work, if they cannot find a job, cannot get to the job, or cannot support themselves and their families on the wages offered, they cannot work.

rituals in a location which provides the materials for an identity of "learning to be a specific type of worker" that can be evaluated and has validity in the wider society; however, no recognized identity of "worker-to-be" or "future worker" is embedded in rituals and ceremonies in a social service program. Worker-to-be is an abstract concept that needs a content and context. One must be created in programs such as the one discussed here.

As cultural creators in this situation, it is the staff's task to help develop the materials from which this "future" identity can be constructed so that the stigmatized identity of welfare recipient can be minimized until a new identity can be located and validated in "real" work. The staff have significant power to construct, communicate, and serve as the only external audience who can validate its performance, if it must be bounded by the program walls and schedules. The worker-to-be role constructed specifically for programs such as this one probably cannot eliminate the identity as a welfare recipient outside of the program; thus, issues about moral character remain. The client/staff and student/teacher relationships need not be as closely linked to moral character; however, the issue of moral character makes not only the content of the role important, but also increases the salience of the worker/worker-to-be relationship. The manner in which the staff claim authority reflects directly on the young women's moral character.

With the staff divided as it was, it is not surprising that two distinctive worker-to-be identities developed; the arbiters developed rituals designed to increase interviewing and job-holding skills, and the mediators constructed an identity by developing rituals and symbols that changed the meaning of welfare use. While the arbiters' approach appeared to be practical on the surface and the mediators' approach attacked the use of welfare directly, the arbiters received many more challenges from the participants than the mediators. The staff may be able to create new identity contents and serve as evaluators; nevertheless, the participants heavily influence the process. The worker-to-be identity must be negotiated or bargained for (Blumstein 1975). This chapter focuses on why the participants challenged the arbiters more than the mediators, despite the mediators questioning of welfare support.

While studies show how powerful institutions can stigmatize powerless individuals and how some people can escape such a label, few efforts exist which explore how relational inequalities affect the identity construction process. Some research suggests such effects; researchers found that perceived inequalities in marriage relationships have an independent effect on self-concept (Schafer, Keith, and Lorenz 1984). Equality/inequality is one aspect of an asymmetrical relationship, but how people express that difference and how others interpret it may also be important.

The manner in which the asymmetrical relation is constructed to try to entice or compel the young women to go along communicates something about the identity of the "future worker"; it communicates something about the kind of people who are future workers but are still welfare recipients. The practical information provided, for example, about how to get a job, what is available, how to keep a job, and how to be a good worker-to-be are only part of what is communicated about the kind of person who *is* a worker-to-be. The arbiters and mediators not only communicated different practical information, they constructed distinctive styles of worker/worker-to-be relations, which communicated different messages about staffs' appraisals of the young women as welfare recipients. This chapter explores the communication of the content of the "future worker identity" and the processes of the construction of the worker/worker-to-be relationship. I suggest that not only the content of the identity proffered but how the staff attempted to compel the participants to do as they wanted and how they dealt with worker/worker-to-be inequality affected the acceptability of and the commitments to the identity offered.

Staff Disagreements on Welfare and Jobs

Although all of the workers wanted the young women to get off welfare and find a job, there was no agreement on how that should or could be accomplished or how they should deal with the use of welfare. One of the most heated discussions between the arbiters and mediators concerned whether welfare should be discussed with the young women. The arbiters wanted to discuss only jobs, while the mediators decided it was critical to discuss the welfare system—how the participants used it, why, and what it meant. Intrastaff discussions of welfare revealed conflicting views of the meaning of welfare use.

The arbiters' code expression was the "cycle of poverty," which meant to them that these young women grew up in poverty and on welfare and would continue in that path unless they were taught how to behave appropriately in the middle-class world of work. Moreover, their definition of the "cycle of poverty" had a moral dimension that characterized those who received welfare as not quite as "good" as those who worked. This became clear in the arbiters' comparisons of program youths with other youths.

When a summer youth jobs program was announced, Mr. Harrison said, "The kids who are in school deserve the jobs more than these girls." Roberta agreed with his statement. It was not unusual to hear similar statements about who "deserved" something more than someone else. Moreover, they distinguished between the "deserving" and "undeserving" participants. Those who were deserving were those who were closest to achieving their GED, behaved in the correct manner, that is, dressed neatly, were pleasant, and talked most vehemently about getting off welfare. These were the young women who were called in for special conferences with Roberta, rewarded with prizes, and who Roberta counseled to attend when Georgia was expected to evaluate the program. The "undeserving" would be unable to complete a GED, dressed inappropriately, and did not behave according to the arbiters' standards. Moreover, they were loud and wore old clothes.

There were several staff discussions about whether welfare should be discussed with the young women. The arbiters felt that it should not be discussed collectively. Ivy explained that it was a private affair and that she talked about problems with welfare individually during counseling sessions. She worried that by explaining their rights as welfare recipients she would be encouraging them to continue on welfare; therefore, she concluded that the workers should not discuss welfare. Any public discussion might be regarded as legitimizing and encouraging welfare use. Ivy never saw a way out of the dilemma she had created for herself.

The mediators expressed different views on welfare. Jenna was much more concerned about discussing how it affected participants' lives and with working with them to make sure that they could at some future point stay off of the rolls rather than pushing work immediately. She believed that the young women must be directly confronted with the issue of living on welfare and the way it affects their relationship to the wider society, to each other, and to their children and families. She argued with other staff and, as they began to ignore her and tried and failed to get her into trouble with the state agency, she started talking more about welfare in her classes.

The Experiences of the Stigma of Poverty and Welfare

Experiences in the wider society continually remind these young women not only that they have few resources, but that others stigmatize them for their poverty and use of welfare. They are often subject to what they experience as humiliating situations and are very sensitive to others' actions that appear not to give them the respect they think they deserve.

When someone emphasizes economic differences to those who lack resources, the latter interpret the communication as indicating their inferiority and as a lack of respect for their struggles. For example, one of the participants who had attended a parochial school felt that her classmates treated her with a lack of respect because, in order to be someone, "Your father had to be in real estate or construction." Ella's efforts to be friendly with an aunt only a few years older than she who worked as a secretary for a major corporation were spurned. Ella said, "She really talks funny, real exaggerated like and won't take me anywhere in her car. She thinks she's better than any of us but she ain't got no boyfriend." Steele went into a long discussion one day about her brother's fiancée. "She thinks that she is better than us because my brother gave her this fur coat and she won't accept anything but the best." The participants often appeared to experience others' actions as indications of "being better."

The arbiters were not always sensitive to the young women's feelings of not wanting to be seen as poor. Ivy showed them how she files and saves all available coupons and sends away for any free goods or money from the manufacturers. They were fascinated by her complex filing system and the large amount of money she saved at the supermarket and the actual cash she accrued through the collection of rebates. What had been an interesting session turned to exclamations of "I would never do that" when she explained how she routed through garbage bags to find coupons and proofs of purchase. Several of them wrinkled up their noses and Randy said, "I couldn't possibly do that." Tanya asked, "What would people say if you started picking in the trash. You would be like those bums with no place to live." They all shook their heads in astonishment over Ivy's willingness to engage in such behavior. Most would only buy new clothes, were embarrassed to be seen in the Goodwill Store buying used garments, and bought items there "only if they look new." On the day I went to a secondhand store with five of the participants, no one bought anything because, they explained, the clothes looked "old and nasty." They did not want to expose their poverty.

When asked what was important to them, the young women responded, "having money." Money was often a topic of conversation—usually the lack of it. Several of the young mothers explained that they had to toilet train their children early because disposable diapers were too expensive and they never had enough money for them at the end of the month. Food frequently became a luxury toward the end of the month; those who brought their lunches everyday brought less, those who bought them at the store existed on a small bag of chips and a soda, and others who ate hot dogs at the program promised to pay later. Some thought that Val was boasting when she explained that her boyfriend gave her $50 a month for their baby and she did not even have to go to court to get it from him. Most did not have that extra source of money and thought her rich. On the trip to the car assembly plant, the young women were not very enthusiastic about working in the dirty noisy environment of the plant and saw the office jobs as more desirable until the tour guide explained that the factory workers made much more money than the office personnel. Then several said that they would like to fill out applications for the factory jobs, but Rickie cautioned them that it would be a long time before they hired again. Her aunt, who worked there, told her they were being laid off for several months to ready the plant to assemble a new car. Clearly the young women experienced their economic situation not just as a lack of money to buy necessities but as degrading too.

Discussions of dreams for the future were held largely by the mediators, but the young women also expressed their views of the future in compositions and workbook exercises given to them by the arbiters. Their dreams are consistent with most of the dreams of people in this society; they want well-paying jobs (more than minimum-wage jobs with no benefits) and nice homes for their children. When they took "values" tests in their job training workbooks, most appeared suited for the "helping" professions and they said they wanted teaching, medical technology, and nursing jobs. Several admired nurses who had helped them out more than they had expected during prolonged hospital stays.

Even their dreams were largely practical. They did not fantasize about fancy clothes or marrying a rock star. When someone brought in a fashion magazine and a woman came to speak to them about how to put fashionable outfits together inexpensively, they were less interested than they were in a discussion of finding and paying for housing. They took more notes and asked many more specific questions than usual because they wanted to know their rights and how to find a decent apartment without having to put down two months' rent. To rent an affordable apartment with a separate room for their children was a priority. Several had been on the waiting list for public housing for over a year, but the larger families and employed heads of households were always ahead of them. Some examined the newspaper every day for a place to rent, but that seemed unrealistic with the limited and expensive local rental market. In a discussion about dream houses, Rickie told the others that she had ventured into a model apartment once and, continuing in a hushed tone, said, "You won't believe it, but they had wall-to-wall carpet in all the rooms and it was so thick that it was unbelievable!" When asked to make collages about themselves by cutting out pictures from magazines, several included photographs of new homes. It appears that the realities of everyday life are so overwhelming that they do not have time to weave elaborate fantasies. They want a job and a decent place to live with their children.

Authority Claims and the Worker-to-be Role: The Arbiters

Roberta developed a series of exercises for learning what she viewed as necessary skills for getting and keeping a job: filling out applications, writing a resume, dressing for interviews and work, interacting on an interview, and acting appropriately on the job. The correct demeanor was dramatized through role-playing, filling out job workbooks, listening to people talk about jobs, and some discussions. More consequential to the young women were the arbiters' efforts to dramatize their power over them to caste them into the role of worker-to-be. The young women directed their challenges toward the arbiters' construction of the worker/worker-to-be relation, not at the activities they were asked to perform.

Obedience to the Boss: Learning to Fill Out Forms
Filling out a workbook was an activity that established one aspect of an identity as a future worker. They spent much time in the job readiness classes after Sarah left, independently answering questions about job scenarios or personal interests from workbooks. It seemed like days upon days were spent on those workbooks and Roberta initiated little discussion. One of the books was directed toward planning for the future and focused on constructing five-year plans; a second contained tests for establishing job suitability and several sections on filling out applications and writing resumes. The third included short scenes of "on-the-job" interactions and questions about the appropriateness of the employees' behavior.

Little of this required any class discussion and Roberta often did something else behind her screened-off desk area, left them alone in the basement room while she went upstairs, and often used threats of failure to keep them working. "You won't get through the front door unless you can fill out an application without erasing and with all the words spelled right" was a typical admonition before she left them on their own. Most of the time they worked hard for about forty-five minutes. Secretly, the more advanced students helped the others. They were learning, Roberta told me, that she would refuse to answer questions just as a boss would do and that one must become independent and not ask for help.

Roberta also dramatized her power and the need to obey the boss by changing the rules when she replaced the first job readiness coordinator. To withdraw benefits from the young women, she prohibited them from writing in the workbooks and from taking them home. This was an area in which the participants attempted to test Roberta's power. A week or so after Roberta started, Sandra asked if she could finish the assignment at home and Roberta replied that it was not possible. In a very aggressive voice, Sandra explained that they had written in them already and that they had been permitted to take them home. Roberta stared at her and stated that her rules were in effect now and they could not take them home. Her claims were generally honored, but on several occasions the young women took the books home, telling others that they wanted to finish their work and did not care what Roberta said. The books were theirs and they would bring them back.

Obedience to the boss was not only dramatized directly in the worker/worker-to-be relationship, but in discussions about on-the-job interactions with the boss. Workbook scenarios were used to generate some discussion of problems in work settings and how they would resolve issues faced by characters in the stories. Topics discussed included attendance, dress, demeanor, and submitting to on-the-job authority. According to Roberta, if an employee does not obey, thereby failing to indicate deference to an employer, the employee should and does get fired.

The training centered on how to become an obedient worker. In every scene discussed, the boss was correct and the worker who obeyed all of the rules was rewarded. There were no discussions of ambiguous situations, such as the possibility that it is sometimes practical to give in to your boss even when the boss is wrong, or when it may be worth it to pursue your own views. The only message was that the boss is always right and rules are to be obeyed. One guest of Roberta's, who was an old friend and worked in community relations for a large company, explained, "They pay me a lot to do what they want me to do."

No Respect for Workers-to-be: Role Playing Foiled
Obedience to bosses, which demonstrates proper deference, does not mean that employees are owed the same respect. The students took role-playing games very seriously; however, some of the staff appeared not to have any respect for them as a group and favored only those who had, in the arbiters' view, the potential to succeed. During one session in which they role played in an interview situation, Mr. Harrison and Ivy passed out some rules about interviews. The workers were annoyed when Marge (the best student) would not volunteer to be first, refusing by shaking her head and looking down. Yet they skipped Ella, who had few educational skills but who very much wanted to be asked and eagerly looked around at the staff. Selma finally volunteered to be first. When she was done, they told her she had a good smile. The others also had their turns and when it was Hilda's turn (a participant who may have been slightly retarded but who always tried very hard), Mr. Harrison talked while she answered questions and Roberta laughed when she said something that was inappropriate but not funny. Ella asked to be excused prior to Hilda's turn but had been turned down. Ella told me afterwards that she had been afraid she would laugh at Hilda's constant references to religion, and she thought Roberta had had no right to laugh. She had been successful in refraining from laughing, while Roberta had failed. The young women viewed this demonstrated lack of respect for the individual as demonstrating lack of respect for all of them as future workers. Later that afternoon Marge cried as they waited for the bus. Between sobs she said, "I don't think it's fair that they humiliate us when they tell us to respect them." Respect was a one-way street; arbiters expected it but did not grant it.

Competent Authority through Association: Follow the Rules
Roberta, Ivy, and Mr. Harrison sometimes attempted to indicate why they should be believed and obeyed. In discussions of interviewing techniques, job relationships, and the importance of presentation of self, these staff members always used their own and their friends' successes to try to legitimate their power in order to inform the young women of the proper way to obtain and hold a job. According to Roberta's model of the job world, there were specific rules that had to be followed to have a successful job interview and to remain on the job and she expressed these to the young women in terms of her successes and those of her friends.

Roberta always used herself and friends as models when talking about how to be successful. On one of her first days in the program she explained, "I'm going to bring in a lot of my friends who are very successful. You must be realistic and learn how to conduct yourselves in public. You must start in entry-level positions." Then she went on to list all the local influential and public people who were her friends. She expressed concern for projecting the correct image at an interview (dress and demeanor) and gave very detailed instructions. She discussed how *she* sat, shook hands, and looked into the interviewer's eyes. She advised them that *she* never asked about salary first and always had a few questions to ask at the end of the interview about the job. She always had reasons ready and detailed the ways in which *she* was most qualified for the job. One day she showed them a dress chart that lists what all employers use to judge employees. It was appropriate to wear a suit, a skirt and jacket, or a dress. When someone said that she did not have a dress, Roberta said that *she* always had a dark dress or suit to wear for interviews. She told them she always looked appropriate for the situation and had had her color analyzed so she would know what looked best. Having money and spending it on maintaining a public image was very important to Roberta, and she spent it where it was important to do so, for example, on clothes, cars, and what "looked good." She explained to Ivy and me between the two sessions: "They [the young women] don't know how to dress and their manners are terrible. They should wear skirts to the program."

Frequently, when Roberta asked her friends to discuss their jobs and the work world, they would talk a great deal about friends and social events they had attended. Roberta tried to communicate her success as well as her friends', one of whom came to analyze colors. The young women were unenthusiastic as she explained that women were throwing out their wardrobes when they discovered they were not projecting themselves as leaders and successful people because of the wrong colors. Women became more successful when they changed their wardrobes. Those workers-to-be who had brand-name clothes were complimented and told they dressed well. She chose to analyze my colors even when I tried to refuse. No one asked questions during the presentation and several put their heads down on the table as the woman spoke. Not only was wardrobe replacement an impossibility for these young women, but they were aware that most of the jobs that they were being told were possibilities required uniforms (food service, nurses' aides). While waiting for the bus, they complained vociferously about the talk. Again, the young women were being reminded of their lack of resources and the low status of any jobs that they might obtain. But this time it was the content of the communication that offended them, rather than the dramatization of the relationship, thus there was no direct confrontation, just sleepy indications that they would not respond to questions.

Roberta did not claim friendship with all of the guests and some of those who were not labeled as her "friends" had the most success with the participants. Their talks were interesting and they did not dwell on their authority over the participants. One was a woman firefighter who answered all questions directly and gave a straightforward and interesting presentation about her job and what she had to do to earn it. She never gave any indication that she was better than any woman who was not a firefighter. When they asked her if she took drugs, she responded it would not be fair to the people whose houses were on fire if firefighters took drugs. She did not hesitate to respond to personal questions and always explained why with a minimum of moralizing. Her enthusiasm for the hard work of the job was obvious to everyone. They asked questions throughout the lunch hour and stopped only when she had to leave for work. The second woman was head of housekeeping in a motel and quietly and somewhat timidly explained how she had started cleaning rooms. It was clear to all that she was very proud of doing a good job and very pleased with her promotion to supervisor. Several participants wanted to invite her as the graduation speaker. On the one hand, emphasizing one's successes and those of one's friends dramatizes to the worker-to-be that they have not had any successes. They see it in a comparative mode: staff successes versus their own failures. On the other hand, real enthusiasm and honest responses to questions generated excitement and interest in jobs.

Competent Authority of Personal Perfection: Keep Your
Dirty Laundry Private
According to her accounting, Roberta had never had any failures or made any mistakes as the young women had. In one class when we were talking about how to dress, I explained how I had learned to check out my clothing from making a mistake by wearing a skirt that did not stay sufficiently wrapped when I sat. Roberta gave me a very stern look when I mentioned the mistake. She told me afterwards that we should always state a rule "in the positive." People should not make mistakes. She felt that they must learn the skills of impression management as a means to keep their faults in the private world and away from the public; however, what she communicated was that she had no faults and that they did.

Roberta's discussions of friendship were not simply discussions of what to say at work but also implied that aspects of their personal life, such as their use of welfare, were unmentionable in public and, therefore, stigmas. Roberta told the group that if you think you have more friends than you can count on one hand, you are wrong. People with whom you work are not your friends and you should never tell them about your "personal business," which included one's children, male friends, and social life, along with one's economic past. Particularly in job-readiness classes, Roberta told them over and over, "I don't want to hear your personal business" and "I never tell anyone at work my personal business." Work and the program were public places and welfare belonged with personal business, outside of the public's view.

On one occasion, Roberta told the participants: "You shouldn't mention welfare in public because it makes you feel uncomfortable and everyone likes to gossip. Don't give them anything to gossip about." This statement confirmed for Paula her idea that Roberta, Ivy, and Mr. Harrison spent most of the time gossiping about them and their problems behind the partitions and that welfare was something people, including the arbiters, gossiped about. Emma said that she was not going to talk to them anymore. They felt that their private lives were evaluated as deviant by the arbiters. Moreover, it appeared as though, with Ivy's counseling, these staff had a right to enter the clients' private worlds but that the clients could not enter the arbiters'. While waiting for the bus, Marge explained to the others that Ivy and Roberta did not want to hear about their problems in order to provide help but only to gossip and that they did not understand them or their problems anyway. They should talk to Jenna if they needed something. Sandy remarked that Ivy did not even know what an "upper" was. They were convinced that the arbiters supported the separation of their lives as welfare recipients and as workers-to-be and their interaction with the arbiters had to be as "workers-to-be" with "welfare recipient," along with girlfriend and mother, hidden from view.

Manipulation and Coercion: Secrecy and the Threat of the Last Chance
Efforts to control the timing and type of employment after completion of the program through secrecy created further fear and rebellion among the young women. Roberta thought that she alone was responsible for deciding what would happen to the young women after the program. She met privately behind her partition with each of the participants and talked about what they would do next. After those meetings, many said they did not understand what Roberta had told them, were confused about their futures, and were afraid of failing.

Most were told only about fast-food restaurant jobs, nurses' aides positions, and cleaning jobs, not about more education or training. They took seriously the notion of "the last chance," which was what they were told each time Roberta thought they were not paying enough attention.

Secrecy about the process of finding employment backfired when students who were so afraid of not getting what they wanted went out on their own for a job or other training. Marge knew that she wanted to go into a medical technology field and applied on her own to attend a training program. She enrolled prior to the end of the session and left the program. Roberta was not pleased and spoke poorly of her after that. When Marge returned on a day she had no classes, she was ignored. Julia left during the first session to enter a construction skills program. When I saw her on the street two months later, she told me she was very pleased with the training and was attending classes regularly. I confirmed this with her supervisor. Roberta thought that she had been encouraged to leave by other staff members and should have tried to get her GED. Julia, however, had no interest in increasing her writing or reading skills and was reading at about a sixth-grade level. She loved working with her hands.

Roberta was also furious when Esther offered and several clients accepted temporary jobs at her agency after the first session instead of applying for the fast-food restaurant jobs Roberta offered. Roberta would no longer help them with preparing for their GED tests, while she kept in contact with other clients, whom she continued to help with GED preparation. She wanted to be in control, but the workers-to-be maintained some independence.

Failure to Develop a Meaningful Role: You Aren't a Good Worker Yet
The arbiter-created identity of worker-to-be was one of a person who knows how to fill out an application, how to dress and act appropriately on an interview and at a job, how to keep private life private, be obedient, and remain subordinate to others. It is an identity, however, that can only be played out within the boundaries of the program or a similar setting. It has no importance to the world outside and ends with the termination of the program. The one situation where the identity might have had some connection to the external world and received dramatic validation was the job site visit. "They weren't ready to be taken out in public," she declared to the other staff members. To the workers-to-be she explained, "You embarrassed me by your misbehavior. You were impolite and showed you were poor." Their current state was considered shameful.

The job site visits served as a direct symbolic link with the world of work. This was the only occasion when they left the boundaries of the program and ventured into the real world of work to talk to people who held jobs. It was more than the experience of talking to employed people, as most had friends and relatives who worked. While they could not perform as workers yet, it linked them symbolically with that experience. They wanted to be seen as workers and were excited and enthusiastic about the encounters.

Not only was the identity created limited by time and place constraints, but the relational conduct of the arbiters communicated messages about the type of people they thought the participants were as workers-to-be. Not only could worker-to-be only be enacted in the program, but the arbiters' efforts communicated messages that the participants saw as granting them little respect and indicating that they lacked the moral qualities of the arbiters and their friends. Demanding respect and then not giving any in return indicated to the young women that the arbiters thought that they were better sorts of people: efforts to establish authority by touting the success of their friends and their own implicitly compared their success with the participants' lack of success, thus indicating to the young women that they were considered inferior.

Showing only their successful selves and indicating no errors while telling the participants that they must hide their dirty laundry (welfare, boyfriends, and family) affirmed the moral superiority of the staff. Participants began to see from the cues that the arbiters were dealing with them as clients, students, or workers-to-be, people who lived in a separate moral universe. They were able to read beyond any one particular clue that the arbiters thought of them as deviant. Within this context of moral inferiority, it is understandable why there was little commitment to program identities and many challenges to the arbiters' efforts to control and direct their actions. Most of the direct challenges to the arbiters arose in situations in which the young women appraised the arbiters' evaluations of them as morally inferior, not in situations in which they disagreed about instructional content.

Welfare as Scholarship and Moral Equality: The Mediators

The young women were having a discussion with Mrs. Sims about children and training them early when the discussion turned to men and the welfare check.

> *Mrs. Sims* . . . We think we have to give in and have his baby.

Bette He still doesn't stay around much [much under-the-breath laughter].

Mrs. Sims They tell us that they love us but we've got to put the brake on otherwise we'll end up staying on welfare. You got to control your own body. I always used the rhythm system. Do it yourself. A nice man won't want four or five kids and some day a nice man will come around.

Bette and August [simultaneously] The only time they come around is when the check comes [several nodded their heads in agreement].

Ana I'm glad *you* said that.

The mediators confronted the issue of welfare directly: they dealt with the stereotypes, the inconsistencies in the young women's views of independence and dependence, and provided demonstrations of responsibility. They wanted to show the participants how to fend off society's powerful definitions of reality. They were less concerned with developing a worker-to-be identity in terms of skills to get jobs than in developing a way the participants could validate themselves as currently responsible welfare users; the mediators did this by communicating the means by which this is possible in a relational context of common experience and moral equality. This relational context is dramatized by the use of "we" by Mrs. Sims in the above discussion.

Links through Personal Experience and Use of Persuasion
Most of the mediators began their classes with tales of their own personal experiences, which they linked to the experiences of the young women. Invited by Jenna, Dr. James and his assistant, Mrs. Sims, came twice a week for two months. In his first session, Dr. James told his life story; how he had been poor, went back to school to complete his education when he was much older, and struggled with a family, a job, and his schooling until he achieved his Ph.D. He talked for well over an hour and everyone listened carefully for the entire time. He kept emphasizing that "*we* are all poor" and never said that "*you* should do it." He emphasized only that it was possible and that if he could do it, even so late in life, they could as well. Everything about his past was not perfect. An alternative life pattern was possible, the merits of which they could confirm with other information or from other sources. He used persuasion.

The mediators' discussions included both events evaluated as positive by the wider society and those that were not approved of. In order to develop a relationship with the young women while dramatizing her views, Jenna told them about her own experiences on welfare. She had had a child at nineteen but knew that the father was not worth marrying and that she needed more education to obtain a better job to support her daughter. Welfare checks paid for college and provided support for her child. She explained that while the system often tried to get her down, she always tried to maintain her self-respect and always thought of her child first. Her technique was not to establish herself as a measuring rod but to establish membership in the same community.

To develop a relationship with each of the participants in order to demonstrate that they are all important persons and to incorporate them as members of the same group, Jenna learned names and something about each young woman in the beginning of each session. After introducing herself to Ana, a new student that day, the following discussion occurred.

> *Jenna* What do you think behavior modification is?
>
> *Ana* Your behavior in public.
>
> *Jenna* Partly. It's to change your behavior or attitudes. In this program we try to give you the skills to get ahead and get off welfare. We want to look at what welfare is and what it does to you.
>
> [Ana grins to all of those at the table and appears to wrinkle up her nose.]
>
> *Jenna* Why are you smiling like that?
>
> *Ana* I don't get welfare.
>
> *Jenna* Everyone can learn something new but you have to participate and you can't put other people down for what they do in this class. We can talk about everything but we can't be nasty to each other.

With many of the details of Jenna's personal life made public, the young women felt that they could be much more open with her and admit their fears and also accept her sometimes tough criticisms of their use of welfare and their conduct. Not only did she work to bring each new young woman into the group, but she set the stage for critical, open discussion of difficult issues and feelings among equals.

After successfully establishing themselves as the same kinds of people as the participants, the mediators typically encouraged the young women to raise issues and criticisms on their own. They used their experiences to indicate the possibility of alternative behavior patterns, that is, they made use of persuasion (Wrong 1988), which involves presenting arguments that the others can check out against alternative sources of information and experience and does not depend for compliance on the relationship with the speaker. While the arbiters tried to claim authority and the participants tried to evaluate what the arbiters communicated without giving into their feelings of humiliation and entirely rejecting what the arbiters told them, the mediators tended to express arguments that depended more on the participants making sense of them in terms of their own experiences and following them because they made sense.

Critical Attacks on Behavior: The Independence and Dependence of Welfare
The mediators' view on the meaning of welfare and work differed substantially from that of the arbiters, as did their approach to the topic. In their view, the young women were struggling and fearful and one had to be sure not to destroy strengths. They had to be convinced, however, that long-term welfare use might destroy them and their children and that current welfare use could be socially and morally responsible, if used correctly.

The first step to permitting the participants to examine their situations clearly was to point out the contradictions between the independence that welfare gave them from their mothers and boyfriends (Piven 1985) and the increased dependence on the government and on their own babies. Tension developed when the young women who viewed welfare as a means to obtain independence from both their families and from the fathers of their babies were confronted by evidence provided by Jenna and Dr. James: Welfare *also* means dependence on the system and on your child. These staff members never denied the independence that welfare receipt provided, but they did reveal the contradiction with the dependence on the system and the frequent public degradation that dependence involved. Generally, the young women were left to evaluate this contradiction on their own.

An independent source of money, even if it was welfare and too little to live on reasonably, was significant to the young mothers. It was theirs and not their mother's or their boyfriend's. Welfare permitted some independence from their mothers, who tried to control their lives by taking care of their children and trying to regulate with whom and when they went out. Several explained that they still had to sneak out of their bedroom windows when they wanted to see their boyfriends. Welfare permitted independence and equality validation through spending what they wanted on their children (new clothes and toys) and eating the kind of food they liked while buying few or very inexpensive clothes for themselves. Several proudly announced that they had given their mothers money for groceries.

Money from welfare also meant they could be independent from the fathers of their children and could date whom they chose. Many no longer went out with the fathers of their children, many of whom were unemployed. If the fathers did not provide money, they could not demand anything, June explained to the others, who nodded in agreement. Having money permitted control in her own life and gave her the opportunity to control others. One young woman argued that if you gave some guy money, it meant that you could control him, but Glenda replied that many of the guys "ain't got no pride and they take what they can get from you and do what they want anyway." In these discussions, Jenna frequently permitted and often encouraged the young women to critically evaluate the behavior being discussed but would not allow anyone to criticize others in the group. By encouraging discussion among the participants, the young women were encouraged to validate or invalidate the points she made and to critically examine their own experiences.

While receiving welfare may provide a sense of independence from mothers and boyfriends, as a link to the wider society, it is problematic. A welfare recipient is a client and stigmatized rather than respected. Experiences with representatives of the wider society are uniformly negative. All have stories about how others look at them as they wait in separate lines in the bank to cash their checks on days designated by the bank or when they pay with food stamps at the supermarket. Additionally, receiving welfare creates many situations which permit officials to scrutinize private actions.

Most admitted that they were dependent on the system and criticized anyone in the program who tried to deny it. One "check day" (when welfare checks arrive) most of the young women who had attended during the morning left at lunch to pick up and cash their checks. Ella said, "I don't have to cash my check today because my boyfriend gave me money." According to Liz, "She was just trying to show that she was better than the rest of us who have to live on that check. Don't ever let anyone tell you that they don't need to cash that check." There were too many opportunities to check statements against that of experience for anyone to escape criticism if what she said made little sense to others.

Jenna and a guest, Louisa, were able to encourage the young women to talk about the relationship of welfare to having babies without directly bringing up the subject.

> *Louisa* What do you want for your child? You must think of him. The kid may need his (the father's) social security number if he dies and can get some money.

Ronda I turned in his name and work to the welfare. They
can collect what they can.
Val I'm worried that welfare will find her father, then there
will be less money.
Sara That baby is supporting you. [They admit it themselves, it does not come as a criticism from staff.]
Louisa Parents live on their children.
Val I'm not thinking of marriage. I got to get things done
first but we need the money. When we get married then
we won't need the money.
Louisa Not getting married until later is fine but you would
be doing it on your own without your daughter.
Val Yes, I know that.

The discussion that followed about depending on your baby for
money was one of the longest and most difficult, but no one looked
upset or seemed to want to leave when the afternoon was over. These
staff members helped to point out the contradictions in the use of
welfare, but they never resorted to claiming power through threats,
negative sanctions, or comparisons with their own successes. They
relied on raising issues and arguments which the participants could
assess on their own.

*Attacking the Stereotype: New Ways to Perform Responsibly
and with Independence*
If a person is to remain on welfare until she has gained sufficient skills
to work, the mediators argued, she must strive against fulfilling society's stereotype of the welfare recipient as lazy producers of babies
who remain dependent too long. The mediators argued that the
young women must demonstrate responsibility and suggested some
means by which the young women could remain on welfare and dra-
matically distinguish themselves from the stereotype. This permitted
these staff members to validate a positive welfare identity and suggest
the means to act responsibly while remaining on welfare.

Attacking circulating stories about the "whore on welfare" high-
lights the problems of misusing welfare without attacking the participants. In sometimes heated arguments, the young women rejected
others' designations of them as lazy and as voluntarily remaining on
welfare. They distinguished between those who really need welfare
and those who try to rip off the system. Many discussed examples of
people they thought misused the system, but argued that most need
it and have no alternatives. They claimed that one young woman,

whom several knew at least by reputation, had additional children to get more money. She was in her mid-twenties and had about six kids. Every time I heard the story, her age and number of children varied. While the details changed, the story served to dramatize that there was a difference between those who really needed welfare and those who abused the system. They discussed the links between having children, keeping boyfriends, emotions, responsibility, and welfare:

> *Jenna* I heard girls upstairs discussing a woman with five kids and five different fathers. What do you think?
>
> [Several said "money."]
>
> *Sharon* That's dumb to gossip.
>
> *Rachel* It's dumb to have five kids.
>
> *Lisa* It's a shame to gossip and to have five kids.
>
> *Jenna* I'm not saying that the girls were laughing, they seemed sad.
>
> *Rachel* She thinks that the man will stay, but he won't.
>
> Lisa: It's bad for the kids.
>
> [All agreed.]
>
> *Jenna* Let's set the scene. If she were your friend, would you say anything? What would you say?
>
> *Rachel* If you could find out what's the guy like, you could tell her to leave if he's no good.
>
> *Jenna* What would she think of herself as a person?
>
> *Rachel* She be a whore.
>
> *Jenna* Do you think she would see herself that way?
>
> *Rachel* She might be getting back at the father of her kid.
>
> *Jenna* She's a bit of a fool because her feelings and emotions get the better of her. You've got to learn to deal with them and control them. You got to learn the difference between the heart and the head. This is what we've got to discuss.

The mediators linked getting off welfare to demonstrations of responsibility toward their children. Dr. James's major thesis was, "You must want to get off welfare for your kids" not because their use of welfare was embarrassing for him as it appeared to be for the arbiters. Adults have to plan, he argued, and the ones who are not doing so are the ones who need to plan. That plan must include getting a GED and turning skills into making a living.

In her discussions of welfare, Jenna tried to show that the system has the clients in its control, but also that the clients need to use their own initiative to take a stand and get off. The system does not want you off, she claimed. The following occurred at the end of a very heated and emotional discussion.

Jenna Do you want your kids to go through the same hurt as you do waiting at the end of that month for the next check? It's not easy livin' 'til the first of the month.

Karen I don't depend on nobody. Your baby, that's your responsibility. [She gets welfare but was referring to help from the father of the baby.]

Rachel I wish I had a degree.

Jenna The system wants to keep you in ignorance.

Glenda They act like they are taking money out of their pockets.

Janie It is.

Karen I don't want to be on it in five years. The system wants to keep you in ignorance . . .

Jenna Because you are poor, you don't have to be dirty, or ignorant. You must carry yourself with dignity and respect . . . Do you want your kids to go through the same hurt as you and always living to wait for the first of the month? . . . You have to elevate your thinking and say, "Welfare I don't need you anymore."

August My cousin cusses them [welfare workers] out. They have you where they want you.

Glenda I went with a smile and I never got one in return.

Jenna Some are nice and some are not.

August I don't want my daughter to go through the same thing my oldest sister does to her son. He was on the honor roll but she doesn't get him up for school any more and he's been missing. One day he got up, ironed his pants and went out on his own.

Jenna Waiting for a check is depressing and can get you down.

Glenda There's nothing to look forward to.

Karen Well, at least I can pay my bills . . .

Jenna had them use their own experiences to evaluate their own behavior.

Responsibility also meant knowing something about politics and some demonstration of involvement in the community in addition to keeping up with new information. They needed to use welfare, but that was no excuse for lack of participation in the political process and keeping track of what goes on in the world. Jenna gave them the responsibility to find out who their representatives were and, for those who were eighteen, to register to vote. After that discussion, three of the young women went on their own and registered. Jenna explained to the group:

> You must take responsibility for your actions. You've got to know what you are doing. It's a big bad world out there and you have yourself and your baby to protect . . . You must learn from your mistakes. There is too much information around to be innocent today. Read the papers and watch the news on TV. As mothers it is important to know lots to protect your kids.

She was providing an additional link to the wider society.

She linked responsible use of welfare to talk about their successes in reducing the need for services. The young women liked to juxtapose stories of the misuse of welfare with their own successes in reducing their need for services. Discussions of their children frequently concerned their health. Most had received or were receiving resources from a program which provided funds for nutritious foods for young children. If the children surpassed a certain size prior to the expiration of the time limit, they were dismissed from the program. When Val's daughter passed that size much before the required age, Val proudly announced it to the group. Everyone was properly impressed and the others, whose children had also been terminated from the program, told of their successes but complained of the price of milk and other products. No one ever expressed the sentiment that she was pleased to be receiving money from the government and would not be more pleased to be working.

The mediators suggested ways to gain control of interaction with welfare workers. On several occasions, the group discussed with Jenna the importance of not fulfilling the stereotypical expectations of welfare workers who sometimes become annoyed when those expectations are not met. Here she used some of her own experiences. For example, they talked about the importance of keeping the apartment neat and spotlessly clean so that the worker has nothing to complain about. Jenna explained that when she received welfare she would not wake the baby when the worker demanded that she do so. She told the young mothers that she had explained to the welfare worker that regular naps were an important part of her childrearing practices and, if the worker wanted to see the baby awake, she could return later. The young mothers loved this idea as it permitted them to define themselves as responsible and as in control of the situation. They chuckled and passed knowing looks around the table. Jenna used her personal experience to support her position and provided them with a way to act responsibly and control worker access to family life.

The mediators emphasized making a plan and organizing oneself to head in that direction. "You need to look to the future and if you want to attract men who are responsible, you got to be the one who is going somewhere," explained David to the young women. Rachel replied, "They want a woman who is about something. You got to know what you're about . . . A woman is learning to take responsibilities. They only thinks they are women if they got kids." David answered, "The key word is responsibility and raising the baby. You got to stand up and take responsibility, then you'll have respect." They could do this while remaining, for the present, on welfare.

When Jenna discussed the issue of responsibility, she let them make their own evaluations without being critical of their points. One time they discussed the black Miss America who lost her crown.

> *Jenna* I'm not going to give my opinion. What do you think and feel about the Miss America?
> *Selma* She shouldn't have to give it up because it was before she got the title and she may have needed the money.
> *Di* She shouldn't have taken the picture because she knew she might want to be Miss America.
> *Liz* How did she know that?
> *Hilda* It's not her fault. I feel sorry for her.
> *Bobbie* Your past always comes up. She shouldn't have. It wasn't very smart.
> *Darleen* It was her own fault.
> *Cindy* People were jealous of the photos.
> *Selma* It was a set up.

The group is now split on the issue of responsibility and Jenna interrupts.

> *Jenna* The publishers made money and I hope she got part of it. Don't forget that she put herself in that position. The facts are that she was an only child, her family had money, she had education and talent. She posed at nineteen.
> *Di* She had nothing better to do.
> *Liz* Someone put another face on her body.
> *Jenna* No, she admitted it.

Liz She knew she had her clothes off. [Her opinion has changed.]

Jenna She sold her soul. You got to be responsible for what you do.

Selma I guess it was her fault. She was the one who took off her clothes and she got to live with it.

The staff encouraged the participants to initiate and discuss the topics which allowed them to check out what others say. Responsibility was encouraged by suggesting behaviors that dramatize it publicly and that contradict their dependency as clients of the state welfare system.

Taking a Political Stance: Welfare as Scholarship
Ivy's inability to reconcile how to alert the welfare recipients to their rights and the cycle of welfare dependency led her to think that there was a causal relationship between telling the young women of their rights and encouraging them to stay on welfare. Jenna resolved this difficulty. In discussing her own experience of early pregnancy and using welfare so that she could attend college, she was able to link welfare to educational scholarships. Welfare should be regarded as a reasonably short-term source of income to receive further education and training, the same as the receipt of a scholarship to attend a college or university.[2]

By linking welfare to symbols that more closely represented middle-class status and activities, the young women were accorded some of the respect they needed; by linking it to symbols of a transitional activity—schooling—the rights to short-term use were emphasized. This unconventional meaning to welfare receipt placed it clearly in the conventional cultural world. It permitted some independence from their parents and the right and responsibility of young people to obtain training for future work.

The identity that the mediators proposed and the participants largely accepted was that of a responsible, active, independent user of welfare. This was done by providing ways of dramatizing independence and responsibility while using welfare and connecting its use

2. The mediators never went as far as some feminists might and did not argue that the state ought to provide continuous benefits in order that women need not depend on either the labor market or men. The mediators wanted sufficient benefits so that the young mothers had sufficient time to mature and obtain training to become employed in well-paying jobs. They should be entitled to these benefits as citizens (see Orloff 1993) for a reasonable period. Their education would probably take more than two years.

to a scholarship. The staff constructed a relationship with the young women that placed everyone in the same moral universe. Their judgments arose from the same moral universe as that of the participants and, therefore, were seen as having validity and worth consideration. The mediators provided them with reasonable options that could be considered independently, which, in turn, encouraged independent assessments. With that new definition of welfare use, they could actively confront the community who wished to stigmatize them.[3]

Discussion: Moral Universes

The workers as cultural creators had different models of how to communicate what the culture of worker-to-be should be. Although position in the organization provides that workers and participants play different roles and have different access to the tools of power, the worker/worker-to-be relationships that developed were not dependent on that position or available tools. The staff members had significant freedom and power to develop the relationship as they wished and to create the culture of the worker-to-be identity in interaction with the participants.

Although everyone had the same general goal of freedom from the use of welfare, the arbiters and mediators approached both their relationship to the participants and the path to "working" differently. The mediators were much more successful in enticing the young women to go along with their model of what a worker-to-be should be and the rituals necessary to affirm one's identity as such. The young women liked to see themselves as responsible scholarship recipients. While it might be difficult to persuade the external world to validate them in their performances, they saw it as possible and Jenna was able to provide them with some examples of how to do so.

In addition to the more general applicability of "responsible scholarship student" than "worker-to-be," I have suggested that the acceptance of the identity and staff suggestions is linked to the relationship developed between staff and participants. The participants generally accept what the arbiters tell them because they see some of the skills as necessary; they know from their own experiences that interviewing techniques are important and that they should learn how to fill out an application. In order to obtain the desired skills, however, they

3. This may not be a major new involvement in politics (see Nelson 1984 for an analysis of poverty, women and politics), but it is a potential basis as clients begin to demand respect and resources from the state and others.

must endure rituals of dependence and subordination, threats of negative sanctions, and invidious comparisons. They comply not so much because of the authority of the arbiters, but because they have evaluated the skills as necessary to obtain a desired goal—a job.

The arbiters, from the perspective of the young women, were claiming to be a different kind of people than the young women. While their authority was not totally accepted, much of the experience of the young women was consistent with the arbiters' treatment of them as dependent and subordinate. Consequently, they suspected that evaluation of them as morally inferior might be correct. The participants often took offense to the actions of the arbiters, which they viewed as indicating that they were morally inferior persons, that is, as placing them outside of the moral universe of the arbiters. They often challenged the arbiters' actions for just this reason. Despite the challenges, the young women did not have sufficient confidence that they inhabited the same moral world as the arbiters to disregard such aspersions on their character. The arbiters often used force and manipulation as guardians of morality.[4]

The mediators brought their own family problems and issues into the public discussion. This allowed them to establish a relationship embedded in equality of moral character. This authority is not merely a suspension of judgment (Lukes 1978), a seduction (Sennett 1980), or manipulation (Hall 1985) but is embedded in a critical assessment of moral equality. The young women assessed the mediators and their arguments. When both parties agree that they are the same kind of people, any attacks on the behavior of the other are not as likely to be taken as personal moral attacks because the speaker also would be attacking herself. Moreover, as the young women saw that the mediators' criticisms were not intended as personal attacks on them, they began to respect these staff members for the things that they had accomplished, that is, they gained authority through competent performances and experience. The mediators did not try to claim authority, but the participants granted them authority. Their insights were considered important. They created a cultural community[5] of status

4. Here the arbiters are using what is typically part of the male sphere of public life (power) to do what is typically done by women in the private sphere—guard morality (see Pateman 1989, chap. 6).

5. Part of Jones's (1990) argument for engendering citizenship is that the organization of political life should be transformed "to make it more consonant with principles of equality and face-to-face relationships" (p. 807). This is in part what the mediators tried to do on the microlevel. Though they were not trying to turn all relationships beyond their own with the young women into familial relations, they required intensive commitment and solidarity. They also encouraged autonomy and critical judgments in their use of persuasion and in the development of the critical self.

equals (Kemper and Collins 1990), in our sense, a moral community, and they were attempting to link individuals to collective life (Pateman 1989). They were able to compel the young women to critically examine their own behavior and to check it against real-world experience when they would rather not do so and, as cultural creators, provided dramatic means by which the young women could take some control over their lives and link their identities as welfare recipients to respectability rather than stigma. More broadly, they were teaching the young women to be creative in defining their own place in the social world and to critically question the categories that others use to position and evaluate them.

The young women were not totally passive victims of powerful social workers whose authority they unthinkingly or blindly accepted. They made assessments about the staff's claims for superior judgment and insight. When the person in power claims to be of the same moral character by revealing personal, potentially stigmatizing actions and creating a situation of reciprocity of deference, then the claims for authority may be accepted. However, if the claims are made based on membership in a moral universe in which they are not included, the clients become skeptical of such claims. The young women were not, however, immune from the power of these staff members. If they were, they might have been able to disregard slights or not interpret actions as impugning their persons and thus challenge the request or criticism.

PART THREE

Is Welfare Reform Possible?

CHAPTER NINE

Backstage Links to Public Empowerment

Roberta came out from behind the partition separating her desk from the main room and called to Val, who was heading out the door with several of the others. Val walked over and Roberta gave her money to buy a sandwich from the sub shop across the street. Ronda and I agreed to split a sandwich, because she did not have enough money and said she was not that hungry anyway. Laughing and talking about the parties attended over the weekend, we walked to the store but returned to the program to eat because of the cold.

On our return, Val walked up to the partition and knocked on the wall. Roberta waited for what seemed to be more than a minute before she called "come in." Val handed her the sandwich and change and joined the rest of us, sitting as far from the partition as possible. One young woman who had bought a large bag of potato chips and had offered it to us yelled, "Roberta, want some chips?" Roberta did not reply and later chastised the young woman for yelling and interrupting her lunch.

Sandra cried during Jenna's afternoon class because she was upset with the way her boyfriend had treated her that weekend. He did not show up for their date after he had borrowed the money she planned to use to buy more "Pampers." She had not shown up in the morning and Roberta had given her, in Sandra's words, "an evil look." Jenna calmly explained that she had to make a decision whether her personal problems or her work were more important in terms of where she wanted to go. Then she talked about boyfriends and how a woman needed to demand more from her boyfriend. All of the young women listened quietly and contributed to the conversation. Several spoke sadly of having had their boyfriends fail to do as they promised they would. Jenna turned the discussion to where they wanted to be in five years.

In the routine struggles to develop and establish trust, to communicate ideas, information, and skills, and to develop and establish relationships with each other and the clients, the staff provided models of what social relationships are and should be like and how and where the young women fit and should or could fit into the society beyond the confines of the program and the local neighborhood.

Woven into their daily interaction were the mediators' and arbiters' differing views of the larger social worlds and the individual's relationships to those worlds. That is, embedded in their interactions with the participants, they communicated theories of society, ways of making sense of the social world, and ways to make or take a place or path in the envisioned social worlds. These are the cultural maps or "folk theories" the staff think necessary for survival in the wider society and for creating some semblance of social order.[1] In a sense, they provide the social theory that permits people to think about the social institutions and, one hopes, to participate fully in the social world beyond the local neighborhood.

Staff members' interactions are embedded in their theories of how the social world is ordered and how individuals should fit into or create that social world. That is, through their interactions with the young women and discussions about the social world, they communicate and create a "cultural picture" of how social worlds relate and what individuals' relationships to those social worlds are and should be. The mediators and the arbiters hold different views of the relationship of the program to the worlds of work, family, politics, and community and how to organize their own lives and those of the young mothers both inside and outside of the program. Within the program these positions are communicated through what they will and will not say and do with the young women and each other and the symbols they develop and emphasize.

The arbiters' emphasis on conformity to and dependence on hierarchial authority arises not only from emphasizing membership in and identification with a single community (Hewitt 1989) but from the singular importance given the staff role.[2] The arbiters' work links

1. According to Hewitt (1989), social order is a vision of society and its constituent groups, organizations, and institutions. This sense of social order not only constitutes an important part of social reality, but provides a necessary basis for a sense of an orderly self (p. 110).
2. Hewitt (1989) refers to the identity derived from the role being played at the moment as situated identity.

them precariously to their social identity as "middle class." Even as "professionals" none had a long-term job and all received low salaries. Class is their larger community identity, but it is limited as a community as membership is not clearly defined and people who define themselves as middle class are not very likely to think, feel, or act alike, and they are not always identified as middle class by others. This central focus on work as creating class membership is embedded in a relatively straightforward view of the social order—the total separation and hierarchical ranking of public and private worlds.

The mediators' emphasis is on conforming, but not on being a conformist, and on independence that takes account of the perspectives of others. They have membership and identity in a variety of communities and are involved in many situations of importance to them as workers, mothers, women, activists, girlfriends, and wives. They generally espouse no one particular hierarchy of priorities, but emphasize making choices. Their view of social order is one of continually shifting and evolving front and back regions and of working to adapt to and make changes in those regions.

The arbiter's division of social life into public and private worlds reflects an issue raised in political theory. Many people accept the view of liberalism (individualistic, egalitarian, and conventionalist) that describes and advocates the distinction between public and private worlds.[3] Generally, women are relegated to the private domestic sphere of family while men participate in civil society. Consistent with this view, women, ethnic and racial minorities, and the poor must fight for inclusion in public and political life so that they can be included on the same terms as male middle-class participants, largely through work. This public-private division by the arbiters has strong implications for the organization of daily life for teen mothers and is reflected in the arbiters' interactions with them and the other staff members. The separation of the social worlds into the public and the private constructs a series of oppositions and leads to a hierarchical arrangement between the two worlds.

Generally, the public world is that of work, politics, community involvement, and rational thought; the private world is that of family, friends, nurturing, and emotions. The public world is impartial and governed by rationality apart from particular interests and desires (Young 1987, 60). Cognition stands above emotions or sentiment. The moral person stands outside and above the situation and uses impartial abstract rules to treat all situations and persons alike. The public

3. See Pateman (1989, chap. 6) for an excellent analysis.

world is one of rational calculations, making money, and the place where a person achieves importance in the social world. The public sphere is often regarded as the man's world.

The women's world is that of the private sphere where emotions prevail and one is concerned with the family, childcare, and nurturing. The private sphere is the place where men can retreat and feel comfortable after fighting the battle for financial gain and status in the world of work.

A hierarchy is embedded in this opposition between public and private; the men's public world of business and politics is better or more highly valued than the women's private world, where emotion holds over rational discourse. One's life as a citizen contributing to the larger social system may be segregated from one's life as a virtuous person. A person's standing in society is based on her activities as worker, which is unconnected with the world of family and friends. And, without work, an individual has no standing. "One is what one does in such a world" (Shklar 1991, 68). The arbiters reproduce the separation and hierarchy of the public and private world in their construction of the personnel/participant relationship.

What is particularly problematic for the individual excluded from or living on the periphery of the public world is discovering the rules so as to know how to fit in to the public world of work. While traditionally, membership in public life or civil society was defined on the basis of property ownership, today it is more broadly based in work. But those who do not have jobs, regardless of the reason, are considered second-class citizens. Additionally, there is little in this model to entice or push a person to move into the public sphere except a desire not to be a second-class citizen. Few actual supports for participation exist, however, for the single mother in either world—be it for work or for maintaining a family.

The mediators reproduce a model of the social world more closely resembling that of the front and back regions of Goffman (1959). They try to communicate how to move between these regions and how to prepare in the back stage for front stage activities. For Goffman, back regions are places to prepare for front stage performances "where the impression fostered by the performance is knowingly contradicted as a matter of course" (1959, 112). There is a back stage area to prepare for any front stage performance, whether the bathroom (back stage) is preparation for the bedroom (front stage) or the private office is preparation for the big meeting. Front regions are generally more formal than the familiarity of back stage area; however, what was a back region can become front stage when the audience in attendance changes. The division between front and back is always relative to a specific performance, and it is possible to have many different degrees of front and back regions.

There is no implicit hierarchy between front and back stages and what goes on in the back regions in preparation for a performance is as interesting and significant as the performance on the front stage. Often people must pass rapidly from one area to the next. Emotions are part of both worlds and the types of emotions and feelings expressed do not necessarily distinguish the regions.

> In saying that performers act in a relatively informal, familiar, relaxed way while backstage and are on their guard when giving a performance, it should not be assumed that the pleasant interpersonal things of life—courtesy, warmth, generosity, and pleasure in the company of others—are always reserved for those back stage and that suspicion, snobbishness, and a show of authority are reserved for front region activity. Often it seems that whatever enthusiasm and lively interest we have at our disposal we reserve for those before whom we are putting on a show and that the surest sign of back stage solidarity is to feel that it is safe to lapse into a sociable mood of sullen, silent irritability. (Goffman 1959, 132)

Goffman's idea of front and back regions implies notions of public and private worlds, but it is not equivalent to dividing the world into *the* public and *the* private realm. People may prepare back stage for what is really a very private performance but is front stage for the persons involved. That is, this is a process and relative from one staging area to the next.

A problem for people is controlling the regions. This can be accomplished partially through audience segregation by space and time, but management problems occur when intruders enter, and it takes considerable skill to resolve transitions. A well-rehearsed and perceptive actor can learn the skills to manage transitions more successfully. A more difficult problem for the people who view the world and interact on such terms is a moral issue—to know what their priorities are so that they know what front stages they should become involved in and when to try to maintain one front stage when another is trying to intrude or someone or something is trying to turn it into a more back stage arena or vice versa.

A third problem is developing the type of person who best survives in such a world. The Goffman person is an actor who belongs, moves easily from region to region, is very adept (Hewitt 1989; Hochschild 1983), and whose self is structured by the situation. "Actions happen to the self; but the self does not do them" (Hochschild 1983, 217). This is not the individual the mediators have in mind; people are more active, are more independent, and work to construct a place of their choosing. The mediators offer an alternative to the public/private dichotomy where politics, emotions, power, and community can play a role in any region.

The Public and Private Worlds of the Arbiters

The arbiters communicated a model of social order through their actions and talk in the program that completely separated the public world of work and the program from the private world of family and local community actions. Movement from the private to public sphere and back again is viewed as not only difficult but as something that must be done in a painstaking manner with priority given to the public world. The message that status and legitimacy accrues with success in the public world of work and the program is clearly communicated.

Establishing Separation

The program, like the world of work, is a public place, and, therefore, the staff must act like those in authority, namely, the bosses, and the young women must act like line-workers in the program as clients, students, or workers-to-be. The staff try to communicate that it is necessary to adhere to specific rules in order to succeed in these roles. As the bosses, the arbiters do not want to know anything about the private world of the person. In the public world of the program, it is inappropriate to assert one's identity as a mother or woman or to give it priority; that is part of private life and of secondary importance.

The arbiters reacted negatively on those occasions when the world of family and emotions entered the public world of the program or the public world of work visited by program participants. They objected when mothers brought children into the program, whether invited by other staff or involuntarily, when day care failed. The young women's visits to the public world of a work site made it clear to the arbiters that the young women did not see the strong dividing line between the public and the private world, as they failed to conform to the rules of public impression management and play the role of the quiescent visiter from another world. They brought too much unruly behavior into the public arena. Feelings (anger) were expressed toward the speaker at a job site and they were inappropriately dressed for another job trip. Finally, the arbiters told the participants that since they behaved inappropriately by bringing their private selves into the public arena, there would be no more visits outside of the program. The young women were not yet ready to be seen in the real public world outside of the program.

The arbiters were careful to distinguish their public and private time and space within the program. They defined the public program time and space as oriented toward accomplishing tasks in the order set by the staff and in the space defined as public space. Public program time was dedicated to the development of cognitively oriented skills: reading, filling out applications, dressing, and learning on-the-job rules. Public program time and space were so narrowly defined as task-oriented that the arbiters included almost no organized relaxation, fun, or celebration, especially after they took control of the program during the second session. The staff's private time for relaxation and informality took place behind the partitions during lunch. Their private time excluded the participants, which dramatized not only the staff/participant difference but the public/private separation.

These staff dramatized the hierarchy between public and private: public life and success in it was more important than success at home. Rewards were only for school or job-related skills. The arbiters continually brought up the public successes of their friends. Friends of the arbiters whom the participants met were successful business persons and came to the program only to discuss their business experiences. The absence of informal discussion about family life and feelings was obvious to the participants. We discovered little about their families or other non-job-related experiences. Exclusion from discussion indicates not only separation but lack of importance.

The arbiters were successful in constructing an atmosphere where personal revelations were discouraged during the second session and were pleased with the participants who did not talk about their families or boyfriends. The first group failed, but Roberta continually tried to "teach them a lesson" by starting the graduation exercises when many were buying sodas at the store across the street. They were frightened, excited, and confused over what to do next, but the arbiters disregarded these feelings entirely and continued the program without them. On the one hand, when emotions took over, separation failed. On the other hand, the young women learned the separation of family life from work so well that when Ivy wanted to discuss "private" matters, the participants would not.

Reproduction of the Public World of Work
These staff members informed the young women on how to be seen as safe interactants in the public world. They instructed the young women as to how to behave in the world of employment and provided them with information about the publicly visible symbols needed to be seen as safe players by those who control that world. By setting the rules and attempting to organize the actions and activities according to rigid categories and procedures, they reproduce the public world as they see it.

Symbols of the work world were dramatized. The arbiters created many situations of public competition: prizes for cognitive skills—the best speller, the best student of the week, or the student who attends most regularly. Important symbols were also those of public order: the sign-in charts and posted program schedules, the posting of the best composition of the week, the frequent forms they were asked to complete, and the demands that the students knock on their partitions and wear particular types of clothes. These emphasized the important rules of the work world: competition with fellow workers, attendance, importance of schedules, and deference to the boss.

The arbiters emphasized the importance of obtaining the symbols necessary for entrance into the public world and for legitimation in the work world, symbols such as the GED. "You can get a job then," Roberta frequently told them. Many of the discussions that we had after classes and that Roberta had with the participants concerned fitting into and conforming to middle-class expectations, particularly office etiquette. "The girls," according to Roberta, "must conform to the society whether that is shaving their legs or looking into the eyes of the interviewer. If I am going to refer someone to a job they must be able to act right." Those who were unable or did not perfect the appropriate front were not highly evaluated.

The envisioned public life of the arbiters was very narrowly confined to the world of work. Absent from any discussion or activity were considerations of political and civic life. They never talked of political action or social change or involvement in the community that might challenge "the way things are." What was permitted into their public world was limited. Moreover, the work they portrayed as available to the participants was narrowly defined—the social world of unskilled labor, especially food service and nursing aide jobs, in which the GED is just a symbol that may legitimate one as a good potential employee, similar to a neat application form. This public world is even more circumscribed than originally envisioned by contract theorists and enlightenment philosophers who, while adhering to a strict split between public and private, nonetheless envisioned the public as a utopia of "equals" and a forum for political debate. The arbiters want to "fit in" and be perceived as belonging in the economic sphere.

Compliance with the Rules of the Public World
How do the arbiters obtain compliance with their definitions of public and private worlds and how do people fit into those worlds? Conformity is critical in the public world in which people are not equal; some have more education, better jobs, or more money. This is what counts and formal structures of authority where some people, those who best meet success criteria, exist to tell others what to do. In communicating this model of social relations, the arbiters developed relationships of hierarchy, dominance, and dependency in which the young women were at the bottom of the hierarchy, subordinate to the demands of others, and dependent on others for help. They were subject to manipulation by the arbiters. The daily rituals of deference and the requirement of petitioning for help supported these structures to the extent that it became clear to the young women that the arbiters thought they belonged in the "order-following" group and in a different moral universe.

Additionally, when the clients did not automatically accept the rules of the arbiters, they threatened them with "this is your last chance" or with suspension from the program. Prizes were the only positive incentives given for conformity and very few could win them as those who had the most skills when they entered the program always won. The young women expressed dislike of these staff members but stayed largely because they wanted a GED.

Full compliance was never achieved. Revolts by the students did occur and were typically directed at the arbiters, not at the tasks of the program. Those young women who remained and attended on a regular basis were, in fact, very task-oriented. They wanted their GED's and jobs and were convinced that the arbiters could and would help them pass the GED and get them jobs, despite resenting how the arbiters treated them. Like the workers in factories, they wished to set some of their own priorities and rules for working; they did not wish to avoid work (Burawoy 1979; Roy 1952).

Usually in discussing power in organizations, the focus is on compliance within the organization. The issue here may be more complicated, as compliance within the organization may be only loosely coupled to the mission of the organization, which involves helping the young women affect changes in their lives outside of the program.

The power to create compliance within the organization may be separate from the power to lead them to a reordering of their lives outside of the organization. Furthermore, the power to maintain regular attendance may be different from either, as one can attend without listening or learning. The most power the arbiters had was to develop a definition of the situation within their segment of the program and to try to compel the participants to accept that definition. While they were not successful in maintaining attendance or in generating much enthusiasm, those who came regularly generally followed the rules. The staff's power was limited as they had neither exclusive rights over these young women nor did they offer a unique service; some of the young women did come to the program voluntarily and those who remained were aware of alternative programs for obtaining a GED, but they were aware that those did not include day care. For many, this limited their choices. The question remained, who has the power to do what and how can it be done outside of the program?

The arbiters sometimes failed to generate the conformity they expected within the program, and the young women were not as dependent on them as they would have liked. While the participants revolted occasionally, they were still affected by the relationship; it stigmatized them further and appeared to reinforce the possibility of failure. It was difficult to measure up and they had never been able to do so according to the arbiters' criteria. Moreover, if the arbiters were successful in increasing their dependence and subordination, what was provided that would enable the young women to leave their current situations? Is embarrassment and knowledge that one is stigmatized sufficient?

The Presentation and Location of Self

The "impression-managed self" of the arbiters comes under the constant scrutiny of others and is determined by them. There is only one set of rules for assessing self and that is determined by those in power. Consistent with this perspective, the arbiters provide a very specific idea about how that self is supposed to appear in public. Information that others will assess as deviant must be hidden or obscured to maintain the type of presentation required by the wider society—the middle-class, white society. Acting talent to present the public self is essential, as is knowledge of what should be public.

Much of what the young women should do, the arbiters express in terms of what they should not do. In order to manage public impression, the arbiters argued, you must not tell people about your private lives, you cannot dress as a poor person with rubber sandals, you cannot talk back to anyone, and emotions cannot be a part of public presentations. The arbiters viewed the ability to master conformity to the rules as critically important to developing a self that appears trustworthy to others. As a minority you are often not in control and cannot fit right in. The rules are written by other people. No one should ever enter the public arena without checking that everything that belongs to the private world remains there. Bosses, like staff members, expect others, explained Roberta, "to keep their dirty wash where it belongs and out of the program." That is, a less than "real or authentic" self must be presented to the public and identities are imputed by others. Talk and activities from which the authentic self is constructed must be confined to the private world, hidden away from the view of people who count in the public world.

The arbiters wanted to, but were unable to, reorder identity priorities; they wanted the young women to use their public identities as clients, students, and future workers over their private identities as welfare recipients, girlfriends, and mothers. While the young women typically tried to interact in the program as clients, workers-to-be, and students, they did not always do so. Identities as clients and workers-to-be were too situational and risky an investment and "client" was degrading. They often left the program early for their children, their boyfriends, and their checks on check day.

The arbiters' hierarchy of identities was problematic, even for them. Their private worlds were so cut off that the young women, the mediators, and I never were aware that any self existed apart from the "impression managed" public self. To all audiences in the program, they were clearly social workers and teachers first, working hard to present a perfect face. Perhaps Roberta was not totally convinced that such a division was necessary when she stated in a very plaintive voice, trying to limit my access to the program, "Ruth, you don't know who I really am." While assessing people in terms of their performance in public institutionalized roles is the major way these staff members attribute moral character to themselves and others, they appeared to suffer and agonize over the need to hide their private lives.

The culture as experienced by the arbiters constrains them greatly in their choices. Their experiences of discrimination and lack of regard in the middle-class Anglo-dominated society are both impediments to revealing a more private self in public and an invitation to act as they perceive demands of middle-class etiquette to require. Themes of job-related success both constrain the presentation of a more real self and entice actions that lead to some success in that world. The tension remains and the conflicts are not resolved.

Despite the unemotional style of the presentation and the highly developed symbols of order, the constructed program culture communicated an emotionally charged moral message: the private worlds of the young mothers were messy and dirty and they had failed to achieve success and to be regarded as safe interactants in the public world. It was clear that they did not measure up to the standards set by the arbiters about interaction within the public sphere, although some were closer than others. They existed in a different moral universe.

The arbiters have accepted the need to maintain, and compel others to develop, barriers between the public and private spheres and to support the primacy of the public over the private sphere (Pateman 1989). The traditional notion links the private to "shame and incompleteness" (Young 1987, 74), not even to love and affection as opposed to reason in the public sphere. Moreover, the arbiters limited participation in the public sphere to economic endeavors and did not include political or civic participation. This is a very narrow view of citizenship with the major civic duty being to sell one's labor in the free market. The arbiters seemed unconcerned with other civil rights, such as due process of law, political rights, and social rights, such as welfare provisions and education or other duties.[4]

The Front and Back Regions and Multiple Social Worlds of the Mediators

According to the mediators, the theory of the arbiters was too stable, rigid, and inflexible and did not adequately reflect experience to begin to enable the young women to survive in the wider society. Instead, the mediators communicated a view of a social world constructed from a complicated, ever-changing series of relationships between back and front regions. The boundaries between public and private are rarely clear, continually evolving, and intertwined. Situations are always evolving, but it is necessary to maintain a more general sense of public and private. While women's relationships to family and friends are intimately connected with their lives in the work force or school, there are occasions when the two worlds collide, and people must assess priorities. Earning a living may be an important aspect of being a citizen; however, one's virtue as a mother is as important, and the two are connected. What is problematic for the individual is that different worlds make conflicting demands, and regions are always

4. See Somers (1993) for an excellent analysis of citizenship and Marshall's (1964) definition.

subject to change. Moreover, few provisions for facilitating more public participation in the work force exist, an example being affordable day-care centers or centers for after-school care.

Front Regions and Establishing Priorities
In trying to establish their view of social order, the mediators focused on the processes necessary to work out conflicting demands and changes in regions: examining how others might view the situation, making decisions among difficult choices, and setting priorities, while thinking about dreams of the future. There are times in which children and friends will compete with work or school. Kids get sick and friends demand attention, while bosses require attendance. One has to be prepared to make critical decisions, and resources which facilitate a resolution may not exist or may be too expensive.

On the macrolevel, layers of front regions sometimes conflict. One has to learn to assess such conflicts and make decisions. The mediators talked about having to make difficult decisions and the importance of seeing options and assessing them, in part, in terms of who you are and want to be in the future. Sometimes work may keep a mother away more than she would like from her child. If a woman really wants to join the military, it may be necessary to give custody of children to others. On the other hand, having a job means "being about something" so that your child is not supporting you, and you can make demands on your boyfriend for respect and find and attract men who are "about something" too. "Being about something" means that one is beginning to or has established some independence from the state by preparing or being able to sell one's labor and not depending on one's child for income. On some occasions family life can enter the work scene, such as bringing in pictures of your children to show co-workers during lunch. In this perspective, there are close relationships between disparate parts of one's life and they are not and should not be totally separate. However, an individual has to learn under what conditions certain aspects of her life should remain in the back region.

Moreover, the more experiences people have with different groups in the wider society, the more people will be able to see and evaluate their own actions from a variety of perspectives and to respond reasonably, in addition to envisioning more options. From the mediators' point of view, it should be the job of the program to extend the number and types of groups with whom the young people interact; they should be taken on trips and introduced to a variety of people. The opportunities to do so decreased, however, during the second session after the arbiters took control of the program. Learning to take the perspective of others had to take place largely in discussion.

On the microlevel, people continually enter and leave a setting and sometimes private regions rapidly become public or public regions become private. The mediators try to communicate that different audiences demand different behaviors. For example, when the boss enters, a discussion of boyfriends or parties should stop as that becomes back stage talk when the boss creates a new front stage. The mediators discussed this type of change to front stage after an unknown guest entered the room during a graphic conversation about their sexual relations with their boyfriends and they did not stop and introduce themselves. The concept of continually changing back and front stages is presented as a useful interactional tool.

The difficulty lies in developing some general priorities among the social worlds and to use them in ever-changing situations. At certain times, work must take priority over family, but not all of the time. Sometimes family must be treated as back region when the front region is work, but this is not always the case. While family life affects and is affected by work, they generally must remain in separate spheres. What is important according to the mediators is learning to know when and how to leave children and social life in the back region and when they can be front stage. As there are no formulas for this; they must learn how to take the perspective of the others accurately in the situation and to take into account their personal priorities and future selves in order to make decisions about what to do and to sometimes take a stand that may not be popular.

The Power of Persuasion and Dramatization of Community

Frustrated by the arbiters' strategies to gain control over the organization and their own part-time status in the program, the mediators ceded control and withdrew to develop their own organizational culture in their classes. Here the mediators emphasized symbols of community rather than hierarchy and domination. No one was better than anyone else for having more external symbols of middle-class status, such as jobs, correct clothes, or educational degrees. One assessed actions, in part, in terms of the community by understanding the larger community's views.

> [S]ocial process of experience and behavior which the group is carrying on is directly presented to him in his own experience, and so that he is thereby able to govern and direct his conduct consciously and critically, with reference to his rela-

tions both to the social group as a whole and to its other individual members, in terms of this social process. Thus he
becomes not only self-conscious but also self-critical; and
thus, through self-criticism, social control over individual
behavior or conduct operates by virtue of the social origin
and basis of such criticism. (Mead [1934] 1962, 255)

The mediators point to a different definition of power than the arbiters, one forged through connection, cooperation, persuasion, a
strong sense of self, and respect for others, rather than one based on
hierarchy, coercion, threats, and fear. The egalitarian relationship
and sharing of respect in a community of women, in and of itself, was
a source of power. The young women listened because the mediators
made sense and they were able to see themselves as members of the
same community as these staff members. The mediators demonstrated competence by describing diverse experiences, which was
consistent with their mothers' and grandmothers' authority.[5] The mediators negotiated with the individual directly when the few out-
bursts in these classes occurred.

Unlike the arbiters, who saw the program as a place to teach skills,
the mediators tried to focus on developing identities as members of a
community to communicate their view of social order. As women,
all of them, including staff, exchanged information, experiences, and
points of view. The mediators explained what they had learned from
their experiences and how they had continued and changed after
they had made mistakes. Much was negotiated and involved talk
about how others might view particular actions, how dreams might
serve to direct a person's efforts, and the need to make decisions.
Revealing failures or mistakes is not regarded as threatening to one's
self. In this type of relationship, there is less fear of failing to measure
up even when you have "screwed up" and continue to do things that
you know, and you know others know, are keeping you from going
where you really want to go. But you are not a bad person; you may
not be doing your best and you can change that. With an exchange of
personal information, a shared intimacy can develop that permits
criticism of untoward actions.

Even power to define the situation was in part left to the young
women. They were often asked to set the topic for discussion and
then make comments on what was being said. Additionally, the

5. Collins (1990) has argued that "other mothers" are and have been essential to
the African-American community. These are women who help out birth mothers and
make up, with the blood mothers, women-centered networks, all of whom take responsibility for children.

mediators attempted to persuade the young women to reevaluate their positions on various issues. They did this by providing information and arguments that the young women could try to evaluate against their own experiences to see whether or not the information made sense. The mediators created evaluations of actions by asking the young women how they thought others would see their actions. The speakers did not ask for personal authority, rather their power arose from the evaluation of the data or the argument presented, and authority was often granted after someone "made sense" over time.

A Critical Self and Responsibility

In a world in which situations are always changing—in which back regions evolve into front stages and actors inevitably disrupt the region—a highly skilled actor in taking the perspective of the others and making critical decisions is necessary. A person needs a critical self that is independent and, while conforming, is not conformist. To develop a critical self, a personal identity is necessary that is somewhat distinctive from the sum of social identities; it involves an ever-changing biography of past experiences, a sense of future direction, and the ability, while taking into account others' appraisals and evaluations of actions, to make decisions which may not receive much support. This self takes into account how others evaluate actions, but does not necessarily entirely conform to others' expectations.

According to Mead, people often do take a stand against the community and they should, as self-assertion is the basis for development of self.

> [I]t is a matter of taking the attitudes of the others and adjusting one's self or fighting it out. It is this recognition of the individual as a self in the process of using his self-consciousness which gives him the attitude of self-assertion or the attitude of devotion to the community. He has become, then, a definite self. (Mead [1934] 1962 193)

For the mediators, developing a strong critical self is essential for acting as a moral person. If an individual is continually moving between the front and back regions, then she has to prepare constantly for the definition and redefinition of the situation and she must be aware of and be able to assess the perspective of the others and her future goals in each situation and make a decision about how to interact. Everyone is confronted with situations in which he or she is forced to make essential decisions between conflicting messages by others or conflicting or competing paths embedded in decisions.

A person with a critical self evaluates situations and actions, is not totally dependent on how she thinks others will see her actions, and thinks about where she wants to go. A strong critical self can work successfully only if people have an idea about where they are going or would like to go and where they have been so they can reach beyond the immediate situation in making a decision about what to do. They need the cultural tools to see how acts may be connected, where roadblocks may be, what facilitators may be available, and how others may give meaning to those actions. They have to know how to use the culture and to create it. They have to know who they are and what is important to them. This is why the mediators spent time talking about the dreams of the young mothers: to find out what they wanted and the kinds of persons that they wished to be. A critical self is necessary to find a place and create a personal identity separate from social identities in this complex world. Otherwise, she may be a follower whose self is determined by whatever social situations she finds herself in.

To a certain degree, the individual is a product of her environment. Having a baby at fifteen is not the best timing to become a mother, but one is to some extent a creation of one's social world and in that world many young women become pregnant as teens. Being a teen mother does not mean that one is a good or a bad person or mother. What counts is having a direction for the future. An individual must take her life into her own hands and establish a direction and not let others push her around.

Learning to take responsibility for her actions is a key indicator of someone who is establishing her own place in the social world, but one must be ready to stand up and create a new meaning for a stigmatized action and demand that others pay attention. Motherhood is a critical role and it is good to embed authentic self in being a mother, but a woman has to try to do her best at being a mother so that her child will have a chance in a world of class, race, and gender discrimination. Conflicts with work will occur, but work is necessary for independence, even if one must currently postpone work for further education and training.

A critical self can step back, evaluate, and create a new meaning of activities and, if important, must be ready to promote that definition even when others evaluate it differently. Most important, the mediators found a way of giving meaning to welfare use that did not stigmatize. The mediators were political and advocated change by linking welfare to the middle-class standard of educational achievement: welfare was a scholarship for increasing one's training for the future and a short-term solution—a means (education) to help get something else (a good job). One must be able to take action, not just fit into current practices and understandings.

For the mediators, multiple identities are part of the process of developing a self that can negotiate creatively through the complex and ever-changing social worlds we build and inhabit. Motherhood is an important identity; it provides meaning and entails significant responsibility, but it is linked to being a girlfriend, a student, a worker, and a teen. The demands of all of these identities will compete for one's time and attention and situational conflict will inevitably develop. A person needs a self that can stand back and be independent, yet remain responsible for self and others; that can be free to express itself, yet conform to general standards of decency; and that can have fun and experience happiness, yet deals with real problems and remains levelheaded.

This critical self is essential to the creation of and survival in a social world of evolving back and front regions. It can best be developed in the context of a community of moral equals rather than in a hierarchical relationship with conformity demanded by the powerful and by expanding the variety of settings of interaction. A critical self enables a person to actively decide what should or should not enter a more public region and what should be public. Not only will a critical self be able to take what may be traditionally private into a more public arena, but should be able to limit public access to what is defined as the more private region. In this manner, the public/private dichotomy and hierarchy is transformed and the basis for more active citizenship is created. Citizenship should not be limited to or by participation in the labor market. One can be a good active citizen by remaining at home on welfare while taking care of the next generation and working to increase skills. Moreover, citizenship should involve taking stands on issues and active family and community participation, in addition to becoming an active creator of culture.

Are the Walls Thick or Are the Curtains Torn?

The program the arbiters construct with formal rules, hierarchy, strictly defined roles, and the image of the social world they communicate to the young women is one of stout, thick walls between the public and private areas of social life with narrow doors linking the rooms and through which no luggage can be taken. The arbiters communicate to the teen mothers that these walls exist, what shape they form, and how to carefully open the locked doors, just wide enough so that only the best representatives of the group with no baggage can slip through. It is the staff's job to teach the young women to open the door to the public world of work where everyone follows the rules of impression management and to teach them to lock the door after they have entered that world. At night they can go through that door and reenter private life—the dirty laundry, boyfriends, and children.

The world is full of prescribed roles that must be perfectly enacted and rules that must be adhered to by all residents of the rigidly structured rooms. Important symbols communicate only one correct message to others in that public setting and only a narrow range of appropriate symbols exists for legitimate use. These rooms with thick walls are built by others, those with power.

Those who live in a world full of walls see that rules and roles are already very structured and one must learn to fit into them. An individual has no independence to be different or to freely develop a role or construct an independent personal identity, particularly in the public sphere. To do so means risking treatment as a deviant. Therefore, it is necessary to learn the rules and how to follow them. One must learn to play roles structured, determined, and directed by others. As the rules and roles are already set, valid judgments can be made by observers as to the success in playing those roles and in following the rules. Judgments are made based on readily observable objective criteria and by the people in power who give out the roles which permit one to play and who reward for correctly playing them. Activities or characteristics of persons that may violate visibly the rules of the public arena must be hidden in the private world. For these young women, it means that all activities, feelings, and relationships that reveal the real person must be kept in the private world; they might reveal something dirty. Moral worth is judged by ability to meet the demands of public roles and to keep the public areas clear of private "business." It is derived from one's impression management skills.

The mediators communicate an alternative vision of the social world: one without solid walls, structured roles, and rigid rules. Curtains separate the various front and back stages through which one passes, often through rips and tears in thin fabric in need of repair. There are many curtains to pass through, along with some baggage. The curtains often become entangled, and one must deal with many front rooms with different groups of others. In each room is often someone who knows one's past and back stage life, so that an individual must be strong enough to carry personal baggage and not let it drag her around. A person must be able to decide what to take with her and what to leave behind. The social world is constructed by people and those people do make some rules and they do enforce limits to what can be done, but the individual has to seek out and change the shape of the room when necessary.

The mediators communicate that the individual's identity is important and she must be strong enough to control her actions in constructing a front stage identity. Much more variation is acceptable and how well one fits a role according to some general normative principles is not the way people should be judged. Relationships are negotiated, with close attention paid to what the other does and says, and the response is based on that assessment. An individual may not do a good job in developing or completing a task, but that does not necessarily reflect on who she is as a person, that is, her moral worth. Moral worth comes from trying to do things well that are most important to a person. Judgments are not dependent totally on others' assessments but on a more independent personal self-assessment.

The mediators are trying to teach the young women to increase their agency in the social world. They have to make their own pathways in the world and their own decisions about which paths they can carve out for themselves. They must learn to make their worlds. The arbiters, on the one hand, see themselves as having little agency and the young women barely having enough to change their own lives. Others control the world. The arbiters attempt to provide the cultural map for fitting in and thus improving chances in the wider society. The mediators, on the other hand, attempt to communicate a way of developing relationships that will permit the young women to better create their own paths in the wider society.

CHAPTER TEN

The Embodied Reason of Welfare Reform

Both the dignity of work and the public obligation to work are almost universally preached. Seventy-five percent of the American public think that there is something wrong with not wanting to work. A good citizen is an earner, because independence is the indelibly necessary quality of genuine, democratic citizenship [p. 92] . . . Both parties deeply believe in self-discipline, in independence, in work as the primary source of all value and dignity, and in the ideal of a society of self-supporting democratic citizens.

(Shklar 1991, 97)

On the national level, the debate concerning general welfare policies continues unabated, but the focus of the most bitter debates surrounds not those who make claims because of the failure of the labor market but those who make claims as single parents who must raise children alone. This latter form of welfare is for the poor and often young single women trying to raise children (those who qualify for Aid to Families with Dependent Children) and is treated differently than that attached to paid labor, for example, unemployment benefits (Gordon 1988; Orloff 1993). In the public debate, AFDC and teen motherhood are often closely linked. Much of the debate focuses on the complex and ambiguous relationship between teen motherhood and poverty, minority status, and welfare. And many see them as synonymous or part of the same complex of problems.

Some members of the public and some social scientists blame teen motherhood on the welfare system itself; teens become pregnant to get welfare and stay on welfare because it is the easy way out. Some researchers suggest that prolonged use of welfare is linked to the ready availability of AFDC itself (Murray 1984; Mead 1984), which they claim supposedly entices lower-class women not to marry but to have children (Murray 1984). But they do not fully explain why welfare receipt would have this effect.

The data on the effects of welfare on women is mixed, but it seems to be weighted in the direction that it does not encourage women to, for example, have children in order to remain on welfare. There is little support for a direct relationship between welfare availability, childbearing, and prolonged use of welfare. Some studies find that there is little or no relationship between receipt of welfare and increased out-of-wedlock births (Cutright 1973; Ellwood 1988; Fechter and Greenfield 1973; Moore and Caldwell 1976) and that, while real benefits have decreased, the rate of illegitimacy has increased (Cutright 1973; Ellwood and Bane 1984). Moreover, there is evidence that when women are on welfare, they are more likely to use birth control and to desire fewer children (Ellwood 1988; Placek and Hendershot 1974; Presser and Salsberg 1975).

If it is not the welfare system itself that is related to mothers remaining on welfare, it may be that there are few job options available in the wider society to earn sufficient money to, for example, buy medical coverage. The issue is *poverty* that arises from the lack of well-paying jobs, not *welfare*. In this broader socioeconomic perspective, teen motherhood is embedded in the problems arising from the destruction of the inner-city community and its institutions and the lack of reasonably well-paying jobs in the cities and the nation as a whole. Wilson (1987) argues that both those with well-paying blue-collar jobs and middle-class blacks have left the inner cities, thus leaving behind the very poor and few employment opportunities. Few community organizations remain to stabilize the communities and link the poor to the rest of society. This perspective focuses on the change in the market structure from an industrial economy to a service economy and the resulting high rates of unemployment among black men. Additionally, it accounts for the high numbers of teen pregnancies with the lack of eligible (employed) male marriage partners rather than blaming the teens themselves or defining it as a black problem.[1] More narrowly, some focus on the relationship of birth control information to sexuality and motherhood.

One side argues that information about birth control and sex contribute directly to teen sexuality and motherhood,[2] while others see

1. It is not entirely consistent with the black feminist paradigm of race, class, and gender as interlocking systems of oppression (Collins 1990). Wilson assumes that women will remain dependent in the private sphere.

2. A Chicago high school clinic that gave out contraceptives with parental permission, in a school where about one-third of the female students a year became pregnant,

teen motherhood as arising from the lack of knowledge and availability of birth control. Despite very different perspectives on the issue, people from a wide variety of political perspectives view teen motherhood as a social problem.

Different policy implications follow from the different hypothesized relationships between teen motherhood and welfare, poverty, and minority status: embedded in those decisions is a moral rhetoric. Some policies emphasize the need for basic economic changes that eliminate poverty, and many support the need for some social programs that promote self-sufficiency. However, whether to concentrate on the elimination of poverty or on self-sufficiency and what types of social programs are needed to fulfill these goals are hotly debated matters. These policies directly affect women and their relations to their families, men, and the labor market.

Embedded in some policies, such as the prevention of premarital sex and the requirement that all work to receive benefits, are the views that teen sex is immoral and welfare is an indication of laziness. This position has severe implications for the teen mother. "In the extreme conservative scenario, young women who become non-maritally pregnant are doubly responsible and, therefore, doubly undeserving—first, for 'choosing' sex over chastity, and, second, for 'choosing' AFDC over honest work" (Nathanson 1991, 67). Others, who take a "practical" or "medical" approach (Nathanson 1991), view teen motherhood as arising from lack of information or poor access to birth control and favor the provision of birth control services, health care for pregnant mothers, and childcare training after the birth of the child. The moral and economic context of the young women's lives is less significant. What has changed in the new work-oriented comprehensive programs for teen mothers is the substitution of "economic self-sufficiency," what Nathanson (1991) refers to as the "neo-Moynihan" approach, for medical rhetoric. This newer approach assumes that a tight link exists between teen motherhood and welfare and, sometimes, minority status.

The rhetoric used to debate the issues and to justify programs is important. "Economic self-sufficiency" was the rhetoric embedded in the program studied and largely informed the interactions of the arbiters and the participants. The rhetoric surrounding a public issue is suffused not only in the justifications for social programs at the

---

was the scene of picketing (*New York Times*, 4 November 1985). The cry that contraceptive information increases sexual activity occurs even though teens wait an average of eleven months after starting sexual activities to obtain contraceptive advice.

national and state levels but may enter into routine interactions of daily life. Real young people enter programs and real teen mothers have real children and real problems. The rhetoric can impinge directly on interactions in daily life in the wider society, the local community, and social service programs. Partly for this reason, I have argued that it is necessary to study the daily interactions in social service programs to understand the relationship between participants, programs, and national policies and rhetoric.

Not only are there competing views on what the social service programs are and should be doing, but a lack of consensus on more general welfare policy is also created by two, sometimes competing, objectives (Gueron 1990): (1) the elimination of poverty; and (2) the promotion of self-sufficiency. Gueron argues that the dilemma need not exist if funds were available to approach the problem from both sides. Those who wish to eliminate poverty tend to focus more on societal reforms, such as raising the minimum wage, Earned Income Tax Credits,[3] and voluntary training or educational programs, while those concerned with the promotion of self-sufficiency tend to focus on AFDC reform and making work or looking for work a necessary part of receiving welfare benefits, that is, demanding reciprocal obligations between the individual and the state. This means that women must do both the unpaid labor of their family responsibilities and the paid labor of the marketplace.

While the policies based on the hypothesized roots of the problems as defined by each of these objectives may appear consistent on the level of national policy, they may not be consistent with each other on the level of lived experience in the programs and communities. Voluntary educational and training programs—in terms of policy—may be consistent with both approaches. On the microlevel of lived experience, however, all voluntary programs may not communicate the same thing to participants and may in fact communicate messages more consistent with involuntary programs.

Involuntary programs that require something in return for benefits are deviations from the 1935 Social Security Act. When first enacted as part of that act, welfare was intended to provide funding for mothers so that they could stay home and raise their children.[4] Only after

3. "The Earned Income Tax Credit is a tax supplement to earnings for tax payers who maintain a household for one or more children. If a worker's family income falls below a certain level, the federal government funnels money to him or her by cutting his or her taxes. The credit is also 'refundable': If a family pays no federal taxes, it still gets the benefit in the form of a check from the government" (Gueron 1990, 82).

4. The Social Security Act of 1935 provided the first federal support for welfare, including dependent children in single-parent households along with the aged and the blind. They later set up AFDC when aid was extended to mothers in 1962.

1971 did the idea behind the provision of welfare begin to shift to reducing dependency through the provision of work experience or education (Gueron 1990).[5] Policymakers and politicians currently focus on work and educational requirements for everyone who receives welfare benefits. In 1988, the Family Support Act called on the states to develop programs that would impel women to give more information so that support payments could be required from the fathers and to set up programs that would mandate participation in education or jobs programs the states would have to provide. For example, teen parents would have to participate in educational activities. Results of the national policies have not been found to affect significantly what the states have done. Most have been hampered by lack of funds and a reluctance to force programs on recipients (Gueron 1990). This position assumes that a program which compels people to participate can communicate the importance and increase the possibility of achieving self-sufficiency.

Support for nonwelfare reforms to eliminate poverty, such as measures to ensure an adequate income for the working poor and, for example, providing transitional programs for employment rather than welfare, emerged to combat the stigmatizing and degrading experience of AFDC and to provide support for the working poor (Ellwood 1988; Ford Foundation 1989). Participation in educational or training programs was supposed to be voluntary, which would therefore minimize the stigma of the experience. However, this view assumes that the governmental definition of a program as voluntary and nonstigmatizing is what is communicated to and experienced by the participants. In order to develop programs where the elimination of poverty and the promotion of self-sufficiency can be consistent, we must explore the meanings of social control at the micro- and macrolevels. Some theories view welfare and social service programs as increasing social control and repression, whereas others view all programs, voluntary and involuntary, as potentially bringing people into moral conformity. A third position views the provision of benefits and services as a social right of all citizens and voluntary programs as potentially increasing social control through self-regulation.

5. Gueron (1990) argues that this transition has occurred for four reasons: the change in the percentage of working mothers with children under six from 30 percent in 1960 to 65 percent in 1987; the high increase in the caseload in the 1960s and early 1970s and the shift from widowed to never married or divorced mothers; the increasingly high rates of children living in female-headed households and the high rates of poverty in these households increased the desire to collect support from the fathers; and the high numbers who remain on AFDC for long periods—one-quarter of those who ever use AFDC stay on it for ten or more years.

Welfare Programs and Views of Social Control

An unanswered question is whether social welfare programs, particularly those geared toward the poor and women, represent the repression of specific groups without access to resources in our society or whether they are real, if not always successful, attempts to include the poor and the handicapped in mainstream society. According to the repression view (Piven 1985 and 1988; Piven and Cloward 1971; Schram and Turbett 1983), welfare and social work programs for the poor act to repress groups in order to maintain social order so that, for example, welfare benefits increase as a result of insurrections and decline in times of economic expansion to encourage work.[6] Some feminists, critical of the link of repression to the economic system alone, view the intrusion of the state into the lives of women receiving AFDC and the small income that it brings compared with the greater benefits of unemployment or disability compensation and lack of intrusion into the lives of the people receiving such benefits (mostly men) as part of a patriarchal system of domination (Gordon 1988; Nelson 1984).[7] Welfare policies regulate family structure, domestic labor, and the reproductive and sexual behavior of the single women (Gordon 1988). Welfare represents the threat of and use of force to demand quiescence and subordination.

A second view assumes that the poor lack sufficient social control and need to be brought into moral conformity. Some argue that resocialization is necessary, while others view coercion as necessary to bring people into moral conformity. Social control as resocialization through social services reflects the larger community's desire to reeducate the poor and bring them into strict social and moral conformity with middle-class society. In this perspective, social work pro-

6. For a review of several neo-Marxist positions on the relationship between the state and the economy, see Quadagno (1987).

7. "Social citizenship analysts envision social policy as having emancipatory as well as regulatory potential. Even where emancipation is not a manifest objective, social programs may have unintended 'independence effects'" (Orloff 1993, 305). However, policies on the macrolevel do not always predict what will occur on the microlevel of everyday experience.

Some feminists dispute Piven and Cloward's (1971) view of the origin and social control function of welfare policy as the control of excess labor. Moreover, Gordon (1988) argues that feminists who advocate welfare rights activism of welfare recipients and Piven and Cloward underestimate the recipients political understanding and activism (Gordon 1988, 625). Not only are women choosing to remain single, help-seeking is a political action (Nelson 1980). Despite this activism, Gordon (1988) argues that the social control function of the welfare state is paternalistic and works to keep women out of public-sphere activities, thus reinforcing dependency and domesticity; however, they do not need to depend on men but on the state.

grams and welfare represent a failure of social control by the traditional institutions of socialization. Social service programs must serve to resocialize those whom the society considers unworthy, disruptive or deviant, but benefits may, if too freely offered, support or even exacerbate dependency. This latter emphasis may advocate mandatory work or educational programs to bring welfare recipients into moral conformity. This places women in the position of doing unpaid labor in the home and paid labor in the labor market.

Third, the provision of benefits and social service programs may represent society's efforts to control itself (self-regulation) by increasing its ability to regulate itself through the elimination of misery and the reduction of coercion and by increasing a subgroup's ability to regulate itself. Welfare benefits may be an extension of mass society and may help to resolve some of the problems of misery by giving people access to resources such as money, food, and shelter, that is, such benefits are an extension of social rights. The boundaries of society are expanded outward (Grønbjerg 1977; Janowitz 1975 and 1978).

There are several questions that arise in all perspectives on social control. First, what are the goals of social control? Second, what is the relationship between subgroups and the larger or more powerful group? Third, is it possible to have increased social organization or order and some collective stability without a reduction in authenticity, personal freedom, and creativity? This third question, in particular, points to the microlevel of experience.

While the first view of welfare policy argues that all social control is repressive and all must bow to the needs and desires of the powerful state, market, or gender hierarchy, the second or moral conformity perspective sees social control as necessarily strong and total for moral and social order to be achieved. For the social control as self-regulation perspective, dilemmas and tensions always exist in situations in which the society's efforts to control itself appear at odds with the subgroup's efforts at self-regulation.

Janowitz (1975 and 1978) specifies goals for social control from a self-regulation perspective. The welfare state is embedded in the idea that the citizen is better off with resources generated not only by the marketplace but by grants or resources provided by the government through the political process of negotiating demands, not by coercive authority. It is legitimate for the government to intervene and assist citizens in the achievement of personal and household needs (Janowitz 1978). Policies (Janowitz 1975, 84) must be designed to enable a social group to regulate itself in accord with a set of norms consistent with a reduction in coercive control (some always remains in a legitimate system of authority), "the elimination of human misery" (some inequality always remains), and a commitment to procedures to "enhance the role of rationality" (Janowitz 1978, 30). These policies should enable groups to regulate themselves in terms of a set of legitimate moral principles and result in a reduction of coercive control if the experience is consistent with the rationality of the policy. Social control is effective if it motivates human groups. However, these policies only hint at how daily life should be organized, as there are many ways to translate these "principles" into action.

The view of welfare policy as repression and the view that it represents efforts to achieve moral conformity share the assumption that social control implies suppression of individual choice and authenticity. In the case of the first of these perspectives, the agency of that suppression is an elite group or the state itself. In the alternative perspective, the agency that effectively delimits the range of choice is the general value system. The third view of welfare does not share this assumption. Rather it sees social control *as* self-regulation that includes the possibility of a delicate, ever-changing balance between social control of a group and the group's ability to regulate itself. It does not imply that tensions between the individual and the group do not exist; they remain, but social control is potentially a dynamic and interactive pattern even when some inequities and imbalances exist among the parties.

Many studies of social services and welfare focus on macrolevel analyses and infer the intent or effects of such programs from the changes in rates and types of available funds and efforts invested in such programs in relation to larger economic successes or failures (Piven and Cloward 1971; Schram and Turbett 1983), from state-market relations (Quadagno 1987), from power resources (Orloff 1993), or from the extent of urbanization as representative of an increase in secondary institutions (Grønbjerg 1977). While measuring the increases or decreases in available services against a changing economy or comparing the effects of welfare policies on gender among nations (Orloff 1993) tells us something about the meaning of the programs to those in power or group-level effects, such studies are limited in their capabilities to help us understand what the service providers communicate to their users or how the users experience programs and react to them.

Can these macrolevel theories help us understand the experience of recipients? If so, how? The welfare and social control debate revolves around the issue of whether citizenship in the form of welfare benefits and social services (social rights) serves to incorporate the poor as citizens, thereby lessening class conflict, or does it, in this form, serve only to try to keep them quiet so that there remains a potential for conflict? Do programs confirm a group's position on the periphery and increase its dependency or can they begin to move people more toward the center with increased participation in the organizations of the wider society? Do they predict that people will be confirmed on the periphery by provision of welfare, which allows them to live in the style the poor value (lower-class culture), by failing to provide the "cultural codes" necessary for inclusion or by failing to provide the type of resources that permit and/or encourage equal participation of all classes, races, and genders? Policies and programs may, however, further include people by resocializing them to the norms and values of the wider society, thereby further insuring moral conformity, or they may increase options and provide for increased diversity, freedom of choice, independent decision making, and authenticity of the individual.

Much of the research on social service programs in this country focuses on the macrolevel and some view welfare as an additional instrument of the capitalist system to maintain surplus labor quietly in a subservient position or as part of a patriarchal society to keep women out of the labor market and with less benefits than men. They fail to confront issues of social control except as repressive mechanisms emanating from bourgeois capitalist or patriarchal society that will wither away with the fall of the capitalist/patriarchal state.

Even perspectives that greatly sensitize us to the differential effects of the welfare state on men and women[8] are not directly able to explain how they operate to control people at the microlevel of experience. They are able to show how welfare policies that distinguish between provisions based on paid labor market involvement, available largely to men, and those based on family, that is, unpaid labor available to women, are less generous, stigmatize recipients, and create and reproduce the hierarchy between men and women. However, this perspective is not able to inform us on the microlevel about how the programs may differently affect women, either increasing their capacity to maintain households or obtain work or confirming them in dependent relationships.

Some cultural studies suggest ways that culture is part of the process of domination and that the ruling class maintains its position not

8. Orloff (1993) provides an excellent analysis of gender and the social rights of citizenship by using a power resource model and carefully documenting the literature on gender and the power resource model.

only through economic control but also through cultural hegemony. Society is held together through "voluntary" adherence to dominant ideas. Power and class are embedded in cultural codes (Bourdieu 1974 and 1977; Bourdieu and Passeron 1977). For Bourdieu, the ability to perceive is unequally distributed in society and can be attained only by those who have the cultural codes to do so. This is the cultural wealth of the society—the family and schools are the institutions that communicate these codes and all environments are not equally able to communicate the necessary codes. Schools attended by the poor or by women would be less likely to transmit this code—that would be critical of the system. Social service institutions also would be unlikely to do so, given the low status of those who work there and the cultural milieu that emphasizes that lack of economic success is related not to social conditions but to individual gifts. Welfare use would be seen as individual failure. Class culture is likely to be reproduced in social service programs as social workers would be unlikely to be able to provide the keys to new class cultural codes.

The moral conformity perspective regards the need for welfare and social service programs as the desire to instill the proper work ethic in recipients, who have not been properly socialized elsewhere, either because they grew up in an alternative culture or adapted to a lack of opportunities. Consistent with this position and providing explanations are the traditional "lower-class culture" and "culture of poverty" arguments (Banfield 1970; Lewis 1966; Miller 1958) where an independent value system perpetuates a lifestyle of single parenthood and unemployment. The desired values can be taught in social work programs or demanded by sending welfare recipients out to work. This latter strategy may be necessary to avoid supporting a value system in which work is not valued.

On the level of lived experience, Mead ([1934] 1962) provides us with an idea of how social control can operate on the microlevel by self-regulation, which can increase authenticity and provide increased freedom of choice. Empowerment is necessary for a group to regulate itself through increased perspective taking, that is, through an expansion of the generalized other that provides more options and facilitates decision making for the individual. By increasing participation in various groups and situations, people will be able not only to see and take into account the way others view the social world, but they can become increasingly capable, by developing a unique creative self through decision making, of transcending a given social order, thus increasing their creative potential (Shalin 1986 and 1988).

They can develop a critical self. But this may not occur. It depends on what is communicated in daily interaction in a particular program.

Involuntary Programs as Nonrational in Terms of Self-Regulation

Involuntary programs that promote "self-sufficiency" are consistent with the moral conformity model but are inconsistent with self-regulation because in receiving benefits an individual owes something in return. A model of citizenship in which citizenship is linked solely to the individual's relationship to the marketplace is congruous with a commitment to mandatory work requirements and implies that people have a duty, regardless of the situation, to provide for themselves and their dependents in the marketplace. Social rights as protection from the free market are minimized (Hasenfeld, Rafferty, and Zald 1987). Thus women on AFDC who cannot support their families are not considered full citizens, and they may need to be coerced into the marketplace by requiring some form of work in exchange for benefits (workfare). Involuntary work is a policy supported by the notion of the importance of self-sufficiency over the elimination of poverty. These people owe the government (other hardworking citizens) something in return for the receipt of grants. It is legitimate to coerce people in order that they meet criteria for citizenship.

The stigmatization and punishment of women with young children for nonparticipation in the workplace dramatizes the public/private hierarchy and clearly relegates motherhood and childrearing to secondary importance and to unvalued, unpaid labor. If people are not regarded as citizens without an active role in the workplace, those who receive direct grants to remain at home to care for their children (not supported by a husband) are even more greatly stigmatized and excluded from full citizenship. This view of social life creates a world divided into two distinct spheres: a public sphere of participation in the workplace and a private sphere of family, home, and local community. Family participation, household maintenance, and the nurturing of children is not an alternative form of participation as a citizen. As discussed in the last chapter, this model of the separation of the public and private spheres leads to dualities in all aspects of life and a hierarchy in which the male-dominated public sphere is regarded as more important than the mostly female/family private sphere where men may also try to control women.

On the macrolevel, policies requiring work in exchange for AFDC benefits are consistent with this view of the strict division between the public and private and the need for participation in the public sphere of work (coerced if necessary) to achieve full citizenship, that is, to engage in public discourse and to receive government-supported grants. People who do not work[9] outside of the household are not included as fully cooperating citizens and, after a certain period, if conditions are not fulfilled, benefits may be lowered. This most clearly affects women and the children they are trying to support. Self-regulation in the sense of the nation trying to reduce coercion and minimize the misery of its citizens and incorporating this group of unemployed and poor mothers into public discourse appears to be decreasing as the welfare bureaucracy becomes more coercive and decreases the ways women may participate in society. In this sense, nonvoluntary programs of work are not rational policies within a welfare state but are coercive and repressive policies. This does not mean, however, that voluntary programs are necessarily noncoercive and serve to increase self-regulation on the microlevel of peoples' experiences.

The Potential Conflict between the Macro- and Microlevels of Policy and Experience

While the development of voluntary programs appears consistent with both the elimination of poverty and increased self-sufficiency, from the perspective of self-regulation, the question of whether such voluntary programs are necessarily effective in increasing self-regulation is debatable. What occurs in the programs themselves on the level of daily interaction and experience may not be consistent with policies developed by administrators and politicians on the macrolevel. They are loosely coupled cultures.

While the program studied suggests that voluntary programs have a potential for enhancing the sense of agency and skills necessary for increased involvement in their clients, it also points out that there is a considerable potential for failure, insofar as such programs aim at integrating the participants further into the wider society and the work world. Assessing the participants' experiences furnishes deeper insights into what actually occurs than when we merely calculate the number of students who take jobs or continue their education after completing the program. To understand what goes on, we must pay

9. In some states, mothers must work or look for work to receive welfare if their child is over one year old.

attention to daily face-to-face interactions in the delivery of the services and benefits and not just to macrolevel policies and the distribution of funding. It should not be surprising that lower-level staff have considerable influence over citizens (Lipsky 1980).

Knowledge of how such programs actually work and what effect they have on program participants should encourage critical self-awareness on the part of program staff, thus helping to increase client self-regulation and to decrease dependency. According to Halton's interpretation of Dewey, "science itself is not 'systematized knowledge' but *living* inquiry" (1986, 21). Free inquiry is essential to the community; it is a principle mode of communication in a democracy. Lived inquiry cannot be replaced by abstract systemization because the latter obscures the differences of individuals and communities. If inquiry is to serve a communicative purpose and facilitate "inquisitive and imaginative human nature tempered through its observations and refined through the self-critical community" (Halton 1986, 22), it must be able to show the unique qualities of that community. We saw how the program emerged on a daily basis and the conflicts that arose among staff members and between staff and clients. By most indications, the staff should have had similar relations with the clients: they had similar jobs and training, they were in the same organization with one mission, and they had similar social characteristics. However, they did not have similar relationships with the clients. The staff communicated very different messages about the individual and society. We saw how policy was transformed and made meaningful by the workers as they communicated their views to the young women in terms of their own experiences in the social world and how they thought the social worlds were organized and operated.

Focus on the level of lived experience does not mean disregard for macrolevel processes. Macrolevel factors help to shape the microexperience, while the latter reinforces institutional patterns. In that sense, this is not just a microlevel study; the examination of daily experience lets us see how the macrolevel world shapes and is, in turn, shaped by the face-to-face relations of lived experience. Economic, gender, and state structures help shape state and federal policies on types of social service provision and funding which, in turn, have an impact on and help to shape not only class, race, and gender stratification, but, more important—as demonstrated in this book—the mission, organization, hiring processes, and the daily running of the program. Most critically for job-training programs, the larger economic market and political forces affect the availability of employment for those who "complete" the program and the support services necessary for women who raise children alone and work at low-wage jobs without benefits. State regulations and policies provide the groundwork for the staff's labor, but what the staff actually do is not wholly determined by the program's manifest ends or the staff's own places in society. Moreover, their actions feed back into the state policies and practices. It is a dialectical relationship.

We have seen how the welfare policies of the state shape the type of social program that is offered and the categories of people for whom they are designated. The separation into "entitlement" and "means-tested" programs shapes the different experiences of those who receive benefits from one or the other. State and federal policies also determine the resources available for these programs and what services are offered, which impacts on those who are available to work in such programs. It was state-shaped policies and local organizations that developed a program for "disadvantaged workers," which separated these young women from others their age and these teen mothers from older mothers and unemployed men. It was the state officials and local organizations who defined it as a "job-readiness" program and not one of teaching specific skills. As a one-year program with poor pay for staff, those who have full-time continuous jobs are unlikely to apply for staff positions. It was the state agents who decided to have two groups for five months each and who wanted to start the program within two weeks of receiving the funding. It was also the state agents who decided that the research component was necessary, though it was some of the mediators who quickly took up the idea of having a participant-observer instead of simply administering a survey before they received the funding. The organization lacked tight supervision, there was no real authority hierarchy among the staff within the program, and each had her own class. This permitted different orientations toward what "help" was and should be and how it should be offered. And it was some of the staff who turned it into a program for women and, during the second session, a program for blacks.

None of the more macrolevel structures exclusively determined what went on in the program, though they did provide broad parameters for its operation and in shaping staff orientations. The staff in interaction with the young women shaped the program organization and culture. What went on inside was not immune to the lives of the young women outside of the program. Issues and problems followed them into the program and daily problems and dilemmas kept them out. Their lives were subject to experiences, needs, and relationships outside of the program that could only be dealt with during program hours. Sick children cannot go to day care and someone has to stay home. These young women cannot afford the money for special services for a sick child, even when such are available, and sometimes their personal networks fail them.

A close examination of the taken-for-granted world of social services revealed two cultures that evolved simultaneously within the program and were differently related to the culture outside, both of the program intent and of the worlds of the teen mothers and staff. Little really was consistent and there were many disagreements among the staff and between staff and participants. The cultures were loosely coupled: the arbiters from the mediators, the young women from some of the staff, and the cultures inside from the different worlds outside. Much occurs on the microlevel of lived experience that is not consistent with macrolevel polices. In order to understand more fully how and why a voluntary program that appears to be consistent with both the promotion of self-sufficiency and the elimination of poverty on the macrolevel is not completely consistent with those policies on the microlevel, we must examine not only the different communications of the staff but also the difference between disembodied reason and embodied reasonableness (Shalin 1992).

Disembodied Reason and Embodied Reasonableness

What we treat on the macrolevel as rational, as cognitive sense making, may not be reasonable on the microlevel of lived experience. "Knowledge uninformed by feelings and stripped of emotive elements can be rational without being reasonable; it achieves certainty by discarding insight from the senses in favor of the rationales laid out by intellect" (Shalin 1992, 256). Voluntary program participation, such as job training or education on the part of an AFDC recipient, on the policy level seems like a rational way to partially alleviate poverty and incorporate the individual further into the larger social world through noncoercive means by providing options. But is it necessarily reasonable on the level of face-to-face interactions of real program participants?

We saw how Project GED operated rather independently from state controls and developed into two, sometimes antagonistic, cultures. The disjunction between policy and practice may be understood, in part, as a result of the loosely coupled relationships among the different groups, the written documents, and actual program implementation: the staff, the participants, the state representatives, and the consortium of agencies, the proposal, the staff-stated goals, and daily interaction. The conflict between the macro- and micro-levels also may be embedded in a distinction between embodied reasonableness and disembodied reason (Shalin 1992). Both reason and formal rationality refer to the way decisions are supposed to be made in the public sphere, with cognitive grounding being given precedence over emotional commitment. This sphere is largely dominated by men. Relations in the private sphere, on the other hand, are embedded in emotions and sentiments. In this traditional model, women are the guardians of emotions. What may be rational on the policy level, based on a model not taking into account emotions, may not be reasonable on the level of program participation in terms of lived experience of the participants themselves, who receive all sorts of messages from their handlers, some highly injurious to their sense of dignity and self-esteem.

The split between formal, cognitive rationality and substantive rationality is the object of inquiry and the source of pessimism about modern life in the Weberian approach and points to a possible dilemma of a national policy that appears formally rational and the actual provision of the services that may not be substantively rational. The Weberian (1958) separation between formal/instrumental and substantive/value rationality makes this point. Formal rationality increases efficiency, helps calculate the future, and is handy to assert control, whereas substantive rationality permits the judging of values and what gives life meaning. In Weber's view, the increase in formal rationality decreases substantive rationality, as bureaucracies and administrative procedures predominate. When a split exists, rationality becomes a force to curb impulse and emotions and, through reason, is embedded in cognition and verbal intellect. Human experience appears here as merely "private and intellectually mute" (Shalin 1992, 225).

A model which sharply separates emotions and affect from verbal intellect provides insufficient grounds for questioning the rationality of a voluntary program as described above or for understanding what the experience was like. Such programs are designed to raise the skill levels of clients so that they are better able to get jobs and, thus, become more involved citizens. Program failure to improve the skills of the participants can be judged rationally by assessing individual improvement in skill level or jobs obtained. If too few receive GED's or jobs or raise their self-esteem, the program may be judged to be a failure because of such factors as failure to provide enough time to complete the services needed, to furnish the designated services, or to recruit the personnel with relevant teaching skills. On the participants' side, blame might focus on such factors as the failure of the clients to exert themselves to complete the program work or on their originally low educational level, which made it impossible for them to catch up. It would not be of concern whether the experience in the program proved reasonable to participants.

In Shalin's terms, what is missing from such an analysis is embodied reasonableness, which pragmatists oppose to disembodied reason. Pragmatists are concerned with lived experience, which includes not only verbal intellect but the human body and emotions, feelings, and sentiments, which are not subordinate to ideas and concepts. "Communication is contingent on minding something together, carrying out a larger act in which participants are engaged bodily as well as mentally" (Shalin 1992, 254). Cognition and emotions are inextricably linked; they are complementary aspects of the same action and breaking them apart is sure to render our official policy pronouncements impotent. We need to communicate our messages not only verbally and linguistically on the conceptual levels but also on the level of nonverbal, emotional intelligence. Emotions and feelings can be "generalized" and "communicated even more readily than ideas."

> Contrary to the rationalist view, reason has a lot to learn
> from noncognitive functions: feelings point to a crisis in experience: sentiments signal when general principles take a
> beating from obdurate reality; emotions provide a running
> commentary on the success of our plans. To divest reason
> from living experience is to disembody it, to leave it helpless
> in the face of perennial indeterminacy and contingency with
> which humans have to struggle in their everyday existence.
> When thinking leaves experience far behind and escapes
> into *theoria*, it is likely to lead practical action astray. (Shalin
> 1992, 255)

There is constant tension between the cognitive and the emotional in everyday life. The two do not exist in separate spheres. On the microlevel, the experiences of the young women are filled with emotions such as fear, insecurity, love, excitement, and ennui. As participants interact with staff, they assess the reasonableness of what they are told; that interpretation is embedded both in emotion and cognition. One can understand the reasonableness of their suspicion of the arbiters when one looks at the fear they have of workers who have the power to take away their children. Many have been threatened by welfare workers or have friends who have been. Fear of the GED test and failure to show up for classes or the exam can be understood as reasonable, for even though they might value the GED for its own sake, they have failed in school too often in the past and are frightened to take the risk again. Investment in the program, when they have failed before, is highly risky, particularly when it has been billed as their "last chance." Based on a purely cognitive rational perspective, they should try harder since this really may be their last chance and they truly want to do better this time around. But it seems perfectly reasonable to limit this emotional commitment when they are so convinced and frightened of failing. Failure to go all out on a job hunt may seem irrational given that it is widely seen in our society as a basis for citizenship and independence. But it also means clinging to that part of their life where they experience the most joy and triumph—motherhood, which is a key to their sense of self-worth. In short, the young women's responses to the arbiters' program are not unreasonable if we use embodied reason rather than disembodied rationality to understand their behavior. Moreover, staff who consider emotions in their interactions are better able to interact with the participants.

It is difficult for several reasons to predict the success of a particular type of policy because of the loosely coupled connections between the policies at the national level and the way they are actually carried out through face-to-face encounters with service recipients. An administrative policy set up purely in systemic terms and on cognitively based precepts does not guarantee in pragmatic terms that it can or will be viewed as sensible or reasonable by the participants. This is not to say that the GED and related exercises are irrelevant. The program provides a means of potentially including this population in the greater debate and increasing their chances to find a place in it in the more public arenas.

Pessimistic Forecast: Disembodied Reason and Continued Dependence

The young women who attended fairly regularly saw the program as a rational means to a desirable end: a GED as a path toward a job. Their experiences, however, did not always make sense to them personally. The young women were afraid of failing and were suspicious of the arbiters. They regarded these staff members' decisions and actions as denigrating their dignity and self-respect. Humiliated by the arbiters, they frequently felt as though their private lives were not only insignificant, but worse, something they should be ashamed of, something dirty; that they would always be dependent on the goodwill and charity of others even though they might be employed and supporting their own families. The arbiters' demands were experienced as attempts to control their lives and deprive them of the rights accorded others as citizens capable of finding and keeping jobs and of participating in the politics of the wider society. Looked at from this perspective, the program appears unreasonable. Even if one sees the rationality of getting a GED or making it through the program, the experience of the staff/client relationships overpowers the cognitive rationality of investing in the program. The program experience is too degrading and the risks of failure appear too great to invest fully in it. The arbiters scoffed at the young women's fear by never acknowledging it as real, as going to the very core of their personhood and undermining the program's proffered goal.

Failure to Encourage Independence and Decision Making
How can a person make a successful transition to the work world when what little sense of agency they have is systematically undermined by the arbiters' efforts to claim strict control of interactions? Voluntary social service programs can and, in this case, did place the young women at the bottom of a steep hierarchy and the arbiters tried to create a relationship which made the young women dependent on those in authority above them. The arbiters created the rules and enforced them. They were determined to model the program space after a typical work setting in which the young women might find themselves. By structuring the interaction so that only some topics could be discussed and only in particular ways, the arbiters affirmed the private lives of family and community as dirty laundry utterly removed from what goes on in the public work sphere, the only place to legitimately claim citizenship in American society.

While the arbiters argued that the young women were supposed to be financially independent from the state, they were reaffirming their dependency on others through the relationships that they created. This is not uncommon in welfare state bureaucracies (Hasenfeld, Rafferty, and Zald 1987, 398). The arbiters organized their relationships so as to make the young women dependent on them in order to teach them what the rules were in each setting outside of the local community. The staff told them what to do and how to behave: there was no discussion, there was no opportunity for the young women to assert their independence, and there was no way to learn how to be independent or to deal with their emotions. They were to follow and obey as individuals without any collective identity and told they could not and should not make independent choices: work must come before family and boyfriends. Nothing they did placed them on an equal status with the arbiters and they were made to believe that they had never quite learned how to use appropriate symbols in public. Social distance was emphasized by the arbiters, whether that meant eating separately or not being seen together in public. When the young women did try to take power or make independent moves, they were threatened, criticized, or kicked out of the program. All of these interactions communicated to the young women that their position in society was dependent and morally inferior to that of the staff members.

There are few choices the young women can make in the social world created by the arbiters, either in the program or in the world of work, the unique path to citizenship. It is imperative in order to survive, if not succeed, in such a world that the dependent individual in the subordinate role learn the rules of the public sphere fixed by those in power. Work is what others care about and give credit for, and, in order to get that work, one must learn not only the skills and rules but the external symbols of membership in the public sphere, such as presentation of self—dress style, rules of etiquette, and the necessity of hiding one's private life. This means fitting carefully and precisely into a subordinate role created by others and accepting identities and rules set by others. The arbiters' messages, however, were not always consistent, which undermined their authority. Despite their efforts to promote rule conformity, undivided commitment to rules, and the importance of impression management, the arbiters sent some conflicting messages when the participants saw behind their public presentations. John came and went as he pleased, came in drunk, and continued to collect his salary. Roberta and the others gossiped and sometimes appeared to be doing nothing. Mr. Harrison spent a lot of "work time" looking for another job and Ivy claimed to know things she clearly did not. It appears that the workers had a lot more freedom to do as they pleased in the program than they were prepared to grant to their clients.

While the young women sometimes demonstrated a sense of agency in interaction with the staff by taking on the role of instructor or changing the topic of discussion or beginning to launch a revolt, the arbiters worked hard to reclaim their authority and to stop any manifestation of genuine independence. In fact, anyone who appeared to be too independent (that is, anyone who did not behave according to the demands of the arbiters) was defined as a trouble-maker or an inappropriate placement and kicked out of the program.

Importantly, the arbiters' view of submission to authority and lack of agency created problems for themselves. When they presented a position and the young women changed the topic or took on the role of instructor, that is, changed the situation, the arbiters had few ne-gotiation skills to renegotiate their authority. They claimed authority and, when it was not accepted, they had no way of reclaiming it ex-cept by reasserting their claims more strongly. The arbiters appear to have only one recourse: threatening to kick out or actually expelling a participant from the program. When people do not follow the es-tablished rules, there is no negotiation to keep them in; they will be cast out.

Without a sense of agency, where does a person find the energy to handle the myriad of problems and dilemmas of everyday life expe-riences or to look for a job? There are too many situations where family and work life will conflict, where acting as a girlfriend and a mother will make competing demands on limited resources, and where no solution can be worked out without a sense of control over one's life. If the programs fail to foster agency, then they negate the very things they claim as their goals—client independence and self-regulation.

Failure to Acknowledge Feelings
Moreover, the failure to acknowledge that feelings, emotions, and values are a part of everyday life, whether in the workplace, the street, or the family is unrealistic and contributes to the experience of unreasonableness. Many of the young women were angry and upset when they discovered that their reading levels were well below the last grade they completed in school and were hurt and angry when a man showing them around a work site inferred that they were lazy. Punishment was the arbiters' response to the expression of negative feelings and all trips were suspended after the job site visit. While instructors teach stewardesses simply to conceal their true feelings and to fall back on rehearsed expressions appropriate to the job (Hochschild 1983), the arbiters told the young women to suppress them as shameful in their essence. There was no discussion about how to manage negative feelings, nor did the arbiters ever acknowl-edge that their own actions might affect the clients' feelings. Indeed, the arbiters systematically eliminated the events and settings where participants could have expressed positive feelings: the parties, the

mother-children days, and on job-site trips. One does whatever the boss tells one to do, or else one is a misfit.

It becomes clear that the young women did not have very reasonable experiences in the program with the arbiters. While they assessed the learning of skills as rational in terms of the need to obtain a GED and a job, there were too many encounters and demands they viewed as threatening, humiliating, or anxiety-provoking and too few they experienced as promising or exciting to encourage greater investments in the program. Bear in mind also that what they learn about social relationships and the world of work is not likely to help much in getting a job that pays enough to support a family or nurturing the social, emotional, and cultural skills necessary for balancing work and family worlds. Dependency is reaffirmed.

Grounds for Optimism: Embodied Reason and the Development of Agency

While the above analysis is pessimistic about the possibility that the provision of education and job-training services will increase self-regulation and motivate groups toward greater participation, there is reason for optimism. Voluntary programs such as the one studied can contribute to the reduction of human misery and coercion. It is possible to motivate and increase the active role of the participants in the wider society. This side was reflected in the mediators' actions.

The young women, as portrayed here, are already active participants in their micro social worlds and skilled performers who know how to take the perspective of the other and protect themselves as less powerful persons. They need, however, to broaden their sense of community and breadth of perspective-taking skills. Within the context of the provision of services, the participants can develop skills necessary to increase autonomy and participation in civic, political, and social life beyond the family and local community. While the mediators lost the battle for program direction, their efforts demonstrate the path toward a reasonable program that has as its prime goals providing clients with a broadened scope of experience, heightened skills at taking control of their lives, and increased ability to handle their feelings. For such a program to be successful, it is necessary that the young women increase their sense of agency, that is, that they view the world as malleable and open to change and view themselves as sensemakers, choosers, citizens of the nation rather than just as wards (Janowitz 1983) of the mediating institutions of society.

For teen mothers, a group with few resources and little experience outside of the local community, being able to take control of one's life in the wider society and create a place for oneself both inside and outside of the local community is difficult. The cultural capital needed for deciphering and the power to manipulate the social worlds in which all of us interact is not equally distributed in American society. This raises the question as to whether the mediators are equipped to help young women decode the social world outside of the local community and move more actively to join the work force. Cultural competence is a matter of experiences that are not furnished equally to all. Yet the social world outside of the local community demands interpretive skills which are sometimes decidedly different from those fostered by a local community. Will the young women do better by learning to follow unquestioningly the rules set by those in power or by taking the perspective of the other, making their own decisions, and changing situations? To put it more provocatively, should we encourage an individual to take a critical stand vis-à-vis a community? This raises the further question of whether the self can affect the larger community. According to Mead ([1934] 1962),

> The only way in which we can react against the disapproval
> of the entire community is by setting up a higher sort of
> community which in a certain sense out-votes the one we
> find. A person may reach a point of going against the whole
> world about him: he may stand out by himself against it. But
> to do that he has to speak the voice of reason to himself. He
> has to comprehend the voices of the past and of the future.
> That is the only way in which the self can get a voice which
> is more than the voice of the community . . . He can per-
> haps change the attitude of the community toward himself.
> [pp. 167–68]
> We know that as we pass from one historical period to an-
> other there have been fundamental changes, and we know
> these changes are due to the reactions of different individu-
> als. It is only the ultimate effect that we can recognize, but
> the differences are due to the gestures of those countless in-
> dividuals actually changing the situation in which they find
> themselves, although the specific changes are too minute for
> us to identify. [pp. 202–3]

People can change the community and others' attitudes toward them.

The mediators emphasized choice, working with and toward one's dreams, community, decision making, taking the perspective of the other, dealing with emotions, and making one's own path in the social world. They worked hard to show the young women that it was possible to change their social worlds and to play an active part in creating new ones. They showed the young women that it was possible to change the welfare workers' perception of them by being in control of the situation, by keeping the house neat, and by not permitting the social worker to wake the baby during a nap. They showed the young women that it was possible to demand that their boyfriends treat them with respect. They could change the meaning of welfare. The participants were encouraged to take an active role in their own lives, always keeping in mind not only the current self but their future selves, so as to engage in actions that take into account who they want to be.

There were, however, few opportunities outside of the volatile, emotional discussions with the group and the mediators to act out their development of a critical self and to try to change their social worlds and enter new ones. Mediators encouraged the young women to set the direction of the discussion, to voice their own thoughts and feelings. They took into account the fears and doubts and understood the self-criticism hidden in the young women's attacks on others' activities. To encourage a critical self and to show how others might interpret their actions differently and that they might have to change actions or persuade others what they "really meant," the mediators questioned actions and their meanings but never attacked the person. The mediators prepared the young women to shed the stigma of being unable to create a place for themselves in the wider society and of being dependent on the state without having them give up their cherished identities as loving mothers and caring women. The young women saw the priorities and techniques used by mediators as reasonable and sensible, as addressing their frequently hidden feelings, and, above all, as responsive to their need for understanding and self-respect. The model,[10] provided by the mediated, permitted them as political actors to begin to change the divisions between public and private spheres and to control the process of region changes.

10. This view is consistent with Somers's (1993) critique of Marshall (1964) in which she shows that the relationship between citizenship and social class is not as tight as generally assumed. She found that "working people with similar categorical attributes displayed different citizen practices" (1993, 610). Here the arbiters and mediators, from similar backgrounds and in similar positions, held very different notions of citizenship. The mediators views were close to her view of citizenship—citizenship "was created by the activities of people in particular situations who interacted with institutions, ideals, and rules of legal power and governmental participation" (1993, 611). The mediators were active creators and worked to involve the young women in that perspective and consequent actions.

The Real World of Unskilled Labor and Unsupportive Policies

Even if they develop a sense of agency and are able to begin to make their way in the social world outside of the local community without jeopardizing their local worlds, these young women are probably going to hit brick walls. Despite strong efforts to achieve commendable goals, many are likely to fail. Supporting themselves and their children on minimum- or low-wage jobs in the service sector and trying to care for their children is an enormous task, especially for teens. Jobs that pay enough to support a family and provide benefits such as health care are in short supply for women who have only a GED and are still under twenty-one. Day care is not a priority of this welfare state, though medical issues have become a public concern.

The mediators' options seem to be more reasonable here; they know that the world is a difficult place in which to carve out a niche for oneself when one has little education, is a single mother, belongs to a minority group, and has to sacrifice part of one's childhood and young adulthood. They provide a way of maintaining self-respect and gaining that of others while using welfare. However, brick walls exist for the young and unskilled and only the most clever and ambitious may be able to negotiate a path for themselves; therefore, it may not be completely unreasonable to follow the arbiters' lead and learn to fit in and follow the rules given the jobs available and the shortness of the program. Both orientations have their limitations.

All of the staff are faced with the difficult issue: how can the program help ready teen mothers to succeed in a world that is competitive, hierarchical, male-dominated, and meritocratic without changing the world or forcing them to adapt to this world? These social service workers have to deal with a world that already exists, and the arbiters feel that the young women have to learn to fit in as carefully and as closely as possible. It may be that these teens do not have the luxury of constructing their own social worlds and must take not only unrewarding jobs but ones where strict adherence to rules is necessary for remaining in the job and in which no freedoms to make decisions or affect the work situation exist (Kohn 1969). Realistically, the types of work the unskilled and poorly educated young women can hope to find require discipline, deference, and tolerance of monotonous and sometimes onerous chores, such as changing bedpans or cleaning bedsores as nurses' aides. Most of those jobs have little room for creativity or possibilities for advancement without much more education. It is possible to argue that the arbiters' image of the world as a place with brick walls is more adequate for describing the social world, particularly the work experience, into which these young women must move. Perhaps it would be better to learn to look like the others, to fit in, and to follow orders.

But how does one become active in pursuing a job or place for oneself in such a structured universe? If one is dependent, subordinate, and stigmatized, as the arbiters never fail to remind their charges, how can one find an exit from this damaged moral universe and find an entrance to and a voice in another one when the chance of failure is so great? Is the desire to rid oneself of the stigma and join the conventional work world sufficient for a breakthrough, particularly when many people in one's own community are in the same predicament? A person cannot live well on welfare benefits, but at least she can have health insurance for her child, which is a great responsibility in and of itself. And will a mother be able to manage as well after entering that world of work? Where will money for child-care come from?

Superficially, it may seem reasonable to fit people directly into the types of jobs available, such as housekeeper or food server, but these jobs tend to increase alienation from labor. In their jobs, they would have to follow rules and obey authority as in the program, but they would do so while losing their identities as thinking and feeling human beings. This sacrifice may be too great.

The short duration of the program raises another issue: is it possible in five months to do any more than to prepare a few to take their GED's and learn some basic tricks for getting a low-skilled job? Given the time limit, it may be the most practical thing to do, because it takes much longer to construct a secure sense of place in the wider society that encompasses more groups and perspectives. During the five months, the arbiters can emphasize adherence to principles, to do what is right, to affirm the need to work, and to follow orders, as opposed to giving in to pulls from home and youthful desires to have fun and goof off. Citizenship means holding a job and paying your own way.

The mediators, on the other hand, examine the circumstances of the lives of the young women and try to adapt their positions to those circumstances. The participants are young, they are mothers, and, currently, they do not have skills that will enable them to obtain "self-supporting" jobs. They need to have time to play as all young people do. And they see in all circumstances that, while one has to use the larger culturally defined expectations, circumstances vary and trade-offs occur. The mediators are not trying to distance the young women from others, but they are trying to show them that there is more than one way to "fit in" and make a place for oneself. They can be a bit creative, thus "fitting in" without losing their sense of self. Like judicial discretion,[11] there is personal situational discretion in making one's own path. The young people have to learn to make difficult decisions as they confront new circumstances. Moreover, most of the young women are aware of the need for employment and manage to get some without being told by social service providers that it is necessary. Indeed, most women who use welfare go through extensive periods when they work.[12]

There is a significant limitation to what the mediators were trying to do. To create a thoughtful citizen who can manage many different situations and can make reasonable assessments and decisions is an arduous, time-consuming, long-term task. To be a successful person able to negotiate her own path, let alone changing the social world, one needs much education and practical skills and creative alliances with others. While it is possible to get started in a five-month program, it is probably impossible to fully educate all but the most advanced when they are so young and need to learn so much about the wider society. While many of the young women are reasonably skilled in taking the perspective of the other when on their own turf and have some sense of their own agency, they have not had many positive experiences interacting in the larger social world of work, education, politics, and social life. Moreover, they have many real problems with money, housing, children, and the lack of income-earning men. With the bleak shape of the national economy, with its shrinking industrial base, and with continued discrimination, even if they make some progress toward greater participation in the wider society, the possibility that a single problem will undermine everything they have achieved is vast. Given the available institutional supports, one

11. Atiyah (1980), in discussing the function of law and the judicial process, proposed that one of its functions is to affirm what correct behavior is. The view was that law was designed to influence behavior. This he calls the hortatory function (Atiyah 1980, 1249). The other function is dispute settlement. These two functions can come into conflict when the tendency of the first is to apply the law in a blanket way to affirm the importance of the rule, while in the second, the point is to achieve justice according to the particular circumstances of the case. That is, in the first case one adheres to principle and in the second the judge makes a pragmatic decision to bring justice to a particular set of circumstances.

12. Several studies have shown that welfare families sometimes add to their benefits with work in the conventional labor market (Pearce 1979; Rein and Rainwater 1978). Duncan (1984) has demonstrated that welfare is often used as a supplement for labor market earnings. Analyzing the work histories of black teen mothers for seventeen years after the birth of their babies, Harris (1991) found that most had extensive labor market experiences and that education facilitated movement off welfare but that the lack of childcare services was often a hinderance.

ill child, another downturn in the economy, or a family member in need could roll back whatever progress they have made.

Both positions are, to a large degree, predicated on the basis that there are jobs available locally, that these young women can obtain them, and that affordable day care and health insurance is available. For the arbiters' position, any absence of viable employment leaves the young mothers in an untenable situation. In the real world when no jobs or day care are available, they will have to stay on welfare. But as welfare recipients, according to the arbiters, they are not full-fledged citizens, not morally upright persons. Work is the indication of moral worth regardless of the circumstances inhibiting employment. They are accepting the model of labor force participation as the only real way to participate. The stigma is automatically affixed to one's moral character and one is relegated to a separate moral universe. A welfare recipient, in fact, risks losing public standing and is publicly shamed. The door to the public world of work is shut. Separating spheres of activity as the arbiters mandated not only makes the specific linkages outside the purview of the young women but indicates which activity sphere is most important and what should remain in the inferior private sphere.

The mediators' position leaves room for flexibility. The mediators communicate that the context of being a good mother is central and thus achievement in this sphere is an important aspect of who a person is. They need not invest themselves totally in the world of work. Placing all of the emphasis on investment in work and schooling is very dangerous for the clients because their records are already poor and, given their limited labor market skills in an increasingly limited and professionalized market, their futures are uncertain. Furthermore, the young women know that the jobs they will have are low status and that there are insufficient benefits available to them as mothers. When jobs are not available, when more time is needed to gain skills, and when supportive services are unavailable, they have an additional reasonable source of identity, motherhood, and receipt of welfare should not stigmatize them or make them less active citizens.

In the short term, the perspective adopted by the mediators makes the availability of employment and the support services that must accompany employment less critical for maintaining a positive image of self and they provide some techniques for dealing with these circumstances and for alternative paths to citizenship. One does not have to be immediately employed to maintain one's dignity as a human being. Welfare support can be regarded as a form of public scholarship for all young people to complete more training and grow up. One must continue working toward financial independence and be responsible to maintain one's dignity, that is, one must act responsibly as a mother, which means not only acting well toward one's child but working toward the situation where the child is no longer supporting you—that is, "being about something." One is a citizen.

Being a mother is not an identity that needs to be hidden backstage in the totally private world of family. It is not a low-priority identity or the dirty laundry that the arbiters want to make it but, rather, the most salient part of self which expresses the young women's most meaningful aspirations. Working at being a good mother and doing it well is what allows many of these women to see themselves as deserving of respect. One has to learn to manage the relation between the more private world of the family and the more public world of work, but family, like emotions, are not unconnected with and unmentionable in the world of work, power, and politics.

Knowledge that one can learn new cultures in different settings and that these cultures are continuously evolving is more important than the teaching of specific rules of behavior for particular social settings. Predicting how interactions will evolve and situations will change is rarely possible as one is frequently confronted by ambiguities and conflicts. It is better to learn how to adapt to new situations, make decisions, and to take the perspective of the other to see "what is going on." Even places of employment vary in their expectations for workers. In some work sites there is much less of a wall between the public and private than in others. Being willing and able to take the perspective of the other is critical to making one's path through the job world and among the worlds of employment, politics, and family.

The culture of the organization may not have been rich, but it does not mean that there was an absence of culture. Perhaps, if there were some explicit rituals and ceremonies of membership in the organization, or ceremonies which connected the young women to the world in which they lived or were supposed to live in when they completed the program, more would have stayed in and those who remained would have remained more committed. The messages from the staff members about how they were and should be connected to the wider society were quite clear and affected how they thought about themselves and their futures. However, the two distinct versions left them confused and uncertain.

Perhaps the young women were convinced by neither or perhaps they canceled each other out. Few seemed to be successful in the arbiters' terms. Several did finish their GED's in other programs, but three had at least one more child within two years of leaving the program, two were in jail on serious charges, and the young woman who was regarded as the best client was working part-time at a minimum-wage job four years after the program. She told me that she was still trying to get herself a better job.

References

Adler, Peter, and Patti Adler. 1987. *Membership Roles in Field Research.* Beverly Hills: Sage.

Allport, Gordon. 1955. *Basic Considerations for a Psychology of Personality.* New Haven, CT: Yale University Press.

Anderson, Alan K., and Omar Khayyam Moore. 1960. "Autotelic Folk Models." *Sociological Quarterly* 1: 203–16.

Anderson, Elijah. 1990. *Streetwise.* Chicago: University of Chicago Press.

Altheide, David. 1989. "Mediating Cutbacks in Human Services: A Case Study in Negotiated Order." *Sociological Quarterly* 29: 339–56.

Atiyah, P. S. 1980. "From Principles to Pragmatism: Changes in the Function of the Judicial Process and the Law." *Iowa Law Review* 65: 1249–72.

Banfield, Edward. 1970. *The Unheavenly City.* Boston: Little, Brown.

Barber, Bernard. 1983. *The Logic and Limits of Trust.* New Brunswick, NJ: Rutgers University Press.

Ben-Yehuda, Nachman. 1990. *The Politics and Morality of Deviance.* Albany: State University Press of New York.

Blumstein, Phillip. 1975. "Identity Bargaining and Self-Conception." *Social Forces* 53: 476–85.

Bourdieu, Pierre. 1974. "The School as a Conservative Force: Scholastic and Cultural Inequalities." In *Contemporary Research in the Sociology of Education,* edited by John Eggleston, pp. 32–46. London: Methuen.

———. 1977. *Outline of a Theory of Practice.* Cambridge, U.K.: Cambridge University Press.

———, and Jean-Claude Passeron. 1977. *Reproduction in Education, Society, and Culture.* Beverly Hills, CA: Sage.

Brieland, Donald. 1977. "Historical Overview." *Social Work* 22: 341–46.

———. 1981. "Definition, Specialization and Domain in Social Work." *Social Work* 26: 79–84.

Brogan, R., and S. S. Taylor. 1983. *Introduction to Qualitative Research Methods.* New York: John Wiley.

Broll, L., A. E. Gross, and I. Piliavin. 1974. "Effects of Offered and Requested Help on Help-seeking and Reactions to Being Helped." *Journal of Applied Social Psychology* 4: 244–58.

Brown, Shirley. 1983. "How Well Are We Serving the Adolescent Mother: A Look at Public Social Services." *Children and Youth Services Review* 5: 135–54.

Burawoy, Michael. 1979. *Manufacturing Consent.* Chicago: University of Chicago Press.

———. 1991. *Ethnography Unbound.* Berkeley: University of California Press.

Bush, Malcolm. 1988. *Families in Distress: Public, Private and Civic Responses.* Berkeley: University of California Press.

Cameron, Stephen, and James Heckman. 1993. "The Nonequivalence of High School Equivalents." *Journal of Labor Economics* 11: 1–47.

Card, J. J., and L. L. Wise. 1978. "Teenage Mothers and Teenage Fathers: The Impact of Early Childbearing on The Parents' Personal and Professional Lives." *Family Planning Perspectives* 10: 199–205.

Children's Defense Fund. 1985. *Preventing Children Having Children.* Washington, DC: Children's Defense Fund.

Cohen, Abner. 1974. *Two-Dimensional Man.* Berkeley: University of California Press.

Collins, Patricia Hill. 1990. *Black Feminist Thought.* London: Harper Collins.

Condie, C. David, Janet Hanson, Nanci Lange, Deanna Moss, and Rosalie Kary. 1978. "How the Public Views Social Work." *Social Work* 23: 47–53.

Cooley, Charles H. 1902. *Human Nature and the Social Order.* New York: C. Scribner.

Cutright, P. 1973. "Illegitimacy and Income Supplements." In *Studies in Public Welfare,* paper no. 12. Washington, DC: Government Printing Office.

Dahl, Robert. 1961. *Who Governs?* New Haven, CT: Yale University Press.

Day, Robert. A., and J. V. Day. 1977. "A Review of the Current State of Negotiated Order Theory." *Sociological Quarterly* 18: 126–42.

Deutscher, Irwin. 1977. "Toward Avoiding the Goal Trap in Evaluation Research." In *Readings in Evaluation Research,* edited by F. G. Caro, pp. 108–23. New York: Russell Sage Foundation.

Devaney, Barbara, and Katherine Hubley. 1981. "The Determinants of Adolescent Pregnancy and Childbearing." Final Report to the Center for Population Research, National Institute of Child Health and Human Development. Washington, DC: Mathematica Policy Research.

Dingwall, Robert, and P. M. Strong. 1985. "The Interactional Study of Organizations: A Critique and Reformulation." *Urban Life* 14: 205–31.

Duncan, Greg. 1984. *Years of Poverty, Years of Plenty.* Ann Arbor: University of Michigan Institute for Social Research.

———, Martha S. Hill, and Saul Hoffman. 1988. "Welfare Dependence Within and Across Generations." *Science* 239: 467–71.

Ellwood, David. 1986. "Targeting the Would-be Long-Term Recipient of AFDC: Who Should Be Served?" Report to U.S. Department of Health and Human Services. Princeton, NJ: Mathematica Policy Research.

———. 1988. *Poor Support: Poverty in the American Family.* New York: Basic Books.

———, and M. J. Bane. 1984. "The Impact of AFDC on Family Structure and Living Arrangements." Working paper prepared for the U.S. Department of Health and Human Services under grant no. 92A-82.

Emerson, Robert. 1983. *Contemporary Field Research.* Boston: Little, Brown.

Fechter, A., and S. Greenfield. 1973. "Welfare and Illegitimacy: An Economic Model and Some Preliminary Results." Working paper no. 963-37, Urban Institute, Washington, DC.

Fine, Gary Alan. 1984. "Negotiated Orders and Organizational Cultures: Qualitative Approaches to Organizations." *Annual Review of Sociology* 10: 239–62.

Fisher, Jeffrey. 1983. "The Parameters of the Field." In *New Directions in Helping,* vol. 1, edited by A. Nadler, J. Fisher, B. DePaulo, pp. 2–14. New York: Academic Press.

———, and A. Nadler. 1976. "Effect of Donor Resources on Recipient Self-esteem and Self-help." *Journal of Experimental Social Psychology* 12: 139–50.

———, A. Nadler, S. Whictcher-Alagna. 1983. "Four Conceptualizations of Reactions to Aid." In *New Directions in Helping,* vol. 1, edited by B. DePaulo, A. Nadler, and J. Fisher, pp. 51–84. New York: Academic Press.

Ford Foundation, Executive Panel of the Project on Social Welfare and the American Future. 1989. *The Common Good: Social Welfare and the American Future.* New York: Ford Foundation.

Ford, Kathleen. 1983. "Second Pregnancies among Teenage Mothers." *Family Planning Perspectives* 15: 268–72.

Friedson, Eliot. 1975. *Doctoring Together.* Chicago: University of Chicago Press.

———. 1989. *Medical Work in America.* New Haven, CT: Yale University Press.

Fry, Lincoln, and Jon Miller. 1975. "Responding to Skid Row Alcoholism: Self-Defeating Arrangements in an Innovative Treatment Program." *Social Problems* 22: 675–88.

Furstenberg, Frank, J. Brooks-Gunn, and S. Morgan. 1987. *Adolescent Mothers in Later Life.* Cambridge, U.K.: Cambridge University Press.

Gans, Herbert. 1962. *The Urban Villagers.* New York: Free Press.

Gartner, Alan, and Frank Reissman. 1974. *The Service Society and the Consumer Vanguard.* New York: Harper and Row.

Gergen, Kenneth J. 1977. "The Social Construction of Self-knowledge." In *The Self,* edited by T. Mischel, pp. 139–69. Totowa, NJ: Towman and Littlefields.

———, and M. M. Gergen. 1983. "Narratives of the Self." In *Studies in Social Identity,* edited by K. Scheibe and T. Sarbin, pp. 254–73. New York: Praeger.

———. 1984. *Historical Social Psychology.* Hillsdale, NJ: Lawrence Erlbaum Associates.

Germaine, Carol, and Alex Gitterman. 1980. *The Life Model of Social Work Practice.* New York: Columbia University Press.

Giallombardo, Rose. 1966. *Society of Women.* New York: Wiley.

Glaser, Barney, and Anslem L. Strauss. 1964. "Awareness Contexts and Social Interaction." *American Sociological Review* 19: 669–79.

Goffman, Erving. 1959. *The Presentation of Self in Everyday Life.* New York: Doubleday.

———. 1961. *Asylums.* New York: Doubleday.

———. 1963. *Stigma.* Englewood Cliffs, NJ: Prentice-Hall.

———. 1967. *Interaction Ritual.* New York: Doubleday.

Gordon, Linda. 1988. "What Does Welfare Regulate?" *Social Research* 55: 609–30.

Granovetter, Mark. 1985. "Economic Action and Social Structure: The Problem of Embeddedness." *American Journal of Sociology* 91: 481–511.

Grønbjerg, Kirsten. 1977. *Mass Society and the Extension of Welfare 1960–1970.* Chicago: University of Chicago Press.

Gueron, Judith. 1990. "Work and Welfare: Lessons on Employment Programs." *Journal of Economic Perspectives* 4: 79–98.

Hall, Peter. 1985. "Asymmetric Relationships and Processes of Power." In *Studies in Symbolic Interaction,* edited by N. Denzin, Supplement 1, pp. 309–44. Greenwich, CT: JAI Press.

———, and Dee Ann Spencer-Hall. 1982. "The Social Conditions of Negotiated Order." *Urban Life* 11: 328–49.

Halton, Eugene Rochberg. 1986. *Meaning and Modernity.* Chicago: University of Chicago Press.

Harris, Kathleen. 1991. "Teenage Mothers and Welfare Dependency." *Journal of Family Issues* 12: 492–518.

Hasenfeld, Yeheskel, and Richard English, eds. 1974. *Human Service Organizations.* Ann Arbor: University of Michigan Press.

Hasenfeld, Yeheskel, Jane Rafferty, and Mayer Zald. 1987. "The Welfare State, Citizenship and Bureaucratic Encounters." *Annual Review of Sociology* 13: 387–415.

Haug, Marie R., and M. Sussman. 1969. "Professional Autonomy and the Revolt of the Client." *Social Problems* 17: 153–60.

Hearn, Gordon, ed. 1969. *The General Systems Approach: Contributions Toward an Holistic Conception of Social Work.* New York: Council on Social Work Education.

Hewitt, John. 1989. *Dilemmas of the American Self.* Philadelphia: Temple University Press.

Hochschild, Arlie. 1983. *The Managed Heart.* Berkeley: University of California Press.

Hofferth, Sandra. 1987. "Social and Economic Consequences of Teenage Childbearing." In *Risking the Future,* vol. 2, edited by S. Hofferth and C. D. Hayes, pp. 123–44. Washington, DC: National Academy Press.

Hogan, Dennis, and E. Kitagawa. 1983. "Family Factors in the Fertility of Black Adolescents." Paper presented at Annual Meetings of the Population Association.

Horkheimer, Max. 1972. "Authority and the Family." In *Critical Theory: Selected Essays.* New York: Seabury Press.

Horowitz, Ruth. 1986. "Remaining an Outsider: Membership as a Threat to Research Rapport." *Urban Life* 14: 409–30.

Hunt, Jennifer. 1984. "The Development of Rapport through the Negotiation of Gender in Field Work among Police." *Human Organization* 43: 283–96.

Janowitz, Morris. 1969. *Institution Building in Urban Education.* New York: Russell Sage.

———. 1975. "Sociological Theory and Social Control." *American Journal of Sociology.* 81: 82–108.

————. 1978. *The Last Half-Century*. Chicago: University of Chicago Press.

————. 1983. *The Reconstruction of Patriotism*. Chicago: University of Chicago Press.

Jones, Elise, Jacqueline Forrest, Noreen Goldman, Stanley Henshaw, Richard Lincoln, Jeannie Rosoff, Charles Westoff, and Deirdre Wulf. 1986. *Adolescent Pregnancy in Industrialized Countries*. New Haven, CT: Yale University Press.

Jones, Kathleen. 1990. "Citizenship in a Woman Friendly Politics." *Signs* 15: 781–812.

Jules-Rosette, B. 1978. "The Veil of Objectivity: Prophecy, Divination and Social Inquiry." *American Anthropologist* 80: 549–70.

Kadushin, Charles. 1962. "Social Distance between Client and Professional." *American Journal of Sociology* 67: 517–31.

Katz, Jack. 1983. "A Theory of Qualitative Methodology." In *Contemporary Field Research*, edited by Robert Emerson, pp. 127–48. Boston: Little, Brown.

Katz, Michael. 1989. *The Undeserving Poor*. New York: Pantheon Books.

Kemper, Theodore, and Randall Collins. 1990. "Dimensions of Microinteraction." *American Journal of Sociology* 96: 32–68.

Kertzer, David. 1988. *Ritual, Politics and Power*. New Haven, CT: Yale University Press.

Kleinman, Sherryl. 1984. *Equals Before God*. Chicago: University of Chicago Press.

————, and Gary Fine. 1979. "Rhetorics and Action in Moral Organization: Social Control of Little Leaguers and Ministry Students." *Urban Life* 8: 275–94.

Klockars, Carl. 1984. "Blue Lies—Police Placebos: The Moralities of Police Lying." *American Behavioral Scientist* 27 (4): 529–44.

Kohn, Melvin. 1969. *Class and Conformity*. Homewood, IL: Dorsey.

Ladner, Joyce. 1986a. "Black Women Face the 21st Century: Major Issues and Problems." *The Black Scholar* (October): 12–19.

————. 1986b. "Teenage Pregnancy: The Implications for Black Americans." In *State of Black America, 1986*, edited by J. Williams, pp. 65–84. New York: National Urban League.

Landry, Bart. 1987. *The New Black Middle Class*. Berkeley: University of California Press.

LeCroy, Craig Winston. 1985. "Methodological Issues in the Evaluation of Social Work Practice." *Social Service Review* 59 (3): 345–57.

Lefton, Mark, and W. R. Rosengren. 1966. "Organizations and Clients: Lateral and Longitudinal Dimensions." *American Sociological Review* 31: 802–10.

Lenrow, P. 1978. "Dilemmas of Professional Helping: Continuities and Discontinuities with Folk Helping Roles." In *Altruism, Sympathy, and Helping*, edited by L. Wispe. New York: Academic Press.

Lewis, Oscar. 1966. *La Vida*. New York: Random House.

Liebow, Eliot. 1967. *Tally's Corner*. Boston: Little, Brown.

Lipsky, Michael. 1980. *Street-Level Bureaucracy: Dilemmas of the Individual in Public Services*. New York: Russell Sage.

Lofland, John. 1969. *Deviance and Identity*. New York: Prentice-Hall.

Lofland, J., and L. Lofland. 1984. *Analyzing Social Settings*. Belmont, CA: Wadsworth.

Louis, M. R. 1980a. "Organizations as Culture-bearing Milieu." In *Organizational Symbolism*, edited by L. Pondy, P. Frost, G. Morgan, and T. Dandridge, pp. 39–53. Greenwich, CT: JAI Press.

———. 1980b. "Surprise and Sense Making: What Newcomers Experience in Entering Unfamiliar Organizational Settlings." *Administrative Science Quarterly* 25: 226–50.

Lukes, Steven. 1978. "Power and Authority." In *A History of Sociological Analysis*, edited by T. Bottomore and R. Nibet, pp. 633–76. New York: Basic Books.

Maines, David. 1977. "Social Organization and Social Structure in Symbolic Interactions Thought." *Annual Review of Sociology* 3: 235–59.

———. 1982. "In Search of Mesostructure: Studies in Negotiated Order." *Urban Life* 11: 267–97.

———, and Joy Charton. 1985. "The Negotiated Order Approach to the Analysis of Social Organization." In *Foundations of Interpretive Sociology*, edited by H. Farberman and R. Perinbanayagam, pp. 271–308. Greenwich, CT: JAI Press.

Manning, Peter. 1977. *Police Work*. Cambridge, MA: MIT Press.

Marshall, T. H. 1964. "Citizenship and Social Class." In *Class, Citizenship Use, Social Development*, pp. 65–123. New York: Doubleday.

Matza, David. 1966. "The Disreputable Poor." In *Class, Status and Power*, 2d ed., edited by Rheinhard Bendix and Seymour M. Lipset, pp. 289–302. New York: Free Press.

McCarthy, J., and J. Menkin. 1979. "Marriage, Remarriage, Marital Disruption and Age at First Birth." *Family Planning Perspectives* 11: 21–30.

Mead, George H. [1934] 1962. *Mind, Self, and Society*. Chicago: University of Chicago Press.

Mead, Lawrence. 1986. *Beyond Entitlement: The Social Obligations of Citizenship*. New York: Free Press.

Mehan, Hugh, and Houston Wood. 1975. *The Reality of Ethnomethodology*. New York: John Wiley and Sons.

Merton, Vanessa, R. K. Merton, and B. Barber. 1983. "Client Ambivalence in Professional Relationships: The Problem of Seeking Help from Strangers." In *New Directions in Helping*, edited by B. DePaulo, A. Nadler, and J. Fisher, pp. 13–44. New York: Academic Press.

Meyer, John W., and B. Rowan. 1977. "Institutional Organizations: Formal Structures as Myth and Ceremony." *American Journal of Sociology* 83: 340–63.

Miller, S. M. 1952. "The Participant Observer and Over-rapport." *American Sociological Review* 17: 97–99.

Miller, Walter B. 1958. "Lower Class Culture as a Generating Milieu for Gang Delinquency." *Social Issues* 14: 3–14.

Moore, Kristen A., and S. B. Caldwell. 1976. "Out-of-wedlock Pregnancy and Childbearing." Working paper no. 999-02, Urban Institute, Washington, DC.

Moore, Kristen A., and L. J. Waite. 1977. "Early Childbearing and Educational Attainments." *Family Planning Perspectives* 9: 220–25.

Moore, Kristen A., L. J. Waite, S. B. Caldwell, and S. L. Hofferth. 1978. "Consequences of Age at First Childbirth." Working Paper no. 1146-01. Washington, DC: Urban Institute.

Moore, Kristen A., and Sandra Hofferth. 1980. "Factors Affecting Early Family Formation: A Path Model." *Population and Environment* 3: 73–96.

Moore, Kristen A., and Martha Burt. 1982. *Private Crisis, Public Cost: Policy Perspectives on Teenage Childbearing.* Washington, DC: The Urban Institute.

Moore, Kristen A., Margaret Simms, and Charles Betsey. 1986. *Choice and Circumstance.* New Brunswick, NJ: Transaction Press.

Morris, Robert. 1977. "Caring For vs. Caring About People." *Social Work* 22: 353–59.

Murray, Charles. 1984. *Losing Ground: American Social Policy, 1950–1980.* New York: Basic Books.

Nadler, Arie. 1983. "Personal Characteristics and Help-Seeking." In *New Directions in Helping,* vol. 2, edited by Jeffrey Fischer, Arie Nadler, Bella DePaulo, pp. 303–37. New York: Academic Press.

———, A. Altman, and J. D. Fisher. 1979. "Helping Is not Enough: Recipient's Reactions to Aid as a Function of Positive and Negative Information about the Self." *Journal of Personality* 47: 615–28.

Nathanson, Constance. 1991. *Dangerous Passage.* Philadelphia: Temple University Press.

Nurius, Paula. 1991. "Possible Selves and Social Support: Social Cognitive Resources for Coping and Striving." In *The Self-Society Dynamic,* edited by Judith Howard and Peter Callera, pp. 239–58. New York: Cambridge University Press.

Nelson, Barbara. 1980. "Help Seeking from Public Authorities: Who Arrives at the Agency Door?" *Policy Sciences* 12: 175–92.

———. 1984. "Women's Poverty and Women's Citizenship: Some Political Consequences of Economic Marginality." *Signs* 10: 209–32.

Orloff, Ann. 1993. "Gender and Social Rights of Citizenship: The Comparative Analysis of State Policies and Gender Relations." *American Sociological Review* 58: 303–28.

O'Toole, Richard, and Anita Werner O'Toole. 1981. "Negotiating Interorganizational Orders." *Sociological Quarterly* 22: 29–41.

Pateman, Carole. 1989. *The Disorder of Women: Democracy, Feminism and Political Theory.* Stanford, CA: Stanford University Press.

Pearce, D. 1979. "Women, Work and Welfare: The Feminization of Poverty." In *Working Women and Families,* edited by K. W. Feinstein, pp. 103–24. Beverly Hills, CA: Sage.

Perlman, Helen Harris. 1979. *Relationship.* Chicago: University of Chicago Press.

Petr, Christopher. 1988. "The Worker-Client Relationship." *Social Casework* 69: 620–26.

Piven, Frances Fox. 1985. "Women and the State: Ideology, Power, and the Welfare State." In *Gender and the Life Course*, edited by A. Rossi, pp. 265–87. New York: Aldine.

———. 1988. "Welfare Doesn't Shore Up Traditional Family Roles: A Reply to Linda Gordon." *Social Research* 55: 631–47.

Piven, Frances, and Richard Cloward. 1971. *Regulating the Poor: The Functions of Public Welfare*. New York: Academic Press.

Placek, P. J., and G. Hendershot. 1974. "Public Welfare and Family Planning: An Empirical Study of the 'Brood Sow' Myth." *Social Problems* 21: 660–73.

Polit, Denise, Janet Kahn, and David Stevens. 1985. *Final Impacts from Project Redirection*. New York: Manpower Demonstration Research Corporation.

Presser, Harriet B., and L. S. Salsberg. 1975. "Public Assistance and Early Family Formation: Is There a Pronatalist Effect?" *Social Problems* 23: 226–41.

Quadagno, Jill. 1987. "Theories of the Welfare State." *Annual Review of Sociology* 13: 109–28.

Rainwater, Lee. 1970. *Behind Ghetto Walls*. Chicago: Aldine.

Rank, Mark. 1989. "Fertility among Women and Welfare." *American Sociological Review* 54: 296–304.

Rawls, Anne W. 1990. "Emergent Sociality: A Dialectic of Commitment and Order." *Symbolic Interaction* 13: 63–82.

Rein, M., and L. Rainwater. 1978. "Patterns of Welfare Use." *Social Service Review* 52: 511–34.

Rindfuss, Ronald, Larry Bumpass, and Craig St. John. 1980. "Education and Futility: Implications for the Roles Women Occupy." *American Sociological Review* 45: 431–47.

Rossi, Peter H. 1978. "Issues in the Evaluation of Human Services Delivery." *Evaluation Quarterly* 2: 573–99.

Roy, Donald. 1952. "Quota Restriction and Goldbricking in a Machine Shop." *American Journal of Sociology* 57: 427–42.

Sahlins, Marshall. 1972. *Stone Age Economics*. Chicago: Aldine.

Schafer, Robert, P. Keith, and F. Lorenz. 1984. "Equity/Inequity: An Interactionist Analysis." *Social Psychology Quarterly* 47: 42–49.

Schatzman, L., and A. Strauss 1973. *Field Research*. Englewood Cliffs, NJ: Prentice-Hall.

Schorr, Lisbeth. 1988. *Within Our Reach*. New York: Doubleday.

Schram, Sanford, and J. P. Turbett. 1983. "The Welfare Explosion: Mass Society versus Social Control." *Social Service Review* 57: 614–25.

Schwalbe, Michael. 1988. "Role Taking Reconsidered: Linking Competence and Performance to Social Structure." *Journal for the Theory of Social Behavior* 18: 411–36.

Schwartz, Gary S. 1987. *Beyond Conformity or Rebellion*. Chicago: University of Chicago Press.

Sennett, Richard. 1980. *Authority*. Random House: New York: Knopf.

Shalin, Dmitri. 1986. "Pragmatism and Social Interactionism." *American Sociological Review* 51: 9–29.

———. 1988. "G. H. Mead, Socialism and the Progressive Agenda." *American Journal of Sociology* 93: 913–51.

———. 1992. "Critical Theory and the Pragmatist Challenge." *American Journal of Sociology* 98: 237–80.

Shapiro, Susan. 1987. "The Social Control of Impersonal Trust." *American Journal of Sociology* 93: 623–58.

Shklar, Judith. 1991. *American Citizenship*. Cambridge, MA: Harvard University Press.

Smircich, L. 1983a. "Concepts of Culture and Organizational Analysis." *Administrative Science Quarterly* 28: 339–58.

———. 1983b. "Organizations as Shared Meanings." In *Organizational Symbolism*, edited by L. Pondy, P. Frost, G. Morgan, and T. Dandridge, pp. 55–65. Greenwich, CT: JAI Press.

Snow, David, and Leon Anderson. 1987. "Identity Work among the Homeless." *American Journal of Sociology* 92: 1336–71.

Social Work. 1977. "Excerpts from the Discussion." *Social Work* 22: 382–85.

Somers, Margaret. 1993. "Citizenship and the Place of the Public Sphere: Law, Community, and Political Culture in the Transition to Democracy." *American Sociological Review* 58: 587–620.

Strauss, A. 1959. *Mirrors and Masks: The Search for Identity*. Glencoe, IL: Free Press.

———. 1978. *Negotiations: Varieties, Context, Processes and Social Order*. San Francisco: Jossey-Bass.

———. 1982. "Interorganizational Negotiations." *Urban Life* 11: 350–67.

Stryker, Sheldon. 1980. *Symbolic Interactionism*. Menlo Park, CA: Benjamin/ Cummings.

———. 1968. "Identity Salience and Role Performance." *Journal of Marriage and the Family* 30: 558–564.

Sullivan, Mercer. 1989. *Getting Paid*. Ithaca, NY: Cornell University Press.

Thomas, Jim. 1983. "Justice as Interaction: Loose Coupling and Mediations in the Adversary Process." *Symbolic Interaction* 6: 243–60.

———. 1984. "Some Aspects of Negotiated Order, Loose Coupling and Mesostructure in Maximum Security Prisons." *Symbolic Interaction* 7: 213–31.

Torres, A., and J. D. Forrest. 1983. "Family Planning Clinic Services in the United States, 1981." *Family Planning Perspectives* 15: 272–78.

Trilling, Lionel. 1972. *Sincerity and Authenticity*. Cambridge, MA: Harvard University Press.

Turner, Ralph. 1957. "The Normative Coherence of Folk Concepts." *Research Studies of the State College of Washington* 25: 127–36.

———. 1968. "The Self in Social Interaction." In *The Self in Social Interaction*, edited by Chad Gordon and Kenneth Gergen, pp. 93–106. New York: Wiley.

———. 1976. "The Real Self: From Institution to Impulse." *American Journal of Sociology* 81: 989–1016.

Van Maanen, J., and S. Barley. 1985. "Cultural Organization: Fragments of a Theory." In *Organizational Culture*, edited by P. Frost, L. Moore, M. Louis, C. Lundenberg, J. Martin, pp. 31–54. Beverly Hills, CA: Sage Publications.

Van Maanen, J., and E. H. Schein. 1979. "Toward a Theory of Organizational Socialization." In *Research in Organizational Behavior*, edited by B. M. Shaw, pp. 209–64. Greenwich, CT: JAI Press.

Vinovskis, Maris. 1988. *An "Epidemic" of Adolescent Pregnancy? Some Historical and Policy Considerations*. New York: Oxford University Press.

Walz, Thomas, and Victor Groze. 1991. "The Mission of Social Work Revisited: An Agenda for the 1990s." *Social Work* 36: 500–504.

Waxman, Chaim. 1983. *The Stigma of Poverty*. 2d ed. New York: Pergamon Press.

Weatherley, Richard, Sylvia Perlman, Michael Levine, and Lorraine Klerman. 1985. "Patchwork Programs: Comprehensive Services for Pregnant and Parenting Adolescents." Seattle, WA: Center for Social Welfare Research, School of Social Work, University of Washington.

Weber, Max. 1958. *From Max Weber*. Translated by Hans Gerth and C. W. Mills. New York: Oxford University Press.

Weick, Karl E. 1976. "Educational Organizations as Loosely Coupled Systems." *Administrative Science Quarterly* 21: 1–19.

———. 1979. *The Social Psychology of Organizing*. Reading, MA: Addison-Wesley.

Weigert, Andrew, J. S. Teitge, and D. W. Teitge. 1986. *Society and Identity*. Cambridge, U.K.: Cambridge University Press.

Wilson, William J. 1987. *The Truly Disadvantaged*. Chicago: University of Chicago Press.

Wrong, Dennis. 1961. "Over-Socialized View of Man." *American Sociological Review* 26: 183–93.

———. 1988. *Power*. Chicago: University of Chicago Press.

Wuthnow, Robert. 1987. *Meaning and Moral Order*. Berkeley: University of California Press.

Young, Iris M. 1987. "Impartiality and the Civic Public: Some Implications of Feminist Critiques of Moral and Political Theory." In *Feminism as Critique: On the Politics of Gender*, edited by Seyla Benhabib, pp. 57–76. Minneapolis: University of Minnesota Press.

Index

Abuse, 157, 161, 168, 177

Aid for Families with Dependent Children (AFDC), 231–35, 241–42

Amy: failure to understand the participants, 151; in family life class, 164–75, 177; identification as woman and mother, 58; as mediator, 8; in parenting class, 146, 147–49; role in Project GED, 6–7

Anderson, Leon, 84n

Arbiters: actions concerning motherhood, 151; on activities with children, 147; attempts to gain control over the organization, 20; authority of, 85–86, 250–51; awareness context mandated by, 177; as bosses, 216; bureaucratic authority used by, 75–78; citizenship viewed by, 222; communication of relationship of individual to society, 45; competent authority claims, 73–75; conformity and hierarchy emphasized by, 212–13; construction of helping relationships, 40; construction of identity of, 20; construction of staff/client relationship, 66–71; cycle of poverty emphasis, 183; on dealing with a world that already exists, 255–56, 258; deference demanded by, 79, 219; defined, viii; dependency of participants on, 17–18, 86–87, 220, 249–51; desire to be seen as teachers, 98; failure to develop staff/client culture, 89; failure to distinguish between

types of rule violation, 81; formal roles and rules emphasized by, 228–29, 230; on future worker identity construction, 182–83, 187–94, 205–7; gossiping about the participants, 129, 192; hierarchy of identities of, 221; identity as middle-class, 55–58; ignoring participants' motherhood, 162–64; impression-managed self of, 220–22; interpretations of the participants, 131–32; language of professionalism and efficiency used by, 59–61, 62; and the meaning of welfare, 21; participants conceal important aspects of their lives from, 130; participants manage interaction with concerning relationships, 123–24; participants' response to, 144–45; on personnel/participant relationship, 60; on public and private worlds, 21, 216–22; on the relation of the individual to the larger world, 21; relationship with the researcher, 11, 12–13; on sexuality as part of program discussions, 116–17, 118–19, 123–27; social distance emphasized by, 250; taking control of the program, 66–71; testing emphasized by, 103; view of the participants, 13–14, 82, 192; on what the project was or should be, 51; on worker-to-be identity, 182–83. See also Harrison, Mr.; Ivy; John; Roberta

271